Breaking Normal

Essays on My Fat, Black, Geek Life

By TaLynn Kel

Credits and Copyright

Cover and author photo
Andrew Michael Phillips of AMP Image

Photo edits
Acdramon's Artist Cove

Essays were written by TaLynn Kel during 2016 and originally published on Breaking Normal (www.talynnkel.com), Black Girl Nerds (www.blackgirlnerds.com), and The Establishment (www.theestablishment.co).

Introduction

I've always loved writing. It's something I've done throughout my life and more than once told myself what I would do as my profession. I thought it would be fiction novels but life had other plans for me. As a teen, I wrote poetry. In college, I wrote papers. As a young adult, I journaled. Professionally, I wrote marketing materials and for many years, I stopped writing. Then, after leaving yet another job, I decided to write a fiction novel. I've tried twice. Both are still in very unfinished states but I keep telling myself that they are worth finishing. I really want to finish them.

All this is to say that writing is a huge part of who I am and it's a part of me that I keep forcing myself to set aside because there are other priorities, like finishing school; finding a job; hiding from the world; managing my emotional pain and expressing my joy.

Then, in 2015, after several years of trying to find joy in writing professionally for other organizations, I decided to write for myself. It took a super shitty boss and some unexpected extra funds to do it, but I was fortunate to have resources available. Technically, I should have used them to pay down my expensive education, but I've never been the most responsible person.

brief pause to be depressed about student loans

So, I decided to write. I had little hope of being published anywhere other than on my personal blog page, but I tried anyway. I wrote about my life and topical things that interested me. I wrote about my interests and my passions. I wrote for me.

I thought I'd find a niche – like pop culture or cosplay but I realized that I couldn't parse my life like that. It was too incomplete and gave too stark a delineation between aspects of me that aren't separate in any way. My life is a glorious stew of personal shineies that keep me in perpetual confused, enraged joy and if I was going to write about it, that mishmash of stuff needed it to continue being chaotic. I needed to share the overlap and the intersections and the ways that my experiences and identity affect each other.

I don't have an endgame. I didn't know if I would only publish to my site, write for other sites, or what. All I knew was that I wanted to write and hopefully find an audience interested in reading it. And I did. I found you.

Thank you for reading my work.

In many ways, this incremental publishing is the fulfillment of a dream. It's the slow buildup of getting to that place I've always wanted – being a published author. Granted, I've been published on websites for years. Never under my name. Never in a way that I could truly take credit, but it's there. With this collection of essays, I will have met that goal. And when I have a short story published in an anthology, I'll meet it again. And then again, when I finish my fiction books. And again, when I finish even more books.

It may not be the path I thought I'd travel. It may not be the path others used to get there, but I'll get there.

Thank you for being interested and invested enough to join me.

Talynn Kel

Essays

My Cloak of Invisibility

When I was in second grade, I had a teacher who took pleasure in humiliating me. I'm fairly positive I wasn't alone, but I remember her questioning me about my family and our financial situation, about my siblings...whatever topic entered her head. Sometimes she would do this in front of the class, other times she'd pull me aside to pry into my life.

At the time, I knew it made me feel bad about myself, but I didn't have enough experience to understand why. She was my first serious lesson about not trusting authority figures. To this day, I struggle to understand why a grown woman would take obvious pleasure in subjugating children.

My dad tried to help me understand. He told me that she was jealous. Again, she was a grown ass woman and I was a 7-year-old. But now, I kinda get it. And it has a lot to do with someone trying to diminish your personal shine.

Learning to be less is something that has to be taught. In the beginning, I was told to do it: "Don't seem too smart. Guys don't like smart girls" "Don't make your teachers look stupid by asking too many questions." "Be careful not to show your classmates up. It'll make you a target." "Don't let them see how much you know; they'll assume you're cheating."

That's some fucked up shit to tell a child. Hide yourself, because if you don't, the world will do it for you.

And that's what you do. You hide. You hide behind silence. You hide behind books. You hide behind video games. When sexuality entered the equation, you hide behind baggy clothes and feigned misunderstanding. And eventually you isolate yourself as you try to figure out all the fuckery around you.

I say "you" but that's actually what I did.

And I was a smart kid. I was a smart teenager. I couldn't mask that shit if I tried. I used to get chased and attacked by older children because they couldn't outwit me. I was kicked out of class for questioning my teachers as I tried to understand the lesson.

Administrators would make recommendations and choices for you, call you the exception for reasons they couldn't understand. Nobody knew why YOU could do these things that the other students couldn't...that you must know some trick that nobody else knew. And you learned that your shine, your abilities, your accomplishments would always be diminished in some way, so you may as well do it yourself.

That was when I made my cloak of invisibility. I spent most of my twenties embracing mediocrity. I actively hid in plain sight. With the chaos of everything around me, I kept my head low and did what I needed to do. Despite my self-made invisibility cloak, I struggled with people. I struggled to hide that I learned things quickly, adapted to change faster, and could understand what was needed faster and more efficiently than my bosses. And when the "real" me peeked though, I learned that it made them insecure to the point that I would be openly marginalized. They shot down my ideas, they perceived my comments as negative, and if I showed any emotion, they told me I was angry and needed to calm down. There was genuine fear of my physicality in addition to the open disapproval of my larger, brown, body.

According to them, I had an attitude problem. I was insubordinate. Despite demonstrating an ability to complete projects within an allocated time frame, I needed to be managed in some way every hour of the workday. And eventually, I became a problem because if I'm going to be punished for the crime, I may as well be guilty of it.

My last gig, my boss tried on several occasions to make me seem like less than I was. She tried to talk to me like I was a child, and once asked me point blank if I could accomplish the same things she'd accomplished. When I looked her in the eye and said, "yes, I could," she was so stunned it made me smile.

Somewhere along the way, I decided to remove my cloak of invisibility. It wasn't an easy process. First, I had to accept who I was and that on a shit day, I was more capable than many of my co-workers. I'd learned that I could accomplish almost anything I set my mind to do. I know how to set goals. I know how to make plans. I know how to organize. I know how to make connections. I am friendly and personable enough to collaborate with others, provided they actually want to collaborate. I know my shit and if I can't make it happen, I'm comfortable enough to admit it.

I've built a pyre for that cloak. It's not lit yet. I'm still learning to love and accept myself for who I am. I'm not sure if it's a process that I will ever complete, but it is a goal...and I almost always achieve my goals.

Because I am amazing and I do amazing shit.

Because I refuse to pretend to be less than I am.

Because I refuse to BE less than I am.

And because I sure as fuck won't let you diminish me. You can't anymore. I know too much.

Shine on.

Hide yourself, because if you don't, the world will do it for you.

– TaLynn Kel, My Cloak of Invisibility

The Reimagining of Self: Why I Love Marvel's Typhoid Mary

In 2006, I fell in love with Typhoid Mary. The character resonated with the way I fragmented myself, the way I felt like I needed to have almost separate identities for my public, private, family, and work life. In retrospect, that's a lot of partitions, but at the time it was what I needed.

Here's a little backstory. Typhoid Mary is a character in Marvel's Daredevil. She has three distinct personalities: Mary, Typhoid Mary, and Bloody Mary. Mary represented what society and family expected of me. She was docile, meek, and prone to bouts of nervousness and fear. Typhoid Mary was everything they tell women not to be – adventurous, lusty, ambitious, violent, and uncontrollable. She went for what she wanted and wasn't afraid to take it. Typhoid represented who I wanted to be. Bloody Mary is the amped up violent side who hates all men. To be honest, it's amazing that I don't relate more to Bloody Mary after some of the relationships I've had. Kidding - that's how you go to prison.

Anti-feminist clichés aside, these three aspects of Mary intrigued me. I saw it as a pathologization of women's choices. It ties into the many ways that society has criminalized aspects of womanhood to control it. For example, birth control was ruled illegal in the late 1800s for approximately 100 years. It wasn't until the early 1970s that people couldn't be criminally prosecuted for having birth control...and because men legislated this law, you can guess who was punished for possession of contraception. To this day, condoms can be considered evidence of prostitution and until 2014, women could be stopped and searched for looking "slutty" and then arrested if they had condoms. Apparently, the desire to have safe sex is considered evidence of prostitution[1].

Women's bodies are legislated to death, literally. We can be arrested for miscarriages[2]. Pregnant women are arrested under suspicion of child endangerment if she engages in an activity that could be considered dangerous[3]. This includes having a glass of wine or smoking. Women's lives are put unnecessarily at risk[4] because of legally mandated "religious freedom."

---

[1] Santora, Marc. "New York Police to Limit Seizing of Condoms in Prostitution Cases." The New York Times, 12 May 2014. Web. 05 January, 2017.

[2] Allon, Janey. "Arrested for Having a Miscarriage? 7 Appalling Instances Where Pregnant Women Were Criminalized." Alternet, 12, November 2015. Web. 05 January 2017.

[3] . Culp-Ressler, Tara. "Woman Who Is Just 12 Weeks Pregnant Charged With Child Endangerment." ThinkProgress, 3 Sept. 2014. Web. 5 Jan. 2017.

[4] Zoom, Doktor. "Miscarrying Lady Almost Dies At Catholic Hospital, But At Least She Didn't Get An Abortion." Wonkette, 2 June 2015. Web. 05 Jan. 2017.

Our mental health is often judged and found lacking. Passion, anger, fear, and sadness are considered a sign of mental instability. Who hasn't heard about the "crazy chick" or the "psycho ex-girlfriend"? Hysteria was a medical condition thought to only affect women. Its diagnosis was predicated on extreme emotional states, sexual desire, defiance, anger, nervousness and they were considered signs of varying psychiatric issues. Female hysteria was sometimes treated in a variety of ways: from inducing orgasm to the removal of the uterus, i.e. a hysterectomy. Women were also institutionalized and underwent electroshock therapy and lobotomies as methods of treatment. All because someone thought their behavior was out of line. And all of it was to deny women autonomy and agency.

Barring the diagnosis of hysteria and hysterectomies, these treatments weren't limited to women. They were used to treat men and children who were considered mentally unstable, and sometimes for the same reasons – their behavior was outside the accepted norm and someone in authority pursued violence as a form of treatment. It's also worth noting that these treatments are discussed solely about the perspective and treatment of white women. Black women were subjected to a much less humane form of medical care and reporting. Despite this racialization of hysteria, Black women are affected by the negative connotations assigned to it – i.e. the removal of autonomy and agency in decision-making.

We see it on the micro-level. For example, when I decided to cut off my hair people asked me if I'd cleared it with the guy I'd been dating for three weeks. When I said it was none of his business, I was called selfish and oversensitive, because, you know, it's just polite to ask an acquaintance's permission on what to do with my hair.

Or when I cosplay – my corsets give me magnificent, attention snatching cleavage. My spouse (the same person from the previous example) initially had some issues with it, but I have made it clear that what I wear is always my decision. He may not like it and that's fine. His dislike does not change my decision about what I wear. We've been together seven years and people still ask me if he's okay with my outfits. And to this day I look at them like they are foolish. It's MY decision.

And that is why I am so drawn to Typhoid Mary. Sure, she's working in a system that has some control over her, but in that system, she's making as many decisions for herself that she can. And most of them are not for anyone's approval. She doesn't try to be normal. Normalcy is for the dispassionately uninspired. She is living the life she *mostly* wants, and sadly, the only way that seems acceptable, even in comics, is to paint it as mental illness.

I don't see Typhoid Mary as someone with borderline personality disorder. I see her as someone navigating extremely hostile waters while trying to maintain a sense of self, a struggle to which I relate. I cannot tell you the number of times I've been in a work environment where I was told that I was too loud, too assertive, too confident, too risk-seeking, too everything. And the proposed solution was for me to be quiet, to fold in on myself, to hide in plain sight. I was explicitly told to reel myself in and contain my energy and abilities. I was told to dim my shine.

And I tried. I tried for years. I moved from job to job, losing a little more of my shine each time. And finally, when there wasn't any more shine to lose, I lost me.

There were a lot of contributing factors to my struggle and there were a lot of people who helped me get out of that hole. Mostly, it was a support network large and strong enough to absorb the shock of my fall. Not only did I fall, I shattered. With help, I put myself back together…most the same pieces, some smaller than before. I am still me, transformed into a more compassionate and nuanced version of myself - one with a greater understanding of my needs and my worth.

I came out understanding that what others saw as failure, I knew was growth. And it gave me the strength to meet life head on, to listen to my body and my mind, and to put those needs ahead of what anybody else wanted from or expected of me. People are always going to want something. And people are always going to tell me how I failed to meet their expectations. Now when that happens, I paint half my face and grab my katanas – because it's time to slay some shit.

My inner Typhoid takes no shit. And the funniest part about Typhoid Mary is that this perception of her isn't that she's not being true to herself – it's the difference between what people want to see verses what's actually there and being able to recognize that. As a Black woman, I am very familiar with what it's like to have people project their expectations onto me, be it the expectation of marriage, motherhood, sexual desire, fragility, or strength. Typhoid is the rejection of your perception and the reclamation of my identity. She is when I take the gloves off and just do me.

Typhoid isn't the partitioned me. She's all of me. All my contradictions, sharp edges, softness, and coldness, my passion, and my rage.

So now, after the fall, the reconstruction, the growth, the understanding, and the forgiveness for not living up to the expectations of others, I don't shine anymore.

I glow.

This story first appeared at BlackGirlNerds.com on January 29, 2016.

I don't see Typhoid Mary as someone with borderline personality disorder. I see her as someone navigating extremely hostile waters while trying to maintain a sense of self, a struggle to which I relate.

— TaLynn Kel, The Reimagining of Self: Why I Love Marvel's Typhoid Mary

Rape Disguised as Romance: Why I Stop Reading Most Romance Novels

Trigger Warning: Rape and Sexual Assault

When I was younger, I used to LOVE romance novels. I'd read at least 4-6 books a month. They shaped many of my ideas around romance, love, sex...I learned a lot from them. So, you can imagine my shame/disgust/horror when I realized these books were romanticizing rape.

Or maybe you can't. Rape is so normalized in society that people don't know what constitutes rape. Is it forced penetration? With what? Does it count if it's just a tongue? Or a finger? What if she says yes, then says no? What if you're naked when she says no? What if you've both been drinking? What if, what if, what if.

It sounds ridiculous, especially once you learn that romance novels are a billion-dollar industry[5] with 84% of its audience being women. One would think that women wouldn't support books about raping women, right? Well, when rape is packaged as romance and discussions around rape in a society centered around protecting men? Then yeah, we get rape books sold as love stories.

I didn't think it was rape at the time. I mean, I'd been conditioned to think that rape was pretty straightforward. If a guy forced you to have sex when you didn't want to, that was rape. But what counted as force? In my mind, they had to pin me down and I would not be able to force them to stop. There would be a layer of violence against me that was a part of it. I was sure I'd have scars, or bruises or something.

---

[5] Romance Writers of America. "Romance Statistics." Web. . 05 Jan. 2017.

But that didn't cover coercion. Or drugs. Or even marriage, where I was under the impression that I can't say no. Because that's the issue, right? That in order for it to be considered rape, I have to explicitly and unequivocally say "no" when there are a crap-ton of non-verbal ways of saying "yes." And as a woman, it is my responsibility to figure out how I am saying "yes" to every guy who shows me the tiniest amount of attention. It is my responsibility. I mean, it's not but that's not what people will have you believe.

It's not something I would learn reading books, watching TV and movies, or listening to the people around me. And let's not forget the romance books that I loved.

I've read books where women are abducted off the street, held captive, drugged, and then raped by the hero, who she later falls in love with and marries, legitimizing everything he'd done to her.

I've read books where the woman was captured, tied up, and sexually assaulted as a form of torture until she is overcome by her arousal and needs to be with the "hero." They later get married and live happily ever after.

There are books where the woman is sold to a slaver, raped, and then marries her "master" because that's the dream, apparently.

How about the books where the male romantic lead threatens physical, emotional, and sexual violence against the female romantic lead...and they, of course, get married and have a bunch of children, because that's logical.

Then there are the books where women are controlled by sex and submissive to men because...oh who cares.

It all comes back to women being treated as property, children, and sex slaves...all at the same damn time, a treatment that supports the perception that somehow women secretly "want it but don't want to admit."

Here is a list of actions that are considered implicit sexual consent:

- Walking alone

- Getting abducted

- Wearing attractive clothing

- Wearing bright colors

- Wearing baggy clothing which creates mystery that must be explored

- Talking to a man

- Drinking alcohol

- Being alone with a man

- Smiling at a man

- Wearing a short skirt

- Kissing a man

- Making eye contact with a man

- Being attractive

- Dating

- Marriage

- Agreeing to go on a date with a man at any time in your life

- Getting drunk

- Falling asleep in the company of a man

- Breathing

Ignorance of implicit consent is not considered to be an excuse. Somehow being sexually assaulted is YOUR fault because you did something that said "yes" even if you never uttered the word. And you can't change your mind because you agreed at some point and that consent is forever.

And that's before we even get into reporting an assault, where all of the above "consent" questions are put on the table and the victim has to somehow prove that none of it was consent.

Did I mention that this is reinforced at every level in American society and is difficult to prove?

So now, when I read romance books, most of which are marketed to and purchased by women, I have to give it the side-eye because what the fuck?

Why are we buying shit that markets the acceptability of rape?

Why are people writing shit that promotes rape?

Why are we promoting and defending rape?

In 2014, California passed the Affirmative Consent Sexual Assault Bill, also known as the "Yes means Yes" law, getting rid of the vagueness around sexual consent. People had issues with the law, claiming that there was gender bias and that it treated all men like rapists, but that begs the question - what exactly makes a sexual encounter rape? And the answer is uncomfortable, even for me.

For most of my life, I considered sexual aggression from men to be normal. As I got older, I tried to mitigate this expectation by only dating men who I knew listened to me and cared what I thought. When I was younger, I didn't think about this and I found myself in situations where sexual attention was forced on me. At the time, I didn't think it was wrong despite knowing that I didn't want it. And, like many women, I felt it was my fault because at some point in the evening I indicated that I was interested and then lost interest. Or I felt like I owed them something for leading them on. And while I didn't want any sexual contact, the normalcy of submitting to something I didn't want with a person I didn't want to do it with was easier to reconcile than rejecting him and running away. And to this day I can't call what happened rape because even though they never asked what I wanted, I never said "no."

I also never said "yes."

So even though I didn't want to do it, I submitted to the social expectation that I believed was a part of romantic relationships. I felt powerless in the situation and was ashamed of it. And even years later, on the other side of that life, I still wrestle with the pain of that time and ask myself if it was rape. I didn't feel physically threatened. I wasn't physically restrained or held captive by anything but my own social expectations. In the sea of what is consent, I don't fit the profile of a rape victim. But I did something I did not want to do, with someone I did not want to do it with and I still struggle with what that means.

The worst part is knowing I'm not alone. When I bring up the issues of rape, so many women tell me a story of this one guy, or this one time where they found themselves submitting to an act that they didn't want. Stories like mine, or stories of partying with someone and waking up unsure if they'd had sex. Or stories of trying to get out of situations where they were interested in getting to know a guy but they felt the expectation of more and just...let it happen. Or stories of women who never indicated anything but he wanted it and was stronger and forced it.

Stories of first dates, boyfriends, husbands, friends, acquaintances. Stories of pain. Stories of unreported rape.

Last year, some guy[6] wrote an article about how he doesn't need sexual consent lessons. He felt they were overkill and that he was smart enough to know what consent is. That same year, Jezebel wrote a story[7] about a reddit thread asking sexual assailants (i.e. rapists) for their side story. The take-away? These men didn't know they were committing rape. They didn't realize they were violating another person, mainly because they didn't see the woman as an individual whose opinion mattered.

Rape is a lot subtler than what they show on TV. It is a form of abuse that can be emotional and physical, gentle and violent, dehumanizing and powerful, coercive and indecisive, subtle and savage. And most of all, shameful. Rape, like everything, is not just one thing, and neither are its victims.

---

[6] Lawlor, George. "Why I don't need consent lessons." 14 Oct. 2015. Web. 05 Jan 2017.

[7] Baker, Katie. "Rapists Explain Themselves on Reddit, and We Should Listen." Jezebel. 27 July 2012. Web. 02 Feb. 2016.

When you grow up reading stories about how commonplace it is for men to talk you into sex, pressure you to have sex, force you to have sex, you think, "well, I guess this is normal. It's what they write about. Why don't I enjoy it like they seem to do in the books, movies, or on TV?"

Now when I read a romance book with a romantic lead who enacts this type of behavior, he's not a romantic lead. He's a rapist. The author is someone who supports rape culture and the abuse of women and the publisher is reinforcing a system that keeps women in danger of sexual violence.

Romance novels have taught me that rape can be packaged and marketed as romance...and is a billion dollar lie.

This story first appeared at BlackGirlNerds.com on February 10, 2016.

...the normalcy of submitting to something I didn't want with a person I didn't want to do it with was easier to reconcile than rejecting him...

— TaLynn Kel, Rape Disguised as Romance: Why I Stop Reading Most Romance Novels

Letting Go

When I decided to attend my first DragonCon, I knew I was going to do Dark Phoenix. At the time, I was going for a traditional look, and I did the best I could do as a fat woman. Back then, you couldn't hop on line and buy custom bodysuits, and even now, there are some serious limitations on thigh-high boots in my size. I ended up making some pseudo boot tops from duct tape and gold fabric. And my "suit" was a burgundy, velour tracksuit onto which I glued a glitter phoenix. I'm fairly positive that the head of my phoenix was turned the wrong way and I left a trail of glitter everywhere I went. Not to mention my $5 wig that was kinda the wrong color. But screw it; it was the best I could do at the time and I let go.

I think back to that time and realize that while it did occur to me that my costume was bad, I really wanted to go to DragonCon in costume. I REALLY wanted to go to dressed as Dark Phoenix. She was a character who spoke to my heart, so I sucked it up, cobbled it together, and went to DCon. While there, we ran into Yaya Han dressed at Lady Deathstrike. She wanted a picture together, which I initially refused because my costume looked so budget compared to hers. She convinced me to take the picture anyway. I let my fear and anxiety of not looking good enough and not having a good enough costume go. To this day, that is one of my cosplay stand-out moments – it wasn't a competition. We were just two fans dressed as characters in the same universe taking a picture.

Because I'm petty, I feel the need to point out that it's easy to be kind when you know you look awesome (which she did), but it was nice to be on the receiving end of that kindness, especially in my bad wig and glitter phoenix, velour track suit. But you know what? I am letting that pettiness go. Mostly. It's a work in progress.

Letting go is a continual process – another thing I've had to come to terms with repeatedly in my life. Most of the time I want to hold on to things until they are perfect, but I have such a strong desire to participate in stuff that my need to participate overrides my desire for perfection. And honestly, that works in my favor. I want to be a part of the madness and in order to do that, I can't get stuck on making things perfect. I need them to be functional and close enough to the target that I can see where I was going.

This has been an interesting experience for me in cosplay because the target is often assumed to be to look as close to the character as possible. That hasn't always been my goal. The first time I did Typhoid Mary, I did my own interpretation of it. The only things even remotely like the character were the red wig, the face painted half white, and the fishnets with ankle boots – in retrospect, that's a lot. But my top was nothing like anything in the comics, nor was the hair style. But I wore it and I loved it.

It was the same with my second interpretation of Dark Phoenix. I remember thinking that I wanted to look like that moment she released her rage – when the light of her energy eclipsed her, and she became a shadow in the glow of her power. So, I had the costume made in black and gold (no more velour track suits and glitter), and I painted my face black, with gold eyes. These days, there are a couple of things I'd do differently, but ultimately, I loved my take on it. I hit my mark. Plenty of people were confused about my interpretation, but that's ok. I hit my target.

In those two instances, I let go of what I thought other people would want to see and I did my own thing. And that's the cool thing about cosplay – you can mix it up however you want. For a long time, I felt like I could only cosplay women or non-white characters. And while those are the ones I gravitate towards, I cosplay whoever I want – man, woman, Black, white, human, alien, god...whatever I feel like. Truth be told, I WANTED to do Black characters, but at the time I had some trouble finding them. That's not the case now – fortunately. That said, I've been pretty focused on Marvel characters, but who knows what the future will bring.

The longer I do this, the more I feel like the quality of my costumes should improve. You know, get closer to perfect. This is an expectation I need to ignore. I admire the people with the dedication and fortitude to be perfect. I really do. There are times when I wish I had the perfect costume, where every seam is straight, every edge is creased, the lines are crisp, the paint job is immaculate, and I manage to incorporate every tiny detail. I mean, who doesn't want to be flawless? But I had to accept several years ago that I'm just not willing to sacrifice the potential fun of the creation and convention experience in order to attain perfection. It just doesn't sound like a good time and the few times when I tried to be perfect were so frustrating and stressful that I felt my joy wither away. Just thinking about it makes me cringe. If everything I did had to be perfect, I'd never leave the house. And with that, I continue the process of letting go and make do with "good enough."

Letting go is more than just saying, "good enough" and putting it out in the world. It's also about listening to yourself. I have found that when I'm concerned about something being perfect, what I'm really worried about is what other people will think or say about it. I am looking for external validation of my efforts and when that happens, it means that I am not doing what I want anymore.

That's the big fear with cosplay – at least for me. The fear that I will compromise myself for attention, when really, that needs to be my lowest priority. I didn't decide to put on a costume because I wanted people to like at me. I mean, it's nice and all, but the real drive was that I wanted to cobble together a costume and wear it.

I am someone who came into cosplay when putting on a costume was good enough for a crapton of attention. I feel the loss as the scene gets more mainstream, and the interest is in the young, white, societally acceptable bodies. The only thing in my favor was my youth, and I'm doing nothing but getting older. I'm not marketable and there is less and less interest in people like me every year. So it's been an interesting journey figuring out how I fit into this scene...figuring out IF I fit into this scene. I asked myself over and over again what I wanted, what I needed, and I built this anxiety about how I could do what I wanted but still be relevant.

Until, finally, I let go.

It doesn't matter if I fit. I'll make my own space. It doesn't matter if people like it. If they do, great. If not, then it wasn't meant for them. It doesn't matter if I'm old, fat, and Black. I belong here for as long as I want to be here.

If there was a piece of advice I could give my younger self...who am I kidding? My younger self got me here and I love who I am now. So, if there's a piece of advice I can give to anyone reading my blog, learn to let go. It's usually not as necessary to hold on to it as you think.

And, as mistakes are how we humans learn, you need to let go enough to learn new shit. I have a number of things on my list that I know I've messed up but next time...next time I'll make it better.

Letting go is more than just saying, "good enough" and putting it out in the world. It's also about listening to yourself.

– TaLynn Kel, Letting Go

Dear Public Health Practitioners

I need you to embrace your flawed humanity in a self-aware way.

You see, I know many of you entered this field to help people. I get that. I mean, that's why I entered the field. I wanted to do work that would actually benefit people in some way instead of convincing them to spend money and make somebody even more rich. That said, I still kind of ended up helping someone else get richer, just indirectly. Damn lobbyists. Damn tangents.

I went into public health because I know from experience that information and support are key to improvement, and I wanted to be in a position to provide that to those who need it.

Now, I admit, my intention wasn't as magnanimous when I went back to grad school. At the time, I was riding the high of losing a bunch of weight and being in some of the best physical condition of my adult life. I felt like I was a walking, talking inspiration and I wanted to go be someone's role model. Arrogant, I know. But I felt like a success story and I wanted to share it.

Then I sat in class with so many arrogant, know better people who were in public health to feed their savior complex or feel authoritative enough to tell other people what to do. I sat through class after class of racist, sizeist, ableist, classist, heteronormative, transphobic bullshit that would consistently send me home hating myself more than usual.

I sat in class learning about health disparities, about all the ways that Black, LGBTQIA, and people with disabilities were failing in health – doctor visits, pregnancy, heart disease, sexually transmitted diseases, cancer, obesity, and general health care. I spent 2 years and thousands of dollars listening to the public health version of the white, able-bodied, supremacist narrative.

And I did not exit grad school unscathed. It beat me down. Then I built myself up with a stronger understanding of how programmed this country, and its education systems are. I wasn't a malleable college student who you could shape to fit your worldview. I grew up living with the socioeconomic factors contributing to your determinants of health pyramid. I was and am those statistics, as is my family, and friends. So while you sat there debating their abstract assumptions of poor health outcomes, I had firsthand experience and a better informed context for it.

What struck me most was everything you didn't say. You didn't talk about systemic oppression. You talked about eating fast "food" instead of fresh vegetables. You didn't talk about entire neighborhoods build on superfund sites, next to oil refineries, and highways - potentially exposing every resident to unknown toxins leeching into the water supply and particulate matter from automobile pollution.

You didn't talk about how the prison industrial complex was just revised slavery and how that financially and socially impacted entire generations. You talked about low income and poor nutrition. You didn't talk about over-policing of Black neighborhoods; you talked about cracks in sidewalks (literally) as you took your white students to predominantly Black populated areas in the city and played your poverty porn monologue.

You didn't talk about white supremacy. You reinforced it. And I came home and cried. I cried as the fat, Black woman who was told she was a burden on the system in every way, simply for existing. I listened to lectures that presented "facts" spun into a convoluted victim blaming. Then I watched as a class of privileged white people bloated from their sense of self-importance and accomplishment moved from the classroom into the public health workforce. People who felt they were better than the people they "helped" because of their hard work and merit, when really it was because their parents, grandparents, and great grandparents had access to public funds, government subsidies, and land grants – wealth building tools that Black people were specifically excluded from receiving.

I watched as they joined the save Africa brigade – feeding like ticks on the idea that they can rescue the brown people of the world with their selflessness.

I listened to self-righteous professors' circle jerk on their textbooks and their research projects, claiming to have solved problems that weren't problems. A twenty-pound weight loss maintained for 2 years is not the key to preventing heart disease, nor does it improve anyone's life long-term in any tangible way. But, you know, fat equals bad.

When I entered grad school, I saw myself going into chronic disease, because I felt like it would be a good fit for me. I like talking to people and hearing their stories. I love problem solving and I know chronic disease – it's a topic I've been drawn to for years. After grad school, I realized that going into chronic disease would be a form of emotional torture. I'd be subjecting myself to bigoted thinking, daily, if not hourly, micro and macroaggressions, in addition to political spin forcefully applied to health topics as the struggle to stay funded is real.

It is safe to say that public health did me the favor of reminding me of the work that needs to be done and showing me that current systems aren't going to address it.

So, public health practitioners, specifically the non-Black public health practitioners, I need you to get your heads out of your asses. You literally ARE the problem. When students sit in class listening to professors shame people for needing to use a motorized scooter in the grocery store, you are the problem.

When students shame people using public transportation and then judge what they are eating and drinking without speaking to them, they are the problem.

When you dictate to people the help they need without asking them what help they need, you are the problem.

When you punish students for not fitting into your narrative, you are the problem.

When you see yourself as the savior of anyone, YOU ARE THE PROBLEM.

And frankly, I need you to save yourself from your arrogance and self-importance. I need you to listen to people. I need you to care about more than your publications and your promotion.

I need you to make a career of actively dismantling white supremacy. Stop making yourself the center of change. Stop making any of this about you. Because it isn't. And when you force it to be about you, you harm the people you intended to "help."

It is safe to say that public health did me the favor of reminding me of the work that needs to be done and showing me that current systems aren't going to address it.

— TaLynn Kel, Dear Public Health Practitioners

Your Approval Is Everything and Nothing

When I was young, like single digits young, I used to dance all of the time. I would go to birthday parties and throw my body around like a discombobulated puppet. And if there was a dance contest, I was first in line to participate. I'd never taken dance classes, never even wanted to, but I loved moving my body and the only guide I needed was the music. When you're a young kid doing freestyle dance, it's cute and funny. Then I crossed the line between "cute" and "know better" where I received different feedback.

Instead of the cheers and encouragement I'd previously received, I heard mockery and scorn. My peers ridiculed me and for the first time I felt ashamed of doing something I loved. And it hurt. Boy, did it hurt. I developed a bit of a complex and stopped dancing.

I had the same experience with costuming. All my life, we'd put on a costume and go out to beg for candy. Then, somewhere around age 11, I was suddenly too old to dress up, a new fact that EVERYONE felt the need to share with me. So, again, I was shamed out of doing something I loved.

This was a trend that would continue. Like to sing? Too bad, you suck. Stop doing it. Like to paint? Too bad, you suck. Give it up. Like to play games? Only kids play games. Stop being so immature. Like to write? Your writing sucks and it's an unsustainable career. Over and over I was informed of what I should and shouldn't do.

After a while that shit got tiring. And I was unhappy. I mean, come on – was my life really supposed to be work, exercise, eat, and sleep? Maybe some dates? Who made these rules cuz they suck!

Occasionally I'd test the water and try out the things I loved. It was usually with a change of environment like college or when I moved to Georgia. I'd dress up, share my writing, dance at a club or party and see what kind of reaction I'd get. Here's the thing, though - as much as I thought I was testing the environment, I was actually testing myself. I didn't realize it at the time, but I couldn't handle the negative response. And it wasn't always negative but that's what I heard and what affected me the most.

It's funny, we are born so malleable, absorbing everything around us before we can realize or understand it. We are imprinted by our families, neighborhoods, and experiences. Nature vs nurture – my nature is to do what I want. I was nurtured to observe and respond to other's reactions. I have a high sensitivity to other people's reactions and had to learn how to work through that.

I know I'm not unique in this experience. I think we all grow up learning how to navigate our environment with minimal damage and obstacles. But imagine growing up in an environment where your interests are accepted and nurtured instead of deterred and discouraged. Imagine being rewarded for speaking your mind instead of being told you're disruptive. Imagine being encouraged to move your body according to your mood and feelings instead of these prescribed steps (I'm looking at YOU Cha-cha Slide).

Over time, I adapted -first by walling off aspects of myself until I could handle feedback, good or bad. I had to learn to trust myself and my judgement. I needed to learn that I'm acceptable as I am...actually more than acceptable. I am awesome and amazing.

I continue to learn how to balance my desire to create with the craving for public acknowledgement and approval. I am the tree in the forest; I make noise regardless of who's there to hear it. I've reached a place in my life where I want people to hear it. I just don't someone hearing it to affect the sound.

While it seems like I may not care what people think about me, it isn't 100% true. What I'm really saying is that I like who I am. That doesn't mean I don't need to learn or keep striving for more. It doesn't mean that I don't hear you or that it doesn't contribute to me feeling good or bad about myself. What it does mean is that I like and accept myself and it's not my problem if you don't.

It's a work in process, just like me.

As children, we learn about the world. As teens, we learn about interacting with other people. As a young adult, we learn about ourselves. And now, I am learning acceptance.

I wonder what I'll learn next.

What it does mean is that I like and accept myself and it's not my problem if you don't.

— TaLynn Kel, Your Approval Is Everything and Nothing

Making Space

When I first started attending DragonCon in 2005, there weren't all these social networks focusing on cosplay. Don't get me wrong, there were tons of people attending and taking pictures and posting them on Flickr, or other, older photo sharing websites, but it was nothing like it is now, where thousands of photos come out each month celebrating cosplay. And back then, it wasn't about "likes" and "followers" and "fans." It was about finding your picture and experiencing what it was like to see how someone else saw you. My friends and I would spend weeks waiting for photo albums to appear so that we could go through the pictures and find ourselves.

Was it vain? Sure was. Am I ashamed of it? Not really. I put a lot of effort into dressing up and at the time, the ONLY pictures I would have were the ones other people took of me. So, yeah, I'd look for myself. I'd also see all the costumes I'd missed during the convention, but that was just a bonus. I was really just in it for me and my friends.

Then cosplay became a thing and you saw cosplay sites popping up all over the internet. Sites with image galleries of their favorite costumes, characters and cosplayers. The convention photography scene changed from people being a fan and loving that someone...anyone dressed up as a character they loved and it became this place where people wanted to see cosplayers who looked as close to their favorite character as possible.

In case you didn't know, the vast majority of those characters have pale skin and fit either a male strength ideal or a female sexy ideal. That is to say, the men are muscular, with trim waists, slim hips and muscular thighs. The women all have hourglass figures, long legs, large, perky breasts, and generally long hair.

Did I mention the pale skin? Most of them have pale skin. And they are slim. Two characteristics I don't have.

So, when people became less interested in the fandom and more interested in seeing their characters in real life, you saw the shift in who had their pictures taken at the conventions. You saw photoshoots pop up looking for canon characters. You saw people having race and body requirements before they'd take your picture. You saw photo galleries showcasing people who fit their ideal of the character, which generated site visits that potentially generated revenue.

In a nutshell, white people sold to white audiences, something that is shoved down our throats at every turn. From movies to religion, we are conditioned to center the white identity in everything we do. Now that people were finding a way to monetize cosplay, white people were put front and center. It's safe to say that my number of photo opportunities hit a steep decline. This community where I'd at one time I'd been sought out now actively marginalized me.

At first I was enraged and resentful. The rejection was so blatant. I'd be standing with friends, talking, and someone would come up and ask for a picture of my friends. The first time you are asked to move out of a photo is shocking, especially when two years prior, they would have taken pictures of both of you without a thought.

Then you'd see people, usually thin, white women, get asked for photo after photo, reinforcing your feeling of otherness in the community that used to celebrate otherness. I told myself it didn't matter, but I felt my attitude changing. I felt myself pulling away to protect myself by saying it didn't matter that nobody wanted my picture, I was there for myself.

For the record, that was a lie. I wanted pictures of me in my costume. I just needed to figure how to make that happen.

I decided to change tracks. I sought out opportunities to be included and started asking photographers to take my picture. That had interestingly negative results. They'd take my picture, but it would happen so fast that I didn't even know if the picture was good. And it was obvious that they were waiting for me to leave so they could grab someone they WANTED to take a picture of. And that picture they took? I'd never see it. I'd go to their pages and it would never get posted. I'd see the photos they took of the people before me, and after me, but none of me.

And it HURT. Oh man, did it hurt. My friends have no idea how much I relied on them to keep me involved in cosplay. They were awesome. They reminded me how much I loved putting the look together. How much I enjoyed the process of trying to make something from nothing. Because as much as I wanted the gorgeous picture, I also wanted to have had a strong hand in bringing that vision to life. Did I mention that I don't sew? Well, I don't. Nor do I measure. I basically look around and figure out if I can build it from the trash and scraps in my house and when I can't, I figure out the easiest way to make it happen without using power tools or killer glue. Or a sewing machine. Or a ruler. I basically use a lot of duct tape and fabric glue. I'm pretty much a hack with a vague plan. Anyway...

I realized that the constant rejection was taking a toll on me and that I needed to recalibrate my expectations and goals if I was going to keep doing this. I had to get real and I had to get messy, but mostly, I had to get honest. And honestly, I was jealous of the attention other people received for wearing a unitard. I was jealous that a Party City costume on a societally approved body held more value than anything I put on my fat, Black body. I was jealous that this felt like Thunderdome and I was always without a weapon. I was jealous and angry that I would never measure up.

So, I stopped trying.

That sounds simple, right? Like I just let everything go and it got better. That is not what happened. I had to forcefully push the considerations of other people out of the situation. I had to really ask myself what I loved about cosplay and conventions and what I hated. I had to re-center the conversation on me - not on the other cosplayers, the photographers, my friends, or anyone else. I needed to figure out what I wanted out of this.

I realized that I wanted stylish and gorgeous pictures of me in my costume. I wanted to take my pictures to the next level. If I could get the money shot, it was all worth it to me. And once that became my goal, that other shit stopped mattering.

If you look at my pictures, you can see the year it happened. In 2011, I took my first picture with Bryan Humphrey[8] in my Blade costume. Bryan is a genius with lighting. That was the first time I'd ever had anyone take the time with me to make sure the lighting was right on a picture and I fell in love. The thing I love most about Bryan is that he takes that time with EVERY cosplayer he photographs. Every. Single. One. After my experiences with other photographers who were clearly trying to get me out of the way, it was so respectful and awesome. Working with him, I felt the same amount of appreciation for my cosplay that I had. He appreciated the people in the costumes and wasn't just trying to be the next big thing. Maintaining that human connection in this hobby is important and when I was treated like an obstacle or a chore instead of a person, I knew that wasn't the photographer for me. It wouldn't be until very recently that I would have any must-see photographers on my roster.

---

[8] Humphrey, Bryan. Blade. 2011, Photograph. Atlanta, Georgia. Bryan Humphrey. Web. 04 Feb. 2016.

The biggest thing I learned through all this is that doing this stuff is about me. It's about doing something I enjoy for as long as it's fun. Once I focused on myself, I became better at navigating the social pitfalls that made me feel bad about myself. I won't say I stopped comparing, but I got better about it and about feeling "othered" in cosplay. People are going to think what they want and seek what they want, but I don't need to internalize their biases anymore.

These days, I'm focused on creating a space for myself.

I stopped trying to get people to care about me and focused on doing my own thing. Anybody can start a blog or create a website and make their own space. It's a bit of work, but it feels right to me. And it's giving me the opportunity to build community and share space with others with whom I share interests. Right now, my space is small and it will probably stay small, but it's something I created and reflects who I am.

I'm no longer waiting for people to figure out if they want to make space for me. I make a space for myself.

I had to re-center the conversation on me - not on the other cosplayers, the photographers, my friends, or anyone else. I needed to figure out what I wanted out of this.

– TaLynn Kel, Making Space

Living Online

I've been a blogger off and on for 11-years. I never did it with the intent to become well-known. I write because it's what I do, whether or not anyone reads it. While I am aware that there are people who make a living doing this, it's not really the norm, nor is it necessarily my goal.

I tend to treat my blog as an online journal, one that I know others will read. Initially, I tried to pretend that it was a real journal. I didn't name any names, but if you knew me in real life, you could figure out who I was talking about online. Needless to say, that had some real-life ramifications. I damaged some friendships and even lost a job, which was more than enough collateral damage for me to rethink what I was doing. That was more than 10 years ago, when hardly anyone was watching. Now, potential employers try to make you reveal your Facebook password so that they can monitor your social media account. That I chose to re-enter this world knowing the kind of scrutiny and harassment I could face says something about my ability to determine acceptable risk and it's not good.

So, in November 2015 I decided to start a new blog. I'm learning the new online landscape as I go, so I'm fucking up a bit, which I'm okay with doing right now. I even reached out and offered to do some guest blogging on other sites in an effort to boost my visibility and web traffic. That comes with some pluses and minuses. My first blog, "The Reimagining of Self: Why I Love Marvel's Typhoid Mary[9]" did pretty well. I received a lot of positive feedback for it and for the first time in a long time, I felt as though my writing had been legitimized. Then I got scared. What if I wrote something that no one cared

---

[9] Kel, TaLynn. "The Reimagining of Self: Why I Love Marvel's Typhoid Mary." Black Girl Nerds, 29 Jan. 2016. Web. 30 Dec. 2016.

about? What if people hated it? What if it just straight up sucked?

I kept writing for my personal blog because it's almost my practice space where I can write about whatever the hell I want and no one cares. The online journal, remember? I have a ton of half-finished essays waiting on me to get over my fear and finish them and post them. That didn't solve the problem of what to submit next. I opted to do a kind of safe, cosplay piece for The Anime Complexium website – "Types of Cosplay Photographers." I'd originally posted this list on my site last year.

The article I chose, "Rape Disguised as Romance: Why I Stopped Reading Most Romance Novels[10]" was one I hesitated to post on my personal site. It was intensely personal and discussed a topic that I was still learning to manage – coercive sex, i.e. rape. I decided to ground the personal narrative in a societally accepted medium – romance books. I chose this mainly because I grew up reading them and learned a lot of my romantic expectations from them. Not to mention, they very accurately demonstrate the disconnect between consensual sex and coercive sex, as many of the male leads actively kidnap, lie, cheat, steal, and force themselves onto the female lead, and it's intended to be titillating and sexy. There are many mass market romance books on the shelves with these "dominant" male leads who are, in fact, rapists. There are authors I used to buy religiously that I eventually walked away from because they wrote sexual encounters that I considered rape, and these depictions blur the line for people to know what's acceptable and what's not.

I wrote about my confusion about what's acceptable in a sexual encounter and what isn't. I wrote about how I'd read things that led me to believe that I'd misinterpreted the

---

[10] Kel, TaLynn. "Rape Disguised as Romance: Why I Stop Reading Most Romance Novels." Black Girl Nerds, 10 Feb. 2016. Web. 30 Dec. 2016.

situation and that to this day I continue to struggle to define it for myself. I was scared to post it because of what I thought it said about me, but then I decided to submit it and see what response I would receive.

I was genuinely surprised that the site planned to publish the essay – flattered, but surprised. So when they told me that it was going out yesterday, I prepared myself for the response, if any.

That day was just the day for me to be surprised because the response was not to the pervasiveness of rape culture. It wasn't to the question of how we define rape. It wasn't about people's ability to define it for themselves.

The response was that I was attacking the romance genre and that I was trying to paint all romance books as rape stories.

Let me say that again, because I'm still fucked up on this one.

- I shared my experience with coercive sex.

- I shared my inability to reconcile it with what I understand sex to be now.

- I grounded my perspective in the muddled depictions of "consensual" sex I found in romance novels, depictions that we also see in movies, on TV, and hear about pretty regularly.

- I acknowledge that our societal norm is to continue to muddle the concept of consensual sex.

- I discuss how California is working to clarify it.

Yet the take away for many readers was that I was attacking the romance genre and saying all romance books are pro rape.

So, yeah, I was surprised by this shit. Especially when people couldn't say that I was wrong – they told me I was reading the "wrong" books or that they'd never encountered any rape-promoting romance novels, but no one could say that these books didn't exist.

In fact, many of the people who criticized the article and me didn't even read the article or if they did, they made up shit that I didn't say. For anyone that's interested, I captured the tweets responding to the article[11] so that you can read through them. Form your own opinions about the response.

In response to the backlash, I felt pressured into writing an addendum adding some context to my essay. Ironic, right? In response to an essay about coercion, I felt coerced into writing something I didn't feel was necessary to write. In the addendum, I stand by my essay. I still stand by it. I'm just sad that so many people missed the point in a knee-jerk response to what they felt was an attack on their literary preferences – to which I feel compelled to say again – IT WASN'T.

Today the website published a rebuttal to my essay. I was going to read it, but in the interest of self-care, I'm going to let it go. If there is one thing I've learned in my years of writing, it's that you can't control how other people respond to it. People are going to run the information through their personal filter and walk away with whatever message that comes through the sieve and it's not my responsibility to change that.

All I can do is trust myself. I shared my experience and put myself out there. If you love it, great. If you don't, great. Either way I'll be fine. What I am not going to do is tie myself up in knots trying to make you feel good about my experience and fuck you if you try to make me. If you want to chat, I'm

---

[11] Kel, TaLynn. "So I Wrote About Rape and Romance Novels…" Storify, 10 Feb. 2016. Web. 05 Jan. 2017.

available on Facebook or email. If you want to try to make me feel bad, fuck off. I'm making my space. If you don't like it, go make your own.

Self-Care

I talked about self-care and that is an important part of living in the information age. Here are some of the things I do to manage this instant gratification, often overwhelming, digital life.

1. Don't allow comments on your blog (If you need to share something, email me. This space is for my thoughts, not yours).

2. Log off of social media.

3. Turn off the phone.

4. Walk away from the computer.

5. Leave the house.

6. Go for a walk.

7. Talk to people.

8. Spend time with offline friends.

9. Eat (sometimes I accidentally skip meals).

10. Talk to my therapist (Yep, I have one and she rocks).

11. Play with animals (the nice ones, unlike that asshole cat that sits in our driveway but won't let us pet him).

12. Take a hot bath.

13. Read books that don't trigger you.

14. Play video games.

15. Hit a punching bag (a real one, not a convenient person).

16. Write (which is what this blog is – me pushing out the poison of other people's bullshit).

17. Dance (because dancing is the best thing EVER).

You don't have to do all these in the same day, but you know, use as needed. Just remember to take care of you.

If there is one thing I've learned in my years of writing, it's that you can't control how other people respond to it. People are going to run the information through their personal filter and walk away with whatever message that comes through the sieve and it's not my responsibility to change that.

— TaLynn Kel, Living Online

Single for Life

For a long time, I thought something was wrong with me because I'd never been in love. In fact, the first time I fell in love I was 28 years old and it was a hard fall. I'd fallen for a guy who treated me like his girlfriend but didn't believe in defining relationships. He took me on dates, introduced me to his friends, and taught me what it was to hate someone for loving them. He told me he didn't want to see me anymore over instant messenger while I was at work. I responded by shutting down my computer, leaving work, and going to his apartment where I knocked on his door until he opened it. I'm not quite sure what we talked about, but I walked away with the understanding that we were still sleeping together, even if we weren't "together." So, basically, nothing changed until the rage set in. It was all downhill from there.

Less than a year later I was seeing someone who I loved spending time with, but found out he was sleeping with another woman and lying to both of us about it. The funny part was that I never wanted to be exclusive, but went along with it because he said he wanted it. Then he cheated. I didn't even care enough to get angry. I'm actually still cool with him today.

A year later I was seeing someone who actively pursued me. We had a ton in common and he actually asked me out on a date, a rarity in my experience. He wanted to have sex pretty early in the association, and I warned him that sex makes me disrespect men so we should wait. He didn't care, so when the relationship evolved into booty calls, he struggled with it. Not because he wanted more, but because he didn't know how to deal with a woman who didn't want more. Eventually, he told me that I wanted too much and he had to walk away. But he wanted to be friends because I was fun.

side eye

That was the progression to me deciding to be permanently single. I was over people trying to force me to play games I had no interest in playing. I'm a very forthright person. I tell you where you stand with me. If you piss me off, I tell you. If you make me happy, I tell you. I do not play poker because I lack the ability to mask my emotions and honestly, while that is a skill that would help in the office, it's not one I want to develop in my personal life.

After the pain of rejection and all that other nonsense, I decided that I didn't want to be in a romantic relationship. Like, at all. I couldn't make sense of it. People constantly lied, expected me to pretend to be something I wasn't, and actively tried to compensate for the lies they assumed I would tell.

What the hell was that?

Even now, I still trip over that realization — that my dates expected me to lie to them and they were internally changing my answers to what they thought I really meant.

Can you talk about something doomed to fail? If this is modern dating, there is no wonder it fails so spectacularly.

And I used to argue about it. The number of times I'd have to tell my date to listen to what I said and not assume they knew what the fuck I meant was staggering. While I am not a true introvert, I do keep to myself quite a bit, mainly because I can't deal with the bullshit social rules that are supposed to dictate my life. Dating and trying to meet new people would thrust me into the middle of a social dance to which I never learned the steps. I was aware the steps existed, but I thought they were bullshit, so I opted not to dance. Occasionally, I'd try dating again, but I eventually realized that it wasn't really for me.

And while I'd decided to stop pursuing dating, I did make one concession. If someone asked me out on a legitimate, no bullshit date, I would go. That meant they couldn't invite me to their place to watch a movie. They couldn't suggest that we "hang out." They had to lay it out there and actually declare interest in dating. Otherwise, fuck 'em. I'd been down the road of asking men out. They treated me like I was disposable when I approached them. Or they were intimidated that I didn't "let them" ask first. Such ridiculous rules.

So, for two years, no one asked me out. That is not to say I wasn't invited to chill; I was. But that wasn't a date so that person wasn't datable. And I was completely upfront about this. I told people that all they had to do was ask me out and I'd say yes. Nobody did and it was actually a relief. I felt free to live my life however I wanted. I dressed however I felt. I participated in whatever I wanted. I gave zero fucks about what anyone thought about my hobbies or choices. I didn't care if people thought I was datable.

I hadn't realized how much of my life had been dictated by my "datability" until I stopped worrying about how my choices would be perceived. It was liberating and amazing. I became friends with my exes, which is all we should have been from the start. And I realized how many of my interactions with men were funneled into sexual or romantic relationships, unnecessarily. The sex was only in the story because that's what men and women did together. Unless they were related...sometimes.

I realized the many ways people try to put you in a box, especially when it comes to male/female relationships. Even now, years later I feel like I am in this constant battle to define myself and my friendships instead of letting others define them for me. It's fucked up that in order to embrace and love myself, I had to tell the world that I didn't care if it loved me. I was going to love myself.

And it is with this attitude that I now navigate the world. And don't get me wrong, the walls of the box spring up with every decision that I make. Like when I met my current partner — suddenly there were rules about who I could hang out with, or whether I cut my hair, and what costumes I wore. Except fuck that. I do what I want and anyone who wanted to be with me needed to understand that. I come first. It is, actually, all about me.

And it's working. My partner and I have an understanding about my independence, my autonomy, and that he has no say over what I do, but we can talk about it. We make the "rules" about what's acceptable in our relationship, and I ALWAYS prioritize my needs during these conversations. The "single for life" didn't stick because I met someone who didn't try to make me fit into some ideal girlfriend/lover/spouse. I am me and I handle my shit and he handles his shit and together, we handle our shit. And they are not all the same thing.

So when people tell me I'm selfish...fuck 'em.

When people tell me I'm not being a good partner...fuck them, too.

Good partners are not ones who suppress themselves and their needs to accommodate someone else. Those are liars. Good partners are people who are honest with themselves and others about their needs and wants. They work with their partners to meet them. Good partners take care of themselves and don't make decisions that build up resentment, or, when they do make those decisions, they check in with themselves and try to honestly and openly rectify it.

Good partners tell the truth and practice self-care. Bad partners lie and pretend everything is fine.

Part of the reason I'm thinking about this is because I have some friends re-entering the dating scene. I'm not worried for them. They are smart and capable people. I just want them to put themselves first. This is not an attitude promoted among women, but it needs to be. We are important and deserve to come first in our lives. You matter; you are the most important person in your relationship. You are your own best champion so when you make decisions, when you make choices, don't think of the other person. Think of what you need and want FIRST. It's not selfish, it's protective. This is your life and it's all about YOU.

This is how I navigate my relationship with my partner. I also encourage him to put himself first. If he chooses not to, I work with it, but he decides for himself how he wants to operate in our relationship and we find our common ground. Our contentment in the relationship is high and our resentment is low, which I am certain is due to the space we give each other to be ourselves. Our contentment fluctuates, because life and all, but we work hard to support each other without getting in the way.

If being single means I put myself first, then yeah, I'm single for life. Even married, I work through decisions as though I only need to worry about myself, and once I know how I really feel, I take my partner into consideration. My marriage doesn't come first. I come first. It's the only way to be sure that I am respecting my needs.

Call it selfish if you want - I can live with that. What I can't live with is slowly sacrificing myself for the comfort of others. I love myself too much for that nonsense.

Good partners tell the truth and practice self-care. Bad partners lie and pretend everything is fine.

– TaLynn Kel, Single for Life

Othering the Self: Learning to Recognize My Anti-Blackness

When I was in high school, we were required to meet with our guidance counselor to discuss what colleges we wanted to apply to. I remember my counselor, after looking at my list, asking me if I'd considered any historically Black colleges and universities (HBCUs). I'd chosen schools with widely accepted, excellent reputations, so his question threw me. In fact, his question offended me. I remember wondering if he thought I wasn't good enough to get into the schools on my list and if he asked white students the same question. And that thought is an example of the pervasiveness of white supremacy.

Let's take a moment to unpack that because there are a lot of assumptions in my reaction to the counselor.

Assumption 1: That HBCUs were not academically equal to the colleges on my list. In all fairness, many of the schools on my list were ivy league, or one tier below. But who ranked these schools? What standard was used? I was using a list developed by people who may not understand the value of an HBCU, specifically the self-esteem and social value one could gain there.

Assumption 2: That the system ranking the schools was trustworthy. These days, the mechanisms behind why some things are considered superior to others is a lot more transparent than in the past, so we understand that these rankings have more to do with who manipulates the criteria rather than the actual worth of the school for students.

Assumption 3: That asking me to consider an HBCU meant he thought I wasn't good enough to attend a non-HBCU. Not only didn't I meet his approval, but I wouldn't meet the approval of these historically white colleges and universities.

My response to him was something along the lines of, "Do we live in a historically Black country? Am I going to work in a historically Black company? Or am I going to be surrounded by white people all the time so I may as well get used to functioning in that world?" Needless to say, the conversation became a lot less productive.

When I look back, a part of me is sad at the anger and defensiveness I felt at the question. I kind of wish I'd looked into HBCUs more, but at the time, I didn't think they would prepare me to live in white culture. And I couldn't fathom a world where I wouldn't live, if not in then side by side, with white culture. But maybe attending an HBCU would have instilled me with the confidence I needed to understand and refute the bullshit of white supremacy earlier in my life. Or maybe I'd be in the same place I am now. Who knows?

What I do know is that that was an example of my belief that Black owned, Black controlled environments were inferior to white establishment. It's a belief I struggle with now, and, unfortunately, I'm not alone in that belief.

We are living in an amazing and fucked up time. That's not saying that the past 500 years have been great for Black people in America. It hasn't. But compared to when I was growing up, we talk openly about racism in a lot more spaces than I've ever seen. I grew up knowing I could only talk about racism with other Black people, mainly because I was living, playing and learning alongside openly racist white people and talking about racism was dangerous. When white kids told racist jokes in school, or called me the N-word, I didn't have the support of teachers when I reported them. When I was excluded from activities by the white kids, I felt ashamed. When I was picked on and called racist names, it wasn't because they were racist – somehow I'd done something to provoke them. Sometimes my skin provoked them; imagine how provoked they'd be if I'd actually confronted their racism? Yet, I was forced to play with these ugly humans who were repeating what they learned from their parents, because integration and diversity and all that.

I silently and resentfully endured teachers picking on me, challenging me, questioning my ability. I learned through a myriad of ways that I was different and would receive different treatment and different punishments than the white kids. And as I learned more, I started to understand that the reason for that difference in treatment was because of something superficial and out of my control. And I learned that for me to succeed, I'd need white approval.

And white approval is ridiculous and terrible. It's arbitrary and conditional. And overall, it's degrading. Many of my authority figures outside my home were white people. People who controlled how I was perceived and therefore, controlled what I learned and was exposed to. Year after year I'd meet a teacher, learn what their assumptions were about me, and learn how to meet their expectations so that I could advance. I'd experience their biases and prejudices in the classroom without context and absorb them into a learned pattern of behavior. The majority of my classes were white, as well as the faculty, so I learned to navigate those spaces, with their invisible land mines, as best I could.

Now, to be fair, I was a smart and inquisitive kid who talked to adults as if they were my peers. I also got bored easily. Unfortunately, this was often seen as insolence, or a behavioral problem and punished. I spent many recesses inside being punished for some classroom infraction, and studies have shown that Black students are often punished more often and more severely[12] for certain behaviors than white students. We are held to a standard of behavior that is higher than our non-Black peers and childish behavior is perceived as an inherent racial defect, not just me being a bored kid.

As I got older, the way to please white people changed. I learned to avoid talking about racism, slavery and anything pro-Black because I'd be socially punished for it. Pushing back on someone's racist comment made me the problem. I was being too sensitive. I didn't know how to take a joke. People would say fucked up shit about Black people then turn to me and say, "But you're different," and I was supposed to be proud of that. My defense was often silence. But it was also isolation. I didn't consider these people to be my friends, because when I did, I got hurt.

---

[12] Moser, Laura. "Schools in the South Suspend and Expel Black Students Way More Than White Ones." Slate 25 Aug. 2015. Web. 20 Feb. 2016.

It was clear that the less I associated with other Black students, the more I was approved by my white peers. I never really boarded that train, but that doesn't mean that I didn't visit the station. I started to internalize the thoughts and actions sanctioned by the white people around me. By the time I hit college — my predominately white, ivy league school — I was surrounded by a lot of Black people who were "not like those other Black people." Interestingly, we simultaneously gravitated toward one another while rejecting each other. So many conversations about how we felt more comfortable together but didn't want to pretend to be friends with each other because we're all Black. Or how we didn't want to be associated with the local residents, who were predominately Black and worked for the school.

And it was in this environment that my belief in my superiority to those "other" Black people was reinforced. This was where I learned how to "other[13,14]" those who looked like me. The line between me and them was so pronounced that I could clearly articulate a difference. I was educated and trying to make something of myself. I was exemplary.

At the same time, I rejected the elitism of my college peers. I often left campus and hung out in town. I went to local bars, moved off campus, got a job in the mall. I was still "different," but I wasn't like those elitist assholes who thought they were better than other Black people. I was better than them, too.

---

[13] Hooks, bell. "Eating the Other: Desire and Resistance." 1992. Web. 21 Feb. 2016.

[14] Zevallos, Zuleyka. "What is Otherness?" The Other Sociologist, 14 Oct. 2011 Web. 21 Feb. 2016.

But that othering never stuck for me. On some level, I was always aware that I was one confrontation away from having my "good Black person" status revoked. I've sat through meetings sorting through resumes and watching the team mock people's names for being too "different." I've participated. I've sat in silence when illness was inexplicably tied to race and didn't challenge it out of worry for repercussions. I've made disparaging comments about predominantly Black parts of town without considering the things contributing to that perspective. And I knew it was wrong.

I'm not sure what finally raised my awareness and consciousness enough to make me speak more openly about these things. I think it's the shift in the public conversation. I feel slightly safer expressing these thoughts and exercising the empathy I feel for people experiencing a reality that's different from my own. Also, I was raised by parents who believed in helping others and taught me about meeting people where they are in life rather than imposing my values onto them. They reminded me of my privilege (we called it *luck* and *fortune*) and that many people didn't have access to the opportunities I had. So, even though I spouted ignorance about Black people needing to do better and get their shit right, another part of me learned why they needed to in the first place. That part of me started paying attention to inequality. I started learning about the systems in place that created this environment — and I started trying to figure out how I could help.

So, what did I do?

The first thing I needed to realize is that I live in a toxic environment that tells me that, as a Black person, I am not important. It is crucial that to refute this lie. I cannot believe what popular culture tells me about Black people - that we do not contribute to society in any meaningful or positive way. It's not true. Regardless of what role we play, popular culture finds a way to malign and belittle it. Black athletes are "thugs." Affirmative action is perceived as a way of advancing unqualified Black candidates and pushing out qualified white candidates from universities and jobs. HBCUs are perceived as less, despite needing to meet the same standards as other accredited universities and colleges. They are ranked on a separate scale than the national college ranking list, implying that somehow they are incomparable to the majority of U.S. colleges and universities. Whether that's a good thing or a bad thing is at your discretion, but when applying for jobs in a mostly white workforce, I have no illusions about how it will be perceived.

Other lies they tell: Black neighborhoods are "sketchy" — dirty, dangerous, bastions of crime. Black hair is ugly. Black hair care is dirty. Black features are ugly. Black actors aren't as capable as white actors, so they can't be cast. Movies with all Black casts aren't just movies, they are "Black movies" so that white people know it's not for them. And if Black people accomplish interesting or fun things, they are quickly appropriated by popular culture and credit is given to the white people who copied it.

Which brings me to the second thing I needed to do: *stop seeking white approval*. I am constantly exposed to a media campaign telling me that I am less. That isn't going to change. I am told that I am not enough. This will not change. I am told that I am less than nothing, through police violence, mass media and daily interactions. If you have managed to carve out a self-sufficient life in the midst of this, you are amazing because the psychological battlefield that is being Black in America is brutal. And deadly. Just ask the many Black women[15] and Black men[16] killed by police. Look at the cities experiencing a constant terror campaign[17] against their daily lives. We do not need the approval of these people through their awards or support of our work. The support these people offer is contingent upon upholding white supremacist ideology. Just ask Beyoncé[18].

---

[15] Abbey-Lambertz, Kate. "These 15 Black Women Were Killed During Police Encounters. Their Lives Matter, Too." Huffington Post, 13 Feb. 2015. Web. 1 Feb 2016.

[16] Swaine, Jon; Laughland, Oliver; Lartey; James; McCarthy, Ciara. "Young Black Men Killed by U.S. Police at Highest Rate in Year of 1,134 Deaths." Alternet 02 Jan. 2016. Web. 21 Feb. 2016.

[17] Berman, Mark; Lowery, Wesley. "The 12 key highlights from the DOJ's scathing Ferguson report." The Washington Post 04 March 2015. Web. 21 Feb. 2016.

[18] Boggioni, Tom. "New York City police union threatens to join Miami cops in Beyoncé boycott: 'Stop portraying us as bad guys'." Rawstory, 19 Feb. 2016. Web. 21 Feb. 2016.

Being told I'm not like those "other Black people" or "regular Black people" is racist. It is a way to justify why they aren't discriminating against me like they would other Black people. It is a form of denial used to separate Black people they like from the ones they can act against. It upholds the idea that overall, Black people deserved to be treated as less, but I am the exception to that rule. If you find yourself generalizing about Black people, really think about that shit. Think about what you are saying and think about why you would choose to promote that message. Why is that negative talk about people who look like you the message you want to share?

Modern day racism is subtle. It sounds like progress when really it's just the same old racism in a less obvious package. Learn the language. Recognize when you use it. I'm working to find the strings that manipulate me so I can cut them and set myself free.

I don't deserve to think like a slave. No one does.

This story first appeared at BlackGirlNerds.com on March 2, 2016

.

And I learned that for me to succeed, I'd need white approval. And white approval is ridiculous and terrible. It's arbitrary and conditional. And overall, it's degrading.

– TaLynn Kel, Othering the Self: Learning to Recognize My Anti-Blackness

Let's Talk Racism in Cosplay

Racism is prejudice plus power. What that means is that everyone is prejudiced, but not everyone has power. In America, white people have power because they create, control, provide access to the spaces where people are seen, and they create the rules and penalties that limit or deny people access to those spaces based on race. We see racism at the industry level and the individual level in cosplay[19] and it affects everyone, but only certain people negatively. That would be Black people and people of color (POCs).

Industry level racism is the current playing field at conventions. Conventions cater to popular fandoms, and popular fandoms tend to be "industry" Here are some ways that racism exists in the comic industry:

1. **Who is telling the story**

    There is a common misconception that white people should be the only storytellers. That they have the ability to discuss nuanced ideas and beliefs shared by cultures with which they have had little experience. It assumes that Black people and other POC are not capable of telling their own stories and erases them from there narratives, also known as whitewashing.

---

[19] Ortiz, E. "The Face of Cosplay: Racism & Cosplayers of Color." 28 Feb. 2012. Web. 04 March. 2016.

2. What stories get told

This is the classic "gatekeeper" issue. Who decides what stories should be told? Who decides what stories should be funded? Who decides where the stories should be shown? When you live in a society that tells you that your stories aren't worth hearing or aren't relatable enough, they aren't shared. This leads to a lack of representation.

3. Character options

If Black stories aren't relatable, are Black protagonists? Anyone Black interested in cosplay quickly learns that that are not a large number of Black popular characters available. In many instances, you'll find more blue or green characters than Black ones. For a list of many Black heroes and villains, check out World of Black Heroes[20]. It's not just Marvel and DC.

---

[20] World of Black Heroes. Web. 4 March 2016.

This industry level racism directly feeds into the cosplay culture by setting the expectations of fans and character representation. People like to stay true to the source material. If all the source material is comprised of a certain body type, gender, skin color, physical capability, etc., it limits who fans expect or want to see. This results in excluding people who don't' embody that expectation[21]. Fans feel justified excluding these people because they are "respecting" the creator with their loyalty to her/his work. It also promotes the idea that by not embodying that work is actually degrading the work in some way. So, my brown skin and fat body in a Dark Phoenix cosplay is somehow disrespectful to the artist because I'm not a good representation of the character. Here are some examples of environmental, individual level racism experienced by Black cosplayers:

1. "Oh, you're the Black *insert character name here*

   Um, no. I'm just the character. Not the Black version. Just the character. Thanks.

2. "This shoot is for canon characters only."

   This response excludes people who don't "look the part" from weight, height, ability to stand without aid, hair type...you name it. But, if you have brown skin, you know you're out.

3. "We need a *insert name of Black character here* - Can you be her/him for us?"

   People will ask you to cosplay Black characters to complete their team. This may be the only time you'll

---

[21] Eddy, Max. "Cosplayers Speak Out on Racism in the Fandom." 13 Oct. 2013. Web. 04 March 2016.

be invited to a photoshoot with white people. People will also assume that you are only interested in costuming Black characters.

4. "Your costume would be PERFECT if your skin was lighter."

    Yes, people say this. It's a horrible thing to say and these folks should lose speaking privileges.

And as painful and frustrating as those experiences are, they don't quite hit the fuckery that is interpersonal racism that happens in mixed-race cosplay groups. This shit is super annoying because the groups are supposed to be a safe space where we can let our geek flag fly free, yet there inevitably is some racist shit that will go down, like a post condoning blackface or some outrage about a Black person being cast as a character who's been white in the comics. I've personally experienced this in online groups that I had to leave, because fuck that noise. It's exhausting.

That leaves the mixed-race cosplayers who you know socially.

How much racism you experience will depend on how often and how closely you associate with white cosplayers. It increases exponentially because each person is a wild card – you won't know how racist they are until it happens and you see how they respond to it. I cannot count the number of times I've been blindsided by racism in this way. It's not the strangers who surprise you. It's the people who invite you into their homes and indicate a level of trust and respect that gets nullified by a simple conversation. Here are a LOT of examples[22] of racism I've experienced:

---

[22] Nigatu, Heben. "21 Racial Microaggressions You Hear On A Daily Basis." BuzzFeed, 09 Dec. 2013. Web. 04 March 2016.

- Being asked "if all Black people *insert mildly disapproved action*"

- Being asked "why do Black people *insert strongly disapproved action*"

- Asking you for the "Black perspective" like that's a real thing

- Asking you how Black people do something, cuz we all do everything the same

- Casually defend other people's racism and accuse YOU of being racist [23]for pointing it out

- Calling you sensitive for calling out their fuckery

- Interracial couples that make denigrating jokes about their race and allow their white partners to do the same

- Point out that you're Black, as if nobody can tell. They will do it in situations where it doesn't matter at all

- Challenging your Blackness when you don't conform to their stereotypes

- Asking you shitty, ridiculous questions as they attempt to shame you into being what they expect

- Exotifying your Blackness - they will find ways to make things seem "Blacker." For example, they'll try to use

---

[23] Utt, Jamie. "'That's Racist Against White People!' A Discussion on Power and Privilege." 20 Aug. 2013. Web. 04 March 2016.

African American Vernacular English (AAVE) to sound "Black" and thinks this somehow makes them cooler

- They will actively seek a "Black card" i.e. validation that they are accepted by Black people. Like that's some kind of universal thing

- There will always be an unspoken expectation of violence from you. When you get really angry, they will be afraid

- They will blame victims of racial violence for their murders

- They will find every reason other than race for the racist shit that happens to you

- They will try to make you validate their racism by denying it. They will try to get you to lie because being thought racist hurt their feelings. They will try to make you console them for being racist

- And if they are actually honest about the reality of racism, they will demand that you educate them on what racism is and help them get better. And when you refuse to do the work for them, they'll blame you for the problem

I am constantly amazed by the mental gymnastics white people will perform to avoid the truth about themselves.

This is the **MOST** consolation you need to give to ANY white person:

American society is 100% racist and has been since before it became "America". Racism is a part of EVERYTHING this country does and produces. White denial is the inability and in many cases refusal to see it. The inability is somewhat understandable, it's all they've ever known. But once they see it, continuing to ignore it makes them a willing participant. They might be a casual racist, but still racist. When they actively deny it, they are actively oppressing people. They are an oppressor.

They also need to understand that the word "racist" is an adjective, like tall, short, pretty, ugly. Disliking the definition doesn't make it less true and it doesn't describe everything about that person. But that racism is a part of them and everything they do and they need to do better.

Racism is such a part of American culture that even those being oppressed will support white supremacy and racist ideology. I've done it. It's hard to shake off everything we've been taught to believe about ourselves and recognize the anti-Blackness in our words and actions. But know, when we don't speak up in the face of oppression, when we don't push back, we are supporting it. And when we deny racism, we are feeding it.

For the record, I don't judge Black people harshly for not pushing back. If there is one thing we've learned is that it is DANGEROUS for us to speak up. It can impact our livelihood and put our lives at risk. It is not always safe to be who you are and that is a shitty way to have to live. So I get it. I do it, too and it sucks. Now, Black people who actively attack other Black people for pointing out racist shit, and who work to undermine my experience? Yeah, fuck y'all. We're gonna have a talk about that shit because something is wrong with you and I'm tired of being part of some bullshit that I know is wrong.

The thing is, these systems, these relationships, these individual acts are tools used to strip Black people of their power. They are used to undermine our self-worth, our self-respect, and the worth and respect we have for people who look like us. And it works, even when we don't realize it. Even when we don't want it to work, it does. Hell, it's working now.

I can't tell you how to manage yourself in these situations. Each one is unique to the individuals participating. While I'd love to tell my boss that she/he is being a manipulative bigot, it's not always realistic. I can't always walk out when my team is making decisions based on old information and white supremacist rhetoric. But I can try to discuss WHY this isn't taking racism into consideration.

If I'm in a bar or restaurant and someone is being racist, I have to assess the situation. If I'm being ignored by a server, I call attention to it. If I'm overhearing an offensive conversation, I will probably just leave. Confronting strangers is hard and potentially life threatening. I don't recommend it.

The one area I have any illusion of control is my personal relationships. I don't remain friends with people who actively try to project their racist assumptions onto me. I don't hang with people who try to capitalize on my Blackness. I don't allow people to use me as social currency and I sure as hell don't co-sign on people's racist beliefs. People who expect this of me are not my friends.

You have that power in your relationships too. Does that mean that you may lose some friendships? Well, if they are trying to silence you and ignore or disregard your experiences, they kinda aren't your friends already. Casual cosplay friends fall into that category.

You have the power to control your personal space and protect yourself from racism. Wield it.

I got your back.

NOTE: Geeks seem to love that Cards Against Humanity game. Avoid that shit like a klan rally. That game is shitty and will cause some issues. Or it'll let you know who your friends aren't, which may be a good thing. I still don't recommend it.

If all the source material is comprised of a certain body type, gender, skin color, physical capability, etc., it limits who fans expect or want to see. This results in excluding people who don't' embody that expectation.

– TaLynn Kel, Let's Talk Racism in Cosplay

My Cosplay is Intersectional

Fat

Let's start by acknowledging the elephant in the room and no, that's not me because I'm not a damn elephant. What I am is fat. I've been varying degrees of fat since middle school. I've experienced the shame, the stigma, the low self-esteem, the insults, and the invisibility, the disordered eating, the doctor fuckery, and the assumptions of poor health that come with being fat. I've also learned that while my fat shapes my experiences, I am not limited by it. The only limits I have are the ones people try to enact upon me and fortunately, I've had the support I needed to deal with those folks...mostly.

Fat Black Woman

It is impossible to talk to talk about my fat experiences without discussing race and gender, because all of these work together to create my reality. I am a Black woman who is fat. These three identifiers are used to keep me in a certain space, usually an invisible, underachiever space. For much of my life, I didn't understand that.

Being gendered as female means being sexualized without your consent[24]. It also means being coerced through advertising and societal "norms"[25] into sexualizing yourself before you[26] even know what that means. Being female means learning that you will not be respected as much as males, even

---

[24] Tatum, Erin. "Think It's Creepy When Men Pursue Underage Girls? You'll Shudder When You Realize How Our Society Encourages It." Everyday Feminism, 11 May 2015. Web. 07 April, 2016.

[25] Pappas, Stephanie. "30% of Girls' Clothing Is Sexualized in Major Sales Trend." LiveScience, 20 May 2011. Web. 07 April, 2016.

[26] American Psychological Association. "Sexualization of Girls." American Psychology Association. Web. 07 April 2016.

when you consistently outperform them. It means that every task you touch loses value because women are perceived and treated as less. Being a woman is to have every aspect of your life centered around some man without your consent, and to have your identity overshadowed[27] by whatever male is closest to you.

Being Black is to be hated, tolerated, dismissed, devalued, and seen as less by everyone. It means being labeled a discipline problem[28] and the angry Black woman[29] for asserting yourself. It means never fitting the Eurocentric beauty[30] narrative that dominates western culture about everything from hair texture[31] to the darkness of your skin[32]. It means constantly being outside of the norm and expected to conform as much as possible to fit the norm. It is to be belittled and ridiculed regardless of what choices you make and to still be considered less regardless of how often and consistently you outperform those around you.

I've been told I'm less for being fat, for being Black and for being a woman. I've been told I'm nothing as being a fat

[27] Boguhn, Ally. "5 Alternatives to Taking Your Spouse's Last Name." Everyday Feminism, 30 Jan. 2015. Web. 07 April 2016.

[28] Grigsby Bates, Karen. "Study: Black Girls Are Being Pushed Out of School." Code Switch, 13 Feb. 2015. Web. 07 April 2016.

[29] Sargent, Antwaun. "7 Lies We Have to Stop Telling About Black Girls." Everyday Feminism, 06 Aug. 2014. Web. 07 April 2016.

[30] Kite, Lindsay. "Beauty Whitewashed: How White Ideals Exclude Women of Color." Everyday Feminism, 24 Nov. 2012. Web. 07 April 2016.

[31] Susan, Trudy. "The Sad Truth About Natural Hair Discrimination." Ebony, 21 May 2014. Web. 07 April 2016.

[32] Nittle, Nadra Kareem. "What Is Colorism - Skin Tone Discrimination in America." About Race Relations, 2016. Web. 07 April 2016.

woman makes me "unfuckable" and being "fuckable" is the whole goal of womanhood. As a Black woman, I'm informed that I'm unfuckable because Black women aren't sexually attractive...unless they are looking for a ride on the wild side[33]. THEN I'm an experience that must be had before settling down.

I've been told that as a fat Black woman, I'm a burden on society. I've been asked if I'm on welfare, how many baby daddies I have, if I'm a single parent, if I went to college for free, how did I become so articulate, how do I have the confidence to put myself in the spotlight, do I have trouble dating, how often do I wash my hair, why are Black women so masculine, why do Black women have to be so loud, why are Black women in such poor shape, why can't Black women keep a man, etc., etc., etc.

I can listen to the news and hear about how Black people are responsible for all the crime in the country or turn on the radio and hear how Black women ain't shit but a receptacle for men's dicks. I can go to church and be told to be submissive and my role as the incubator of the next generation regardless of any risks to my health.

Any identity I have was formed in spite of the constant negative assumptions, projections, and expectations of my environment. It was forged in hate of others, broken by unrealistic expectation, and reformed from a sense of self too resilient to be destroyed.

And while I am not alone in these experiences, I sometimes wish I were, because I wouldn't wish this on anyone. Hell, there are many others who have even worse environments, as I am a heterosexual, cisgendered woman and don't have to

---

[33] Hooks, bell. "Eating the Other: Desire and Resistance." 1992. Web. 07 April 2016.

fight to have my sexuality and gender recognized in addition to my humanity.

Fat, Black Woman Cosplayer

Being a fat, Black woman cosplayer is just another environment where I assert my right to exist and participate by existing and participating. I control my sexuality and reject the racial, gendered, and size fetishization others project onto me. I set my boundaries and push back when I need to do so. And I make a space for myself, and maybe a few others who may feel out of place, in this environment.

The environment is interesting because even though I work to control my presence, I am still affected by others. I am affected by the hypersexualization of women in cosplay and in the past have made some choices playing up to that. I'm actually a little repulsed by it, primarily because that style of cosplay seems to focus on what appeals to men. Cosplay is a lot more than T&A to a lot of people and I support amplifying the other roles cosplay represents for people.

It's a way to support fandoms. It's a way to meet friends. It's a way to build audiences. It's a way to show creativity. It's a way to create businesses and career opportunities.

And for those of us constantly relegated to the fringe of society, it's a form of activism.

Cosplay is a way of loving myself when the world tells me I should hate myself. It is the ultimate self-care. I focus on my needs, my wants, my goals, and I pursue the hell out of them. I don't let other people's definitions of what it is or who they think I should cosplay affect me. It's one of the reasons that I dress as whoever I want - gender, race, size do not matter. I refuse to acknowledge those who say I don't have a place here. To be honest, I don't even know where those people are because that's not my audience. I don't focus on who doesn't want to see me. I want to see me. I have a support network who want to see me. And I have the power to dictate MY terms when I decide to be seen.

This story first appeared at BlackGirlNerds.com on April 7, 2016.

Cosplay is a way of loving myself when the world tells me I should hate myself. It is the ultimate self-care.

– TaLynn Kel, My Cosplay is Intersectional

Oppression: It's the American Way

Do you know who the most destructive people are in the world? Oppressors.

An oppressor is someone who denies humanity and human rights to others. They are someone who benefits from denying those rights. They are a person who is anti-human.

100% anti-human.

This morning I read that Maine[34] is in the process of joining the many states intent on instituting discrimination bills. So far, we have Tennessee[35], North Carolina[36], and Mississippi[37] actively passing laws that make it legal to deny rights to people based on their choice of romantic partner, lover, or spouse.

This is mind boggling to me. I honestly struggle with why people care about this. Like, it doesn't impact them in ANY way. Why do they fight so hard?

Then I really think about it. I think about what people have to gain from restricting the rights of others and I start to understand.

Power. They get to feel powerful.

---

[34] Edwards, David. "Maine approves Christian ballot initiative to strip gay rights from Human Rights Act." Rawstory, 06 April 2016. Web. 13 April 2016.

[35] Fang, Marina. "Tennessee Passes Anti-LGBT Counseling Bill." Huffington Post, 11 April 2016. Web. 13 April 2016.

[36] WBTV. "NC professor explains implications of HB2." WNCN CBS North Carolina, 07 April 2016. Web. 13 April, 2016.

[37] Stewart, Katherine. "Why Mississippi's New Anti-LGBT Law Is the Most Dangerous One To Be Passed Yet." The Nation, 08 April 2016. Web. 13 April 2016.

We live in a culture created by and fostered by colonialism. European history is filled with people who went to other countries, destroyed indigenous culture, occupied the land, and exploited the resources. It's the way white people engaged with the world and you see it in EVERY country that has british governments. The power of these societies is in the subjugating the Native populations. It is in the decimation of Native cultures. It is in the overwriting other cultures, beliefs, and ideologies with their own. Colonialism is about erasure and it is oppressive as fuck.

America was founded in colonialism, exploitation, and hypocrisy. That the american constitution could be written by slave owners is a clear demonstration of that. American history is fraught with layers of oppression – it's written into every aspect of this country and how its citizens interact with the world. Many american citizens view society through a hierarchy, where some need to be on top at the expense of those on the bottom. None of what we are taught embraces inclusivity. It's all about oppression, power, and exploitation.

This is what we teach in our history books. We teach that colonialism is a good thing. A positive thing. We teach that erasing indigenous culture is not just a good thing; it's the right of any european culture. U.S. history is a how-to on being an oppressor, sugar coated to make it more palatable.

The influx of anti-gay legislation should not be a surprise. Oppressors have no power unless they are oppressing someone.

Oppressors also fear being erased if a group surpasses their power, because that's what they do. They sell the fear of being erased, of people doing to them what their ancestors did and what they continue to do. They sell a false narrative of us vs them, when it doesn't have to be one group dominating another. This is an extreme perspective used to radicalize people and incite violence.

So, when we see an uptick in discussions about some group that needs to be "put in their place" what you're really hearing is a rallying cry for power. You are hearing the dominant group pulling together to fight to keep that power. You are hearing the use of fear to incite people to violence against those who are somehow different. And it is ugly.

Watching this happen is amazing to me. I thought we were past some of this but I was grossly mistaken. I'm struggling to hold on to my hope for people to be better, and that is the hardest part of all.

The influx of anti-gay legislation should not be a surprise. Oppressors have no power unless they are oppressing someone.

– TaLynn Kel, Oppression: It's the American Way

Fat Issues

In the past, I've been on the weight loss train. Several years ago, I lost over 50lbs and was in great physical shape. I'd worked out regularly, gained a pattern of disordered eating, and became a huge asshole.

That's right. I became a huge asshole.

Losing weight is hard. It takes a lot of food and activity micromanagement. I had to plan and monitor every food choice and that habit spilled out over into my relationships. I became hyper critical of my and other people's choices. I criticized our meals. I criticized our exercise habits. I became the food and exercise police and I was fucking annoying.

I constantly under-ate and over-exercised. I treated food like a punishment and exercise like air. If the activity didn't burn calories, I wasn't interested. And, after about a year of pushing and punishing myself, I started to burn out. I would cry at the thought of eating. I would hate myself if I didn't walk enough that day. I constantly injured myself exercising and wouldn't give my body enough rest to heal. I had an unrelated health issue that hospitalized me for a week and my biggest concern wasn't that I'd almost died, it was that I hadn't exercised in days and I was scared I'd gain weight.

I was more scared that I'd gain weight than I was for my life.

That was my wake-up call. I spent the next two years learning how to ignore all the weight loss talk. I learned how to eat with less shame (it's still an issue). I had to learn when my body was hungry because I'd stopped listening. And I had to learn to accept my body, fat and all, and to love it as it is.

But when I was on the weight loss train, I was so fucking pushy and judgmental...and I felt like I had to be, as food was constantly being pushed at me. I don't have the same relationship with food that others have. I've been ashamed of my need to eat since elementary school, when I learned that I weighed more than a lot of my classmates. I wasn't fat at the time, but I was bigger and I realized that I was supposed to be ashamed of that. I started being less active because I got teased.

To this day people express amazement at any indication that I am or have been physically active. It's such a fucked up way to live, being scared to eat in public, feeling ashamed at buying anything that may not be seen as healthy. Having people pan your body in disbelief when you talk about working out. Feeling apologetic for not working out. I'm over it. So very over it.

I've gained all my weight back and I try not to be angry at myself for it. I'm not nearly as active as I used to be and that's not actually a bad thing when I was constantly injured and pushing my body past its limits because "pain is gain." I've decided that while there are activities I want to have the strength and endurance to do, my appearance is my lowest priority. That's also a hard one because I cosplay, and how you look is a large part of people liking your costume. Not to mention that people are constantly talking about dieting and fitting into their costumes. I find that talk toxic, but I'm learning to better navigate those interactions. I embrace the fat cosplayer title because fuck it. I'm fat. I cosplay. So what?

It's hard, though. I look at old pictures and miss that look. I miss being on the lower end of the plus size spectrum. I miss having a defined waist. I miss the smaller arms and smaller back rolls. And the worst part is that even then, I didn't appreciate how I looked. I was still not the "after" picture I sought.

Just talking about this reminds me of my hatred of eating, a hatred that makes absolutely zero sense as we need to eat to live. I feel myself struggle against self-hatred and verbal flagellation I want to deliver for failing to hit my weight loss goals. It's a never-ending cycle of abuse, one that I don't want to practice anymore. I was smaller and I still hated myself. I was still unhappy. And I was hungry as hell, which didn't help one bit. The only thing weight loss provided, other than a raging case of obnoxious dieting asshole syndrome was thin privilege (yes, thin privilege is a fucking thing. Work it out).

And the men...if your thing is getting the attention of men, I found that more talked to me when I was fat and not giving a fuck than when I was smaller and looking for attention. Men like who they like and there are men who are into you no matter what size you are. And some will treat you like shit no matter what you look like. It's like a goddamn prize for some of them to treat women like shit. Ugh.

Anyway, being fat isn't a big deal. At least, it shouldn't be. Unfortunately, there are a lot of people really invested in making it into a big deal and it's really hard to ignore all the negative messaging we receive about how fat is bad. It's taken me years to reach this point, and it's still a struggle not to diet, love myself, and believe that I am as worth as anyone else. My weight and size do not define me and even if they did, it doesn't make me bad. Fat is just a descriptor, not a definer.

Fat is a part of who I am, not all of who I am and while I don't love my fat, I don't hate it either. What I hate is how people try to convince me that my fat diminishes me in some way. It doesn't. The only thing that tries to diminish me is other people's fucked up attitudes about it. Why does my fat bother you? Why do you care? Don't like how I look? Stop looking. It's that simple.

When it comes to talking about fat, I put up my shields. I'm just not interested in the hate/pity/fuckery fest that is discussions about weight and fat. I used to be there but now I'm not and I fight like hell to stay out of there. It's a dangerous place – a place I don't think ANYONE needs to visit, much less inhabit. I am fantastic, regardless of how fat I am. We all are.

Health At Every Size (HAES)

Ragan Chastain is a fat activist blogger who consistently challenges the way fat is discussed and promotes the rights for all bodies. I recommend checking out her blog, although sometimes it can be triggering. She pulls in a ton of resources for discussing the barriers that fat people face in life, medical care, and acceptance.

She promotes the Health at Every Size approach to life. The post, "11 Reasons Why I Focus on Health and Not Weight[38]" contains a lot of good reasons that HAES is a much more reasonable approach to weight and bodies that weight loss.

---

[38] Chastain, Ragan. "11 Reasons Why I Focus on Health and Not Weight." Dances with Fat, 29 February 2016. Web. 18 April 2016.

I don't have the same relationship with food that others have. I've been ashamed of my need to eat since elementary school...

— TaLynn Kel, Fat Issues

Love and Gaming: How Playing an MMO Improved Communication in My Relationship

I am not a gamer but I game. I know it's a cliché, but my significant other (S.O.) built MMO gaming into our relationship. I will admit, there was a learning curve for me – I'd never even heard of MMOs before dating him, but once we started, I had fun. Well, not when we first started...

My S.O. was one of the original World of Warcraft (WOW) gamers. He played back when the game was first released and continued playing for six straight years. I, on the other hand, was more of a puzzle gamer. I loved Tetris and played a bunch of match three games where I could zone out. I'd dipped my toe in The Sims only to make the most boring, irritated Sim imaginable, tried Grand Theft Auto but felt bad about killing innocent people. Online PC gaming was not in my wheelhouse.

To address that lack, he gave me WOW. The thing is, WOW is a subscription service, so while he bought me the game, I still had to pay the monthly fee. I was a little put out by that. If you've never played an MMO before, they like to start you out slowly to get you used to playing the character. You always begin play in what's called a starting area, where you learn a bit about the world, get your beginner missions, and start learning your fighting skills. This is a crucial part of the game for new players like I was, but it's a huge annoyance for veterans like my S.O.

Needless to say, that first experience was a shitstorm of epic proportions and to this day I'm amazed that I continued to play. He did everything in his power to get out of the starting area as quickly as possible, while I was still figuring out how to fucking walk and jump. He's darting all over the place telling me to talk to this guy and go talk to that guy. Meanwhile I'm like "Why am I talking to him? Why is the town on fire? Are those werewolves? Why are they attacking me? Are people crying? Who's crying? What's that yellow dot? There's a map? I can't read that shit. Why can't I move forward? How do you jump again? This keyboard and mouse navigation is some bullshit! Is that a wall? What is this looting shit? I can die from falling? WHAT IS ATTACKING ME? Am I dead? How the fuck did I die? WHAT IS GOING ON??!!!"

The whole time my S.O. is yelling at me and getting pissed that I don't know what's happening. After about 40 minutes of this, I logged out. I was ready to choke him and break my computer. After I quit, I turned to him and asked as calmly as I could, "How important is this to you?"

He looked sad and said, "I thought this was something we could do together."

I sat there, angry, frustrated, and ready to go home. "Give me a week to learn to play on my own. Then we can try this again."

So, I did. I made a new character and started the game again. This time I was in a different starting area, one without werewolves. I would ask him questions about gameplay, but basically went through the starting area at my pace, getting a feel for the mechanics of the game. We met up after I finished all the quests and then we started running through the world together.

Despite this, there were still a number of things we needed to learn about playing together. Here are some of the things we discovered.

Be patient.

I will say again, I am amazed that we still play together. My S.O. had been playing MMOs for so long that many concepts were common sense to him. He struggled to understand that I didn't know basic things, like how to target, or how to turn my character's head. Shit, it's been years and I still struggle with that one. I didn't understand bag space, banks, crafting...basic MMO concepts.

Most of the time my S.O. was patient and would explain things to me. Sometimes, though, sometimes he would talk to me like I was a dumb child and that shit was unacceptable. On more than one occasion I'd have to pause the game to address how he spoke to me. He didn't realize he was doing it, and frankly, I wasn't having it.

Accept that you aren't telepathic.

After we worked on how we spoke to each other, still a work in progress, we starting having issues with mind reading, in that we couldn't do it. He'd have this agenda of what he wanted to do in game but wouldn't tell me. Then, when I'd just wander around, doing whatever caught my eye, he'd get frustrated with me for not following the plan he never told me he'd created. We saw this in our day to day life – I'd mention a problem to him, he wouldn't respond, I'd assume he didn't have anything to add and I'd start handling it. Then he'd tell me what he'd planned to do if I'd let him handle it. We finally learned that we needed to communicate up front what we intended – BEFORE we started questing or working on the problem.

Communicate changes in the plan.

The next communication bump in the road came from addressing our individual needs. In game, one of the activities is crafting. You can make stuff you need in game, but to do it, you have to find the ingredients. My S.O. and I always choose different crafting professions so that our ingredient needs don't overlap. At various times, we'd run off to gather some item really quickly, which isn't a problem unless you are going to participate in some big event or fight a powerful enemy and you suddenly realize your healer is off in the forest chopping trees or some shit. Eventually, we'd let the other know we were about to run off to gather some nonsense, but it took time.

Set and communicate your limits.

My S.O. loves MMOs. He will watch videos and read articles to learn about gameplay and how to strengthen your character. I won't read or watch a damn thing. He still sends me videos occasionally, when I start having issues playing my characters, but it's a crapshoot as to whether I'll watch them. This frustrates him but I'm so open about the fact that I have zero intention of learning about this game, that it's become a part of our banter. Also, I'm extremely casual about my gaming. I won't even play every week. He has multiple characters to play on, but he has on dedicated character that he plays with me. It works.

Work together.

I love playing melee, sword-fighting characters – i.e. up close fighters. That class wears heavy armor and is designed to take a lot of damage. My S.O. likes ranged characters, those who fight from a distance and do a lot of damage. These characters wear either medium or light armor, making them easier to damage. We work to compensate for the other's weaknesses. If either of us doesn't play our role, then the likelihood of us dying increases by a lot. It's a balance. We don't always do it well, but we keep trying.

Be honest.

We are honest about our expectations. If we aren't in the mood to play, we just say it. We try not to say one thing and then do another, but when we do, we own the mistake. We admit our limitations. We apologize when it's warranted. We remember to put our individual needs first and try to come together for common goals.

If there is one thing that has been a constant throughout our relationship, it's honesty, even when it hurts. My S.O. had to learn that he has an explosive temper. He didn't like that. I had to learn that I'm not going to be good at everything, especially if I won't put n the work. Sometimes he'll rage quit and often I'll fuck up missions because I won't read them. These things are easier to accept because we're upfront about them.

Remember it's just a game.

In the end, we are playing in a virtual world where we fight demons and monsters and live out a fantasy version of ourselves. And while we learned how to communicate better in real life, the game itself is not real. It's meant to be fun, and when it stops being fun, we try something new. But as long as we remember that this is just entertainment that happened to helped us in some real-world ways, we're good.

Truth is, I appreciate what gaming brought to our relationship. It's something we bonded over and gave us some insight into each other; as well as helping us build communication skills in our relationship. Real life is going to throw any couple plenty of curveballs. Gaming together is a fun way to learn those communication skills before the curveballs really start coming. It's not perfect and it will take a lot of effort, but I am thankful for the ease with which we work through problems. I'm not sure it would have happened as quickly or as effectively if we hadn't learned to work together in a fictional world.

This story first appeared on BlackGirlNerds.com on April 29, 2016.

We are honest about our expectations. If we aren't in the mood to play, we just say it. We try not to say one thing and then do another, but when we do, we own the mistake. We admit our limitations. We apologize when it's warranted. We remember to put our individual needs first and try to come together for common goals.

– TaLynn Kel, Love and Gaming: How Playing an MMO Improved Communication in My Relationship

The Face That Paused a Thousand Meetings

Once again, my face stopped the meeting. Halted it completely because someone felt insecure about it.

I wish I could say this wasn't a common occurrence, but it is. I have stopped meetings at every position I've held in the past ten years. It's getting to be impressive, despite being unintentional. I've been told that my smile makes me look guilty, my frown is frightening, my expressionless face is intimidating, my shifting in my seat is discouraging, my avoidance of eye contact as disrespectful, and my laugh is disdainful.

And while I am sure that at some point, all these things are true, it hasn't escaped my notice that these descriptors usually come from managers during and after team meetings...usually when they want to discuss some other way I've somehow challenged their authority or made them feel less authoritative. This happened so often that a couple of years ago, I started warning people about the faces I make when I'm thinking about what's being said. At the time, I felt like I was heading a confrontation off before it became a problem. Turns out I was just apologizing for being myself and this year I've decided that shit was unacceptable.

No more apologies. That I felt like I had to explain and apologize for my face to avoid trouble is fucking ridiculous to me, but I did. I did it because I like paying my bills – ok that's not true. But I do like being able to meet my needs and have a bit of fun with my income and I didn't want that to stop. So, every time someone gave me some "helpful feedback" on how I'm perceived, I internalized it and tried to adjust.

I sat in meetings with my head in my notebook, avoided eye contact, schooled my face into a non-expression, sat very still, didn't speak, didn't ask questions, filtered my suggestions through better liked co-workers...and found that regardless of whatever technique I employed, they still had a problem with me. I was too assertive, not assertive enough. I looked devious or bored. I didn't offer enough feedback or I was too critical. My laugh was too loud or I seemed like I didn't want to be there. The list of things my body language communicated to them[39] was negative and endless.

Eventually I realized that it didn't fucking matter what I did. Their problem with me was ME. Not actually me, personally, but something about my physicality[40] caused them to see every part of me negatively, regardless of what I did. These people were never going to like ME.

For a while, I internalized that message. I figured I was unlikable...until I noticed that I made a lot of cool acquaintances and some friends every place I worked. People I spent time with outside of the office. Some of these people are still in my life a decade later. If I was so unlikable, how the fuck was I making friends all over the place?

It's no secret that Black people face a lot of racism in the workplace. Black women also have to deal with the Angry Black Woman stereotype[41], where we can't ever express anything that isn't positive without fear of retaliation. I had to realize that this response to me wasn't that I wasn't good

---

[39] Hobson, Janell. "Angry or Complicated? Misrecognizing Black Women." Ms. Blog, 22 Sept. 2014. Web. 28 April 2016.

[40] Yancy, George. "Walking While Black in the 'White Gaze.'" The New York Times, 01 Sept. 2013. Web. 28 April 2016.

[41] Conger, Cristen. "How the 'Angry Black Woman' Stereotype Tries to Control Black Women." Everyday Feminism, 03 March 2016. Web. 28 April 2016.

enough – it was that I was a threat to their perceived superiority. Thing is, I am good at a lot of things I try, and when I'm not, I'm comfortable admitting it. That level of self-confidence triggered a negative response in a lot of people and until I humbled myself (by apologizing or some such bullshit) they felt compelled to do it for me.

That means that in every work environment, I had some boss who tried to take me down a peg and put me in the place they felt comfortable with me. As you can guess from the first paragraph, that shit didn't go well. And the older I get, the less of this bullshit I'm willing to entertain.

Yesterday, a young Black woman colleague approached me about her office experiences. She's fresh out of school and facing her first wave of racist microaggressions[42] in the workplace. I feel for her. Truly. You don't realize the dumb shit people are going to ask you or say in front of you until it happens. And when it does, you think, "Am I making something out of nothing?" Yet, you will continue to hear and be asked things that will put your race front and center in the discussion. People will be openly disdainful and if you confront it, you will be punished. These people will not think they are racist. They will think shit like, "I have Black people on my team. I'm liberal as hell!" when in reality, they are spouting silly ass white supremacist bullshit frequently and enforcing that shit at every opportunity.

My advice to her was, "white people do racist shit all the time and don't think it's racist. They will hold positions of power over you in the workplace and will enact these things both consciously and unconsciously. Your role is to define what you need from this situation and decide how much you can push back while still getting what you need. Your job is to build

---

[42] Boylorn, R. "Working While Black: 10 Racial Microaggressions Experienced in the Workplace." Crunk Feminist Collective, 11 Nov. 2014. Web. 28 April 2016.

coping mechanisms for dealing with this. They can be as simple as calling a friend, or visiting your therapist. Sometimes, you'll have to quit. But don't do that if it's going to fuck you up financially. If that's the case, make them fire you because as long as you follow the correct steps, you can collect unemployment for a little while."

I feel bad telling someone to dim her shine and not rock the boat, but she doesn't have the financial support to leave her job at this time. She can work on creating that support but until then I suggested she figure out how to maintain her independence without sacrificing her self-worth, and that is a difficult dance. You will always take damage and you will always need time to heal.

I wish I knew a better way but this is the reality I see and experience. And while creating your own business, one where you don't have to face the same attempts to disempower you, you will still face this when you deal with white people. You will be told that you won't be trusted because of how you look[43]. You will be told that you will always seem less than white people. You will be perceived as violent despite never doing anything to warrant that perception. People will ask you about "Black" things and be surprised when you refuse to answer. Your contributions will be ignored or dismissed, often publicly, and then implemented in the background – and you will not receive credit for them. Then, when you point out your contribution, you will be viewed as narcissistic.

This is what I face. This is just one of the struggles[44] we as Black women face in the workplace.

---

[43] Woodard, Monique. "The White Elephant In The Room." 13 April 2016. Web. 28 April 2016.

[44] Johnson, Maisha Z. "6 Struggles of Being Unapologetically Black in a Professional Environment." Everyday Feminism, 04 Nov. 2014. Web. 28 April 2016.

Needless to say, I hate meetings. It's hard to keep a semi-smile on your face while listening to people say ridiculous, irrelevant shit for an hour. It's difficult trying to suppress your curiosity and interest in the goings on of the company because your every utterance that isn't "that's great! Love it!" are seen as criticism. Or your problem-solving skills are looked at as a burden, not an asset. As I said, it's not an easy space to occupy. I've failed several times and I will likely fail again. Until I get my independence from this environment, I'll fail and rebound like I always have.

That means that in every work environment, I had some boss who tried to take me down a peg and put me in the place they felt comfortable with me.

— TaLynn Kel, The Face That Paused a Thousand Meetings

My Husband's Unconscious Racism Nearly Destroyed Our Marriage

I wrote this because...well, because I had to. It was cathartic in many ways and it helped me deal with an aspect of my relationship that I didn't want to face...something nobody else seemed to be talking about. And with the way the discussions around racism were changing, how it was so much harder to hide that to not see it meant you were actively looking away, it felt right to talk about how it impacts my relationship. It still feels right to talk about it and we still struggle with it.

People read this many different ways. Some read it as though I am ignorant and self-harming. Others read it as a story of love triumphing hate. It's really just a story about two people who are committed to growing together, but who also recognize that it may not be meant to be. But if it fails, it won't be because we didn't try our hardest to make it work.

*****

When I was in my teens, I figured I'd be married at least three times. The first would be the young, practice marriage. My second marriage would be the passionate one through which I would become a better version of myself, and my third would be the one that stuck. As you can see, I never really had a lot of respect for the institution.

By the time I was 30, after years of never sleeping with anyone for more than two months, much less actually dating them, I'd revised my prediction from three to zero. I'm not religious; I didn't want kids; and I sure as hell didn't want someone in my home that felt like they had any control over my decisions. Why get married at all? That shit looked ridiculous to me.

Then I met *Kevin. We met in the geekiest way possible: He saw a picture of me in a cosplay outfit, wanted to know more, found my blog, and then found my profile on a dating site and asked to meet at DragonCon. Everything about that impressed me. I loved the idea of someone being willing to do a little legwork to find me, especially since exercising my curiosity and putting in some effort to satisfy it is how I engage with the world. His approach spoke to me. Also, he asked me out—no hedging, no game playing. He stated up front that he wanted to get to know me better and asked me on a date. In a society where people are "hanging out" and "chilling" and "hooking up"—meaning anything from a light kissing session to a night of full-blown sex—being direct was important.

There was only one concern: He was white. I'd been in the dating scene for a while and while I didn't think race *should* matter, I definitely knew it *did*. I'd met my share of white men looking for a "Nubian goddess" (their words, not mine). Or the ones who believed that Black women would offer some kind of freaky, wild sexual experience. I'd met white men who wanted to demean and defile me, white men who wanted to dominate or be dominated by me, and white men who just wanted to check a Black woman off their sexual bucket list. Not to mention the ones who thought that being with me somehow made them "edgy" or proved they weren't racist. I mean, not every white guy has a "David Duke cock[45]" right?

---

[45] Clark-Flory, Tracy. "John Mayer's Johnson hates black women." Salon, 10 Feb. 2010. Web. 21 Feb. 2016.

Needless to say, dating white men was tiring. I had to constantly be on guard, preparing myself for their racist comments. And I knew they were coming. I knew there would be a point where I'd have to talk about why I could say n***** and they couldn't. I knew there'd be a conversation about Black on Black crime. I KNEW there'd be some fucked up assumption about Black people that I'd have to dismantle and then beat my white date over the head with—thereby ending whatever the fuck we were doing together. And I really wasn't there for that shit.

But you know how they say timing is everything? Kevin entered my life at a particularly vulnerable point. My father had passed three months before we met. He'd been sick for over a decade with cancer and I spent that entire time blocking out everyone. When he passed, all that energy I'd used protecting myself started to dissipate and my walls softened. I started letting people in. I was willing and capable of giving people opportunities to be a part of my life, and I was also willing to do the work to keep them there.

That's why I let Kevin in, but it's not why I kept him around. I'd always been told to be more feminine, more womanly, and to cater to some stranger's every need, but Kevin didn't expect that. He didn't try to mold me into the perfect woman. He didn't look for me to take care of him. He didn't minimize my accomplishments; we weren't competing, and my success did not undermine his masculinity. And he was nice to me and genuinely interested in me—something I'm sad to say wasn't common in my relationships. He listened and he cared. He also had an important characteristic that I share: the willingness to examine his beliefs and change them when he learns that they're wrong. He doesn't state his beliefs as vocally as I do, but he shares my love of learning and adapting to shifts in our perception and awareness.

Being with Kevin felt like a refuge from sexism. At the time, that seemed more immediate—and easier to address—than the racism that surrounded me. But it didn't negate the fact that Kevin is white—and not just white, *extremely* white. He has ash blond hair and pale, easily sunburned skin. His close friends are all white men and their spouses. His family is mostly white. His co-workers are mostly white men. The more serious our relationship got, the more I was spending half my time—at least—surrounded by white people. While I'd gone to predominantly white schools and worked in mostly white companies, I'd never had so many white people suddenly in my intimate spaces. It's one thing to hit it and split it with a guy and another to interact in my personal time with entire groups of white people, sometimes in my home.

And it affected me a LOT. I was constantly pulled out of spaces where I felt comfortable and pushed into spaces that felt isolating. We live in Atlanta, where multi-racial, multi-ethnic options are everywhere, yet when we socialized with his friends, I was required to visit all-white neighborhoods, businesses, and events. Many of his friends lived in "white flight" zones, suburban areas where white people moved to avoid the "downfall" of urban areas. I was constantly required to go to the one Atlanta county still referred to as a "sundown town"—as in a town Black people shouldn't be in after dark. And while he and his friends were pretty clueless about these things, I was very aware.

It was in one of these predominantly white spaces, a restaurant with a mostly-white clientele, that I first ran headlong into Kevin's unrealized racism. I'd just learned that he and all his friends carried 4-inch pocket knives (or "box openers," as they liked to call them), and I was kinda freaked out by it. My weapons tend to be off-label weapons, like my keys, a pen, or my purse. I only had one friend who carried a gun, and nobody carried knives. Now, I was sitting surrounded by armed white men.

When I pointed out that they were all carrying weapons, they laughed—didn't I know the knives were just for opening boxes? I could have been arrested or killed for carrying something like that, regardless of what I planned to do with it—unlike them. They wouldn't face any consequences for bringing weapons into a restaurant; after all, they were white and the restaurant was mostly white. Kevin shrugged at my observations and said "At least we don't have to worry about being shot."

This was how I realized that I was dating a racist man.

Kevin didn't understand what he'd done wrong, but he knew he'd fucked up; he wanted to know how and why. I told him that his assumption—that we were safe from shootings because we were in an all-white restaurant, that a predominantly Black restaurant would be likely to have a shooting—was shitty, ignorant, and racist. When he pushed back, I pointed out that he and his friends were the ones carrying weapons. What the fuck did they need them for at dinner? Were they expecting a package? But, of course, it's always okay for white people to be armed. If they have a knife, it's probably just for opening boxes. If they have a gun, it's probably for protection—despite all the shootings to the contrary. Kevin stammered and backpedaled, but the damage was done. I'm not sure how far we were into our relationship, but that was the first moment I wondered if this was a huge mistake.

To this day, I look back and question how and why I stayed. I can see now that, this early in my relationship with Kevin and my own personal development, I was still in a lot of denial about what racism is and how it manifests. Ironically, choosing to stay with Kevin after I realized he wasn't immune to racism, and later choosing to marry him, helped me sort that out. Being exposed to so many white people, including some who were now my family, helped me recognize racist buzzwords like "conservative," "social conservative," "Republican," "traditionalist," and "older generation." These code words make racism more palatable and less offensive to those that engage in it. It also makes it easier to lie to ourselves about it.

Being with Kevin also helped me realize how much anti-Blackness I'd internalized. Growing up Black in America, you learn to ignore a lot of racist shit, especially if you are moving in white spaces. I was taught that white spaces were aspirational, that access to these spaces meant success. That's a white supremacist ideology, but we live in a white supremacist society, so it's also true: all-white spaces are where a lot of power brokering happens. This often means that the more power you achieve, the more you face casual social racism. You sit in meetings where people openly say that Black people are lesser—but not you, they add. You're different! That is, you're different until you do something of which they don't approve. Then you're "just like the rest of them" or "you don't know your place." And to teach you your place, they revoke some of your privileges, like a naughty child, until you understand that you are there by their sufferance. To survive in that environment, you learn to stay quiet.

I learned this in school, at work, in certain social groups . . . in order to keep your spot, or move "up the chain," you learn to let casual racism slide. Your ability to stay silent in the face of racist bullshit becomes the norm. So you do it, because you think that's your only feasible option and the price you pay to succeed in white America. The side effect is that this type of talk, this dislike and hatred of Black people, becomes not just the white noise but also the internal harmony of your life. It goes from being something you actively ignore to something you actively hum, and eventually sing. You stop noticing it, and then you stop fighting it, because it no longer sounds wrong to you. It sounds normal.

Dating Kevin jarred the melody. Hearing him parrot anti-Black shit I said helped me hear the discordance in my life. I was suddenly super-aware of my audience, and it forced me to listen to what I was saying—and then to change what I was saying, not from a "fit in at any cost" ideology but from an internal assessment. I started listening to and correcting myself more. Then I started sharing my realizations and pushing back on the bullshit. It's been a shake-up for all of my relationships; I've had more than one non-Black friend express apprehension at talking with me, because I don't divorce personal experiences from the larger, external factors that shaped them. And I don't tolerate racism in my relationships anymore . . . which was scary for me and Kevin.

We hit a point where he had to change or we were going to separate. That point was the Trayvon Martin trial and verdict. From the moment Trayvon's murder became visible, I dismissed the idea that his murderer's actions were justifiable in any way. Imagine my surprise when Kevin said that the evidence supported the murderer's account. It was in that moment, when I saw that the man I'd married believed that a 17-year-old teenager visiting his dad presented a threat to a 30+-year-old man who randomly patrolled his neighborhood with a gun, that I started to fear our relationship was beyond hope.

I talked to my white therapist about it and she commended me for being willing to work through these tough issues. I didn't feel support. Instead, I felt betrayed by the two white people I'd allowed into my intimate confidence. When I was a child, my father had told me never to trust white people, and now I felt that his warning had been validated. If my white husband couldn't acknowledge the humanity of a Black teenage boy who'd been stalked and murdered, if he could believe it was just for this child to be profiled and found dangerous based on nothing but a visit to the store, I KNEW that this person wasn't someone with whom I could spend my life. And I started preparing my exit strategy—exactly one year after our wedding.

I'd realized that, although being with Kevin had helped me to recognize the racist attitudes I'd unconsciously swallowed, he hadn't been able to do the same. He wasn't willing to face his own racism, and this meant I didn't trust my husband with my Blackness. I am not naïve; I do not expect another person to ever understand and accept the whole of me. I think that is highly unrealistic and self-centered. But my Blackness defines how the world engages with me, and it is something that he had to understand and embrace for us to be together. And in order for him to do that, he had to own his racism. He had to acknowledge he was racist, harbored racist thoughts, and said and did racist things. He had to confront this part of himself that he'd denied all his life . . . that he had the privilege of ignoring until he decided he wanted to share his life with me.

The thing that amazes me about him is that he did it, and continues to do it. As I write this, it's been almost three years since I realized that I couldn't live with my husband's racism, and we are still together. It wasn't easy for either of us, but when he realized that I could not trust him, that his inability to admit his racism made him a liar, he knew he had to change. My promise is to give him the space to educate himself and make mistakes, and the time to grow from it.

I also made a fundamental change in how I interacted with him and with the world: I stopped treating my Blackness as a burden. I stopped feeling bad about being Black. I stopped feeling like I had to prove I was different, "one of the good ones." I hadn't even realized I was doing it, and it's still something I struggle with. When I'm in a situation where I feel silenced, or singled out, I don't blame myself anymore. There is nothing wrong with me, my Blackness, and recognizing my skills and accomplishments. I am worthy. I share my experiences and amplify the narratives of others without shame. I invoke the privilege of my intelligence, education, and support network to learn more and write more about the impact of racism in various parts of my identity. I work to center myself in my narratives, instead of the men or the white people who surround me. I have reached a place where I feel safer without all the games I've been forced to play in this society. I'm still not 100% safe, but I'm not sure if that will ever be the case.

This also changed how I interacted with Kevin. Instead of focusing on how my Blackness affected us, we started focusing on how his whiteness affected us. He continues to confront his racism and doing the work to change his thinking and his reactions. He is rewriting himself and learning that his perspective is fucked up and he needs to continually straighten that shit out. It is his job to shoulder the burden of his ancestors and their history of genocide, rape, theft, and destruction of other cultures as they falsely promoted their illusion of dominance. It's his job to check the racism of his family and friends. This is his role he took by being with me. It's not an easy battle for us. He knows when I talk about oppression he doesn't have a seat at the table. He knows that my understanding of racism overrides his.

In exchange, I work to keep our communication about racism as safe as it can be for him—without doing harm to myself. Among other things, this means my anger is accepted without my having to explain or justify it. He knows he is not an authority and that his ally work is in white spaces, not Black ones. He is continually unlearning white supremacy and how to de-center himself in these conversations. It's no longer focused on his hurt feelings or fears that I hate all white people. Instead, it's about knowing that all white people in this country are racist until they take on the continuous task of unlearning what everyone and everything has taught them about race in America.

It's not an easy battle, but it's the one I've chosen. I'm just happy that I'm with someone willing to fight the battle with me.

Name has been changed.

This story first appeared at TheEstablishment.co, a multimedia site entirely run and funded by women on May 26, 2016.

To this day, I look back and question how and why I stayed. I can see now that, this early in my relationship with Kevin and my own personal development, I was still in a lot of denial about what racism is and how it manifests.

– TaLynn Kel, My Husband's Unconscious Racism Nearly Destroyed Our Marriage

Fear is the Mind Killer

A little over a week ago, I published an essay on The Establishment about facing the racism in my marriage. I knew this essay had potential. I wrote it months ago and decided to shop around for places to publish it. I looked at various websites, but ultimately decided on The Establishment because they are intentionally intersectional and they do not have a comments section. Anyone who reads anything online knows to avoid the comments section unless you want to lose faith in humanity. I can only occasionally visit them, and usually only last about 15 comments before I'm too depressed and disheartened. In fact, in April this year the Guardian published a piece called "The Dark Side of Guardian Comments[46]" where they analyzed 70 million comments[47] from 1996 until March 2016 to see what types of comments they received and whether they were worth the existence of the comments section.

What they found wasn't surprising to me, but was surprising to them. They found that the ten most abused writers were either women (8 out of 10) or people of color (6 out of 10). The ten writers who got the least abuse were men.

---

[46] Gardiner, Becky; Mansfield, Mahana; Anderson, Ian; Holder, Josh; Louter, Daan; Ulmanu, Monica. "The Dark Side of Guardian Comments." The Guardian, 12 April, 2016. Web. 06 June 2016.

[47] Mansfield, Mahana. "How We analysed 70m Comments on the Guardian Website." The Guardian, 12 April, 2016. Web. 06 June 2016.

I've seen the vitriol directed at women and Black women who aren't silent. I am very aware of the target we place on ourselves[48] when we step up and dare to be seen, heard, and respected. It's so common[49] that women are expected to figure out how to protect themselves from it before daring to say anything. It sounds a lot like how women are conditioned about rape[50], as if the problem isn't that people decide to commit rape. I am supposed to keep myself as invisible as possible to prevent people from harassing me.

I am supposed to be silent to prevent abuse.

I am supposed to be invisible to prevent attacks.

I am supposed to hide so that I can be safe.

And if I don't hide, if I step up and take my place beside every other visible person, I am inviting abuse.

We all know that shit's wrong, don't we? Like 100% wrong?

---

[48] Starr, Terrell Jermaine. "The Unbelievable Harassment Black Women Face Daily on Twitter." Alternet, 16 Sept. 2014. Web. 06 June 2016.

[49] Hunt, Elle. "Online Harassment of Women at Risk of Becoming 'Established Norm', Study Finds." The Guardian, 07 March 2016. Web. 06 June 2016.

[50] Culp-Ressler. "All of The Things Women Are Supposed To Do To Prevent Rape." Think Progress, 10 June 2014. Web 06 June 2016.

And even though it's wrong, that's the environment I have to navigate. I have to accept that mean and nasty things are going to come my way because I dared to write about and share my experience. I admit, I'm scared. I've seen what happens to people who stand up for their beliefs. We've seen it with people who stand up to their abusive partners[51], activists who fight for environment rights[52], and rape victims who seek justice against their attacker[53]. Our society enjoys finding fault with the victim and then attacks them for being a victim instead of pursuing the attacker. It's ugly. And it's what I can look forward to if I pursue my online writing.

So, I'm scared. I'm scared of being too visible because of what it may do to my life. I'm scared of painting a target on my back. I'm scared that I will say or do something that will result in a backlash so strong that I will be afraid to leave the house.

The question is whether I will let this silence me. The short answer is probably not, which isn't really an answer. It's indecision at its finest but it's the best response I have at the moment.

It's difficult making decision based on what could possibly happen. It's hard to make decisions based on fear. I don't want to be that person, although I do tend to assess "acceptable risk." Is potentially exposing me and my family to the vitriol of the internet worth continuing to write? Is raising my voice worth my safety?

---

[51] Kasperkevic, Jana. "Private Violence: Up to 75% of Abused Women Who are Murdered are Killed After They Leave Their Partners." The Guardian, 20 Oct. 2014. Web. 06 June 2016.

[52]Wallace, Scott. "Why Do Environmentalists Keep Getting Killed Around the World?" Smithsonian Mag, February 2014. Web. 06 June 2016.

[53] Peck, Adam. "Victim's House Burned Down After She Accuses Football Star Of Rape." Think Progress, 14 Oct. 2013. Web. 06 June 2016.

It's super fucked up that writing an essay about my life and my experiences is a scary thing...an emotionally risky and potentially physically dangerous choice. I can live with people disagreeing with me, but they won't leave it at that. It'll be personal attacks about my looks, my life, my family and my choices. I am opening the door for those attacks by daring to speak and be heard. Using my voice is an act of defiance and that is super fucked up.

I might feel differently if I didn't see other Black women worried about increasing their visibility because of the harassment it invites. We see people attacked for doing nothing more than saying, "I love my Blackness," as though loving yourself is some kind of hateful act. It's fucking outrageous that being unapologetically myself is so damn problematic for some people that they feel compelled to try to abuse me for it.

I might feel differently if I felt I had some kind of recourse when it happens but social media platforms have shown time and time again the double standard[54] that exists when it comes to reporting abuse. That double standard is that if a white guy says it, it's fine but if a woman, namely a Black woman says it or even just repeats it, her account gets suspended. We've seen what happened to Azealia Banks on Twitter[55]; it only highlights the double standard that exists.

---

[54] Kutner, Jenny. "This Woman Is Calling Out Facebook's Shameful Double Standard on Sexual Harassment." Mic, 28 March 2016. Web. 06 June 2016.

[55]Hood, Carol. "Azealia Banks' Twitter Ban Reminds Us Freedom Of Speech Is For Whites Only." The Establishment, 13 May 2016. Web. 06 June 2016.

And the thing that fucks me up the most about this is that this is exactly *why* people are harassed. It is to silence them. It is to scare them into hiding. It is to scare *me* into hiding. If people like me never speak up, never speak out, then we can continue with the lie that everything is great and nothing needs to change.

Well, a lot of things need to fucking change and fortunately there are many voices out there sharing that message.

On some level, I've always known that speaking my truth was a kind of activism. It sucks that just being myself is an act of protest. But I've lived with that burden all of my life, before I ever understood what that meant.

I used to think I didn't fit; now I know the world doesn't want me to and that is super fucked up.

Oh, and just in case there was any confusion, this is all about oppression. This is how oppression works. This is how it's worked for years. If you induce enough fear in people, some will stop openly fighting. This is sexism. This is racism. This is white people, white men putting on their anonymous white hoods and attacking Black women for not knowing their place – which is no place.

So, the next time you dismiss some threat or ignore someone's harassment, think about what you're really protecting because one day it maybe you who steps out of line and will need to be reined in.

We see people attacked for doing nothing more than saying, "I love my Blackness," as though loving yourself is some kind of hateful act.

– TaLynn Kel, Fear is the Mind Killer

When the Internet Looks Back

This is what it's like when the internet starts noticing you.

At first, it's exciting. You see your words pop up in random places. If you have a Facebook page, you watch your likes grow and your web traffic increases. You start to receive nice notes on Twitter and via email, messages telling you how much they appreciate your work. You feel validated and appreciated.

Your star continues to blaze. You know better than to read the comments. They can only ruin your joy. You plan for the next submission because this isn't the last. You know that this is just the first of many successes for you, and you plan to run headfirst down that path to greatness. You've worked hard and you earned it.

Then you receive a twitter message. You open the app, one that previously only conveyed positive messages affirming your work, to find someone calling you a bigot. They tell you that you are a racist. That your dad was a shitty father. That you are irrational, hateful, a crybaby. At first, you're confused. Why are they saying these things about you? You feel your heart race and your breath quicken. You worry that this is just the first of many verbal assaults. No, you don't know the people but how can you stop them from attacking you in the first place. You realize you can't and feel helpless.

You take a moment and start to think. You work to calm down. Finally, you remember that you can block people from messaging you. Sure, it's reactive, but at least it's something. You go back and block all the people who sent you messages. You investigate apps that can help block known problematic accounts and ask other Twitter users for advice on handling abusive tweets. The response is unanimous – block them. Twitter doesn't feel safe anymore, but it feels better.

But you are curious. Where did this onslaught originate? So, you google your essay and find a reddit thread discussing it. It's linked to several known anti-feminists and proponents of reverse racism. This is all you need to know but you cannot resist looking at the thread. The comments are...ill informed, but it was what you expected and you move on, occasionally check the feed to ensure the thread has died.

Things quiet down. You live your life, notice a drop in your web traffic, and feel comfortable that the storm has passed either in ignorance or denial of how the internet works. Once you post something, it has the capacity to be spread. And so, a week later, you wake up to find several app notifications from your various social media accounts. Thanks to the previous week's experience, you are apprehensive to look. That much activity overnight feels suspect. Your curiosity gets the best of you and you open Twitter.

Today you are an ugly, fat bitch whoring yourself to the white man. You are nasty looking and desperate for man. Today you are stupid and pissing on your dad's grave. Today you are socially dysfunctional and need to be medicated.

This time, you are better prepared for the onslaught. Again, you are curious what provoked this attack. You google your essay, but the results are the same so you try Bing. There you find a different forum. You click the link to find it is a forum for supporters of a Black man who attacks Black women YouTuber. You look for the post that started the thread and find that the Black man who attacks Black women YouTuber tweeted your essay to his followers starting the influx of negative tweets. You look at your webpage traffic, smile, then look at the forum and frown as they have downloaded pictures of you and are mocking them. A part of you is horribly embarrassed. The rest of you decides to hide your Flickr account and double check your security settings.

You visit your webpage and look for your referrers. You see some referral sites you've never heard of. You follow them and find they are forums dedicated to people against interracial relationships. After being attacked by some groups, you know there is at least one more waiting to pounce. You are just unsure if they will. So as things slow down, you wait. You watch your website hits gradually drop, and with it, so does your tension...kind of. Because you know that at any moment someone will grab your essay and share it with a new audience, potentially reigniting the flame that has been reduced to an ember.

*****

For now, it's just words. It's minimal visibility. It's low hanging fruit ignorance and hate which quickly dissipates as I fade back into obscurity. It is something I can live with, for now.

But there may come a time when my visibility is more frequent. Perhaps even consistent for brief spurts of time. Can I live like this? With this sword dangling above my head?

I don't know. This is the first time I'm dealing with anything like this. I know other people have dealt with much worse, more frequently, but I am living through this and learning how it is at this very moment. I am learning how I cope with anonymous verbal abuse and having experienced in-person verbal abuse, this is a lot less direct, but still hurtful.

And while I feel the pain of being attacked, I don't actually care about the attackers. They are less than nothing. They aren't even a name on the screen. In less than a day, they will be forgotten. What I will remember is that I was attacked, not who or what the attack actually was, just that it happened. And that is the fear they want you to remember so that the next time you think about speaking, writing, or asserting yourself you remember what it felt like when they tried to beat you down. You remember what it felt like to hurt. And you stay down to avoid it.

I've learned over time that I'm resilient. I have broken and put myself back together. I hurt and I heal. All this can do is hurt me in the now.

They will. They have. And I'm still here.

Why are they saying these things about you? You feel your heart race and your breath quicken. You worry that this is just the first of many verbal assaults. No, you don't know the people but how can you stop them from attacking you in the first place. You realize you can't and feel helpless.

— TaLynn Kel, When the Internet Looks Back

Caping for Cops

I grew up surrounded by angry white people.

I went to school with their kids. Wasn't invited to their parties, and learned to coexist amongst people who thought you were good enough some days but would call you a n*gger if you crossed the line.

I was threatened for entering "their" neighborhoods. I was taught to be quiet and ignore their verbal assaults. I was told that Black women weren't attractive and accused of being too sensitive when I demanded respect. I was told I should feel special to be allowed in their white spaces.

And learned that I had no real protections from them or their racism.

After high school, I moved away and vary rarely looked back. I knew these folks weren't my friends and I didn't pretend they were. In fact, I would have no idea what was going on with them without Facebook, the ultimate voyeur's dream application. Now I can peek in on their lives without having to actually engage with them. I can see many of their thoughts and opinions without having to have a conversation. I can see bits of who they are and confirm many of the things I knew, like the fact that they are racist as fuck.

They get really upset when you challenge them about this. Needless to say, I don't know what many of them are up to anymore.

It's always interesting when an event uncovers some of the racism they are in denial of practicing. Not the big shit. Not the abuse and murders of Black people. They are totally against that. But it's other shit like cultural appropriation and how they'll defend it without understanding it. Or supporting the police as an institution not as the terrorist organization it's been for Black communities. Or when they speak up to protect Trump supporters.

It's in the way they get defensive and 100% silent when you talk about racism at all.

I'll be real. I am not interested in creating a public safe space for racism discussions. If you want to talk about it one-on-one, ask me and I'll consider it. Publicly, I cannot and will not tolerate racist fuckery. I'm not going to be some free educational resource unless it's on my own terms and my Facebook feed is not that place. I decide, not you.

And yes, my husband is white. This is not a secret. His being white does not mean I am more tolerant and understand of the racism of others. In fact, being with him made me less tolerant because I was suddenly exposed to a shit-ton more microaggressions than I'd ever had to deal with in my life. I had to learn that this was a challenge I accepted in my relationship; one that many people wouldn't have chosen and that's some hard shit to swallow. But what that also means is that it's helped me see through a lot of the bullshit that comes my way. I don't accept it, people. I don't.

When you come out of the woodwork defending Trump supporters, you show your anti-Blackness. If you are white, you show your racism. When you come out to support the police, you show your anti-Blackness. If you are white, you show your racism. These things are undeniable, regardless of how you want to rationalize it. When you have a ridiculous amount of evidence pointing to the corruption and destructiveness of an organization, supporting it means you support the power, privilege, and corruption, as well as the robbery, abuse, and murder that goes with it. And telling yourself that you can parse that out is a lie. Own your bullshit.

I'm 100% tired of people lying to themselves about this shit. If you're a racist, just own it. I mean, if you're a white American, you are so just own it. And if it bothers you, as it should, work to change it. Make a better world for everyone.

And I do mean EVERYONE.

For the record, supporting the police is more than just supporting the police. What you are actually supporting is an institution designed specifically to harm Black people. You're supporting an institution that routine robs, brutalizes, and murders Black people with virtual immunity. This is an institution that routinely and intentionally decimates Black lives, as well as the lives of many vulnerable populations.

You are protecting oppression and white, hetero, cis, male supremacy.

The police took a Black woman in California to prison because she tried to defend another person from police officers' physical abuse[56]. They arrested and tried her for lynching.

---

[56] Gyamfi, Nana; Abdullah, Melina. "Black Lives Matter Activist Convicted of 'Felony Lynching'": "It's More Than Ironic, It's Disgusting.'" Democracy Now! 02 June 2016. Web. 26 June 2016.

The police beat a 15-year-old Black girl[57] for riding her bike through a parking lot.

The police arrested Sandra Bland[58] for a minor traffic infraction and released her dead body two days later.

The police took a 15-year old girl and started pimping her[59] and using her for sex.

The police routinely imprison people without cause, plant false evidence[60], coerce confessions[61], kill people in police custody[62], lie, cheat, steal, kill and band together to hide their crimes.

There is some shit you really just can't support. This is one of those things. We are not on the same team and fuck you for that.

[57] Agorist, Matt. "Disturbing Video Shows a Cop Brutally Beat a Child for Riding Her Bike, Charges HER with Assault." The Free Thought Project, 14 May 2016. Web. 26 June 2016.

[58] Graham, David A. "Sandra Bland and the Long History of Racism in Waller County, Texas." The Atlantic, 21 June 2015. Web. 26 June 2016.

[59] Sidner, Sara. "Sex, suicide and failure to report: How Oakland police scandal unfolded." CNN, 25 June 2016. Web. 26 June 2016.

[60] Carroll, Jon. "Leaked documents reveal Dothan Police Department planted drugs on black men for years." The Henry Report, 01 Dec 2015. Web. 26 June 2016.

[61] The Innocence Project. Web. 26 June 2016.

[62] Pearl, Mike. "How Many People Die in Police Custody in America?" Vice, 30 June 2015. Web. 26 June 2016.

When you come out of the woodwork defending Trump supporters, you show your anti-Blackness. If you are white, you show your racism. When you come out to support the police, you show your anti-Blackness. If you are white, you show your racism. These things are undeniable, regardless of how you want to rationalize it.

— TaLynn Kel, Caping for Cops

When White People Consume Blackness for Personal Gain

Yesterday I woke up ready to talk about that curly-haired former boy band goofball who pulled an "all lives matter" on Twitter[63]. I was so fired up that I spent much of the day thinking about it, doing research and mentally formulating a critique of popular culture and how it nourishes itself through cannibalism of Black people.

Jesse Williams alluded to it[64]. bell hooks intellectualized it[65]. And Black people have lived with it for hundreds of years. It's morphed some; it's no longer just the physical consumption of our Black bodies. Now it is the intellectual cannibalism of our thoughts, innovations, and inventions. It's the political consumption of our fight against injustice and inequality. It's the absorbing of our ideology as we fight for the protection of our Black bodies. It's the devouring and erasure of our creative contributions to the arts. White people have practiced cultural cannibalism in their colonization of the world. So much so that they have no identity except in their whiteness and the power they built around it, and even that is evaporating before their eyes.

---

[63] Carroll, Rebecca. "Justin Timberlake on Jesse Williams's BET speech wasn't woke, just white." The Guardian, 27 June 2016. Web. 28 June 2016.

[64] Brown, Lauren. "Read the Full Transcript of Jesse Williams' Epically Inspiring BET Awards Speech." Glamour, 27 June 2016. Web. 28 June 2016.

[65] Hooks, bell. "Eating the Other: Desire and Resistance." 1992. Web. 21 Feb. 2016.

Cultural cannibalism. Jesse Williams described it at the BET awards as "mining Black gold." bell hooks called it "eating the other." At one time, cannibalism was the literal ingesting of another's heart in an attempt to absorb their strength and knowledge. In America, it's colonialism, oppression, and white, hetero, cis, male supremacy. It is the utter and complete destruction of a culture that is then picked over for the tastiest morsels that is then shared among the destroyer with the rest being deemed useless and discarded.

To practice cultural cannibalism, the enactor must be so vicious, so savage, and so convinced of their superiority, that the culture they attack, consume, and destroy has to be dehumanized. Seeing yourself in those you destroy is the first thing that must be muted; otherwise the psychological damage would be overwhelming. It is why we work so hard to categorize our differences—it makes it easier to use them to create distance in our humanity. It is how we justify treating people unfairly. It makes it easier to use terrible violence to assert our superiority.

That violence is intrinsic to cultural cannibalism. How can you consume the heart of a culture if that culture isn't decimated? How can vultures feed if their food can fight back? So, you take their tools: their language, their spirituality, their education, their children, their will. You preemptively savage their bodies to demand obedience. You remove limbs, sever spines, mutilate faces, feet, hands. You limit care. You deprive sleep. Provide minimal food. You physically terrorize them until you are the boogeyman they fear. You are the savage you accuse them of being and you tell yourself it doesn't matter because they are different. They are not like you.

You attack them mentally. You make them dependent on you. Deny them language and education[66]. You separate them. Break their families. Deny them livelihood. Deny them community. And you do this for years upon years upon years in hopes that you break them beyond fighting.

That savagery is never far away. It often surfaces when a Black person dares to assert their freedom, think they belong, demand justice. When they say, "Look at me, I am doing everything you are doing and often I'm doing it better than you." It surfaces when Black people dare to demonstrate that we are intelligent and capable. It surfaces when we dare to be seen, when we deviate from the scripted narrative, when we dare to think we are as protected as white people.

I think back to the 2016 Oscars when Chris Rock gave his opening monologue[67]. That monologue was problematic on numerous levels, but the one thing it effectively demonstrated was the eagerness to ridicule and dismiss Black people who demanded to be recognized and how thin the layer of civility is for white people. The crowd laughed heartily at Chris' ridicule of Jada Pinkett-Smith and Will Smith's boycott of the Oscars— even as he used America's violent history of lynching to do it. He used the imagery of a murdered Black grandmother and the audience laughed. The predominantly white, rich, creative, sensitive, liberal, genteel, civilized audience laughed at a comment featuring a Black American grandmother who'd been murdered by lynching.

---

[66] Slavery and the Making of America. Georgia Public Broadcasting. Web. 27 June 2016.

[67] Oscars. "Chris Rock's Opening Monologue." YouTube, 23 March. 2016. Web. 27 June 2016.

I wasn't prepared for that. In fact, I remember being furious with Chris Rock for providing that imagery as a joke. Now I see it for what it was—the stripping away of the veneer of white civility as they engaged in the ritual cannibalization of Blackness.

Hollywood is too enlightened to literally hang someone for entertainment these days, right? At least, not with a televised, live audience. But it is an act they engage in with clichéd regularity in other popular mediums. Movies[68], television shows[69], comics[70]... in all these mediums, they limit the visibility of Black people, murder them, and justify it as necessary[71] for the advancement of the white characters. Sophisticated savagery. Pageant cannibalism. Cannibalism they claim isn't that because Black bodies are different from white bodies so it's not the same.

---

[68] Campbell, Christopher. "Who Else is Upset About the Death in "X-Men: First Class"?" Indiewire, 07 June 2011. Web. 27 June 2016.

[69] Shackelford, Ashleigh. "Orange is the New Black is Trauma Porn Written for White People [Spoilers]." Wear Your Voice, 20 June 2016. Web. 27 June 2016.

[70]Howze, Thaddeus. "On the Death of James Rhodes—War Machine." Medium, 22 June 2016. Web. 27 June 2016.

[71] Nededog, Jethro. "'Fear the Walking Dead' fans aren't happy about the amount of black deaths." Business Insider, 31 August 2015. Web. 27 June 2016.

White people consume everything about Black people—from our slang to our quips, to our hair, to our looks. They condemn us for how we speak[72], then laud some white artist as edgy and cool for speaking the same way. They practice our dance moves[73] and believe that no one will realize where they originated. They practice "blaccents," get butt implants, call themselves rapper artists, and win awards[74] for that bullshit. They call our features ugly, describe Black women as the least desirable women in the country[75], then co-op the parts of us they've exotified[76] and reject the rest.

They mine YouTube, mock our speech patterns, and make songs out of them that they sell on iTunes[77]. They consume our work and repackage it for a white audience that pays them for it. There is a proven market in cannibalizing Blackness. The repackaging is done so they can maintain their distance. *They are not like us. They are not us.* They find us interesting in a way they cannot create themselves . . . but still, they tell us that we do not matter.

---

[72] Paschal, Jaylin. "Smarter Than That: On the Assumptions Made About Ebonics and Intelligence." For Harriett, May 2016. Web. 27 June 2016.

[73]Mangum, Trey. "Hayes Grier's 'T-Rex' dance is cultural appropriation at its finest and Black Twitter is over it." Blavity, 15 Sept. 2016. Web. 27 June 2016.

[74] Zoladz, Lindsay. "Please, Don't Let Iggy Azalea Win the Best Rap Album Grammy." Vulture, 06 Feb 2015. Web. 27 June 2016.

[75] Solomon, Akiba. "The Pseudoscience of 'Black Women Are Less Attractive.'" Colorlines, 17 May 2011. Web. 27 June 2016.

[76] Harriot, Michael. "Black Bodies and the Last Frontier of Cultural Appropriation." Ebony, 20 May 2016. Web. 27 June 2016.

[77] Richardson, Riche. "'The Bed Intruder'—News Video Goes Viral: Antoine Dodson as Internet Celebrity and Commodity." Technoculture: an online journal of technology in society, vol 4, 2014. Web. 27 June 2016.

They tell themselves as they eat us alive that this is "right." They lie and say this is how it was meant to be. They laugh at our pain and try to destroy our wonder, they eat their humanity but pretend that the difference in skin color makes it acceptable. They will lie, cheat, steal, and kill to maintain the illusion of civility and the delusion of sanity while their immortality continues to consume them from the inside.

So keep mining our tweets. Keep digging through our YouTubes. Keep convincing yourself that you are a genius because you have managed to commodify Black innovation. Keep lying to yourself. We see you. We've always seen you. That is why you work so hard to keep us invisible and silent. Truth shines too brightly for you to ignore it, so instead you hide in the darkness of your soul and pretend you are better than you are.

We see you and you are not worth cannibalizing because you are rotten.

***

I woke up crying this morning. Crying because I planned to write about a culture that views me and people who look like me as food. Not literal food, but cultural, exotic, diverse, intellectual food. Creative food. Political food. Ideological food. Sexual food. Emotional food. Exploitable food. Disposable food. We are who they use to feel powerful, because if you do not have anyone to oppress, to whom are you superior? Trying to view myself through the lens of those who do not value me is painful.

That white people think it's easy for Black people to talk about racism exemplifies their ignorance about racism as well as their privilege. That they think we take some kind of special joy experiencing this and pointing it out is ridiculous. As a child, I couldn't wrap my head around racism. It wasn't real to me. I was so busy learning about the world and how to live that the racist obstacles I faced were just obstacles I faced. I didn't understand that they were deliberate. I didn't understand that they had been created specifically to make things more difficult for people who looked like me.

We like to think racism happened by accident, but it didn't. None of this happened by accident. Some of the ramifications, the health issues, are unanticipated side effects, but the conditions that created them are not accidents. It takes many people in a room and numerous years to make laws. That is very, very intentional. And many of the laws being enforced today are designed to prevent the very acts that emancipated America, and it was at the expense of a lot of people.

Thinking about racism, talking about it, is a kind of torture. When I start researching and analyzing it, I take such an emotional beating that it affects me even as I sleep. I wake up with tears streaming down my face from having to ask myself, "Why do people hate me for being brown? Why do white people work so hard to try to convince me that I'm worthless? Why do I have to push so hard to be respected as a human being? Why does anyone have to work this hard? Why are Black invisibility and Black pain the status quo?"

"Why do they wantonly kill people who look like me? Why do they defend it? Why do some people seem to hunger for it?"

I look at the white people in my life and wonder if I can trust them. I wonder if they are imagining what parts of me they can extract to improve future generations. Is it my melanin, because of the protection it provides from the sun? Is it my intellect—my children would probably be pretty smart. Is it the access I would provide to the Ivy League school from which I graduated? Is it the wealth I am slowly amassing for my retirement?

I wonder if they see me as fresh carrion that they are circling, waiting for the opportunity to feed.

I wonder, I wonder, and I wonder . . . until my heart aches, my throat burns, and my eyes glisten.

I wonder and then, just a little, I break inside.

This story first appeared at TheEstablishment.co, a multimedia site entirely run and funded by women on June 29, 2016.

They tell themselves as they eat us alive that this is "right." They lie and say this is how it was meant to be. They laugh at our pain and try to destroy our wonder, they eat their humanity but pretend that the difference in skin color makes it acceptable.

– TaLynn Kel, When White People Consume Blackness for Personal Gain

Loving the Chaos That is Me

"I got demons tap dancing for my soul. I'm allowed to compete but I can't dance."

I wrote those words eight years ago. I was describing my personal struggles with dieting, exercise, and quitting smoking while my father was dying, and I was working at a company that openly hated me. Almost everything in my life was a fight and I was tired of fighting. I wanted some peace, but I couldn't figure out how to get there.

Back then, I looked at my bad habits as demons – evil things actively working against my best interests. I loved them, hated them, fought with them, nourished them, and made love to them. They were the salvation I needed when my world had gone dark. I self-medicated, drank, smoked, and fucked myself through my 20s as I struggled to want to be here, to live. I forced myself through day after day after day until help came prescribed in a little bottle that I fought myself to open.

And things changed. I suddenly had breathing room, some space to look at my demons and some time to figure out how to subdue them. I attacked them with everything I had, using every tactic available. I would place pictures of myself in bathing suits to reaffirm my ugliness. I would call myself names. I would make nutritious food that I didn't like and force myself to eat it. I would refuse to eat if the only food available was off-plan. I would over-exercise on too little food – working out while lightheaded was the norm. I quit smoking because it was affecting my ability to exercise as much as I felt like I needed. Everything I did, loving or not, was to starve my demons into nothing because then I would be in charge. I would have control. My life would be mine.

I fought hard. If a person ever told me I was doing too much, they were the enemy. I picked through the people in my life and pushed out anyone who tried to shift my focus. I pursued friendships that were about my goals – relationships that did not last for obvious reasons. I studied. I planned. I exercised. I hungered. I focused all my energy on straightening myself out. I was going to fix my shit, exorcise my demons, and live a better life.

And as fucked up as all this was, it was an improvement of sorts because I had energy. I was actually doing something. Prior to this, I sat at home and hated the world. I had no motivation to change. I endured. I shut everyone out of my life unless they could fulfill a specific purpose for me. By focusing inward, I was less hostile to people and I could tell myself that everything I was doing was good for me. I was working on the real enemy, myself, and everything was going to be better. I was Buffy and I had demons to slay!

Then my dad died.

It's been seven years and everything in me still pauses when I think about that time. My world stops. I stop.

When he died, everything broke: my world, my life, me...

It is impossible to remain unchanged when you lose someone you love beyond measure. I shattered and had to find a way to piece myself back together. And I did, but the once broken is never the same as before. I went through the motions – I retained the same routines, kept the same friendships but it all felt different from before.

I stopped hearing what people were saying and started noticing how they made me feel. I was this giant, exposed bundle of nerves – it was so easy to hurt me. And when people did, I didn't attack them as I'd done in the past. I also didn't ignore them and beat myself up for being "too sensitive." I looked at them, *really* looked at them and assessed their role in my life.

I realized that life was painful enough without having people inflict it on me. I became less critical and more accepting of people's differences. My empathy grew. I allowed myself to be sensitive and stopped thinking of it as a weakness. I listened more and allowed myself to care about people with less fear of getting hurt. I learned that the potential to hurt was always there, whether intentional or not. I decided to learn how to manage the pain.

I stopped looking at myself and seeing various demons that needed culling. Instead, I finally saw myself as human with all the contradictions, non-sequiturs, irrational fears, and indescribable loves. I am a perfect fucking mess...just like everyone else.

I grew and learned that I am not my enemy. I never was. I just lacked empathy for the most important person in my life: me.

*****

Old habits die hard, though. I still fight with myself, beat myself up for my humanity. I'm getting better about it, though. I don't refer to parts of myself as demons anymore. That narrative was dangerous - I used it to abuse myself. For more than a year I fed myself a diet of frustration, disappointment, and shame. I told myself I was worthless, ugly, stupid, and a failure for things like being hungry, tired, sick, hurt. I gave myself no space to be myself; all I could see were the things I wasn't doing; the goals I didn't meet. I Othered my humanity and I hurt myself convinced that it was for my own good.

Now, I try not to look at my mistakes as damning.

I refuse to lie to myself and say the end justifies the means. If I have to hate myself to reach a goal, that goal is crap. I choose to love myself. I choose to place myself above all the bullshit people say I should want and have.

I decide what I need. I design my own path. When shit gets ugly, I go back to my map and look for alternate routes. I assess the importance of the goal and evaluate the potential outcomes of reaching it.

I work at not judging myself. At loving myself. At appreciating what I can do instead of punishing myself for what I can't. I accept that change takes time. I remind myself that I am worthy and loved, first and foremost by me. Now when I fight, it's for acceptance and inclusion and against the lies that tell us that's wrong.

My demons aren't my demons anymore. I accept myself and love myself as I am and I change to embrace more, not less of myself.

These days I get to be unapologetically and irrepressible me.

I am a perfect fucking mess...just like everyone else.

— TaLynn Kel, Loving the Chaos That is Me

It's Time to Own Our Shit and Change Everything

When I wrote My Husband's Unconscious Racism Nearly Destroyed Our Marriage I decided that I wouldn't defend it. That it would stand on its own and people could interpret it however they wanted, because that's what readers do – they interpret. They filter what they read through their own experiences and decide what they read means to them.

I do it all the time. I recently wrote how Beyoncé's *Lemonade* affected me[78] deeply when thinking about my relationship with America. I don't relate to the unfaithful partner narrative but I understand betrayal. I understand that feeling deeply. I also understand powerlessness, anger, and resolve, which I think were some of the underlying messages of the album, but again, that's my interpretation. Someone else with other experiences may hear it differently.

My essay about my marriage is very personal and from a distinct perspective, that of a Black, cisgender, heterosexual, 40-year-old, American woman married to a white, cisgender, heterosexual, 40-year-old, American man. I wrote it because I see a lot of interracial couples and never hear about that part of the struggle. I remember the pain and isolation I felt while trying to work through these issues. I remember wondering over and over if I'd made a mistake.

My biggest fear was whether I'd married a racist when the reality was that I had. My mistake was believing that it wasn't possible.

---

[78] Kel, TaLynn. "My Lemonade Tastes Like Black Resistance." Breaking Normal, 11 July 2016. Web. 08 January 2017.

I'd asked a bunch of other people if they thought it was possible that my husband was racist. The general consensus was that if we were together then he wasn't a racist. "A racist wouldn't date a Black person, much less marry them," they'd said. I laugh looking back on those responses. Even then, I knew they were wrong. That wrongness was why I kept asking over and over again.

I knew it was possible because I'd been courted by several racists – men who at some point in our association would try to get me to cosign on some "Black people are bad" bullshit. I don't know if they approached me to prove to themselves they were "different" or to check off a box on a list, but I knew they weren't interested in me. They were interested in my Blackness.

I'd had white men approach me who thought I was some special magical Black person in a sea of worthless ones. That I didn't talk like the rest of them or dress like the rest of them made me different...better. For a while, I bought into that. Like many non-conforming Black kids, I was teased by my peers for how I talked. I was never popular and in fact, I was recently reminded that I spent much of my senior prom sitting under a table. Needless to say, I was more than a little weird.

My weirdness made it easy to accept anti-Blackness[79] because in my experience, Black people rejected me for being unconventional. If you spend any time in the Black geek blogosphere, you quickly learn that many of us felt like outsiders among other Black people[80], including our families, and that many of us sought acceptance from people who shared our interests. That acceptance of our interests was usually in white dominated spaces. What was also in those spaces was rampant racism, sexism, and anti-Blackness, but because we are lonely, we learn to adapt. Loneliness is brutal. And while the internet helped us create spaces where we found other people like us, remember, I'm over 40. The internet was born around the time I started college so many of those networks didn't exist for me.

I felt alone in my idiosyncrasies, isolated by my inability to fit in, and struggling to embrace it. I had no known identity and it affected how I navigated my life. I struggled with dating, with figuring out how I fit into the very gendered, extremely sexist roles that women were supposed to occupy. It was much easier to have sex than to date, so that's what I did. I figured a lot of things out about myself as I learned again that I didn't "fit." I'm smart, vocal, and assertive - a combination that seemed to turn men off. I'm fat, which made some men think I was desperate for attention. I also have a dominant personality, which made some men want to control me. I continue to fight being defined again and again.

I am a Black woman because that's what the world tells me I am but I break that mold daily to create who I want to be.

---

[79] Kel, TaLynn. "Othering the Self – Learning to Recognize My Anti-Blackness." Black Girl Nerds, 02 March 2016. Web. 20 July 2016.

[80] Rhodes, Isabella. "Growing Up a Blerd." Black Girl Nerds, 09 July 2016. Web. 20 July. 2016.

I accept my womanhood but reject what people tell me it should mean. I cannot deal with anyone trying to put me in a box. When I was single, I proudly proclaimed myself a slut and fucked whoever I wanted...and a few people I didn't - I own that and all its complexities. I reject many of the approved roles for women – Madonna, whore, mother, good girl, bad girl, submissive, quiet, nurturing. I am a woman because that's how I look, not because that is who I am.

I accept my Blackness but reject the components I'm told go with it. I do not accept religion as the only time my belief mattered was when someone was trying to convince me to devalue myself. Religion is a tool to control people – their money, their sexuality, their choice to forgive...It is a form of control I reject and that rejection distances me from the popular "Black American identity." Just because I'm unpopular, doesn't mean I'm not real. It also doesn't mean I'm alone.

I am a Black woman in America. I fuck, but am not less for it. I refuse to wear heels. My marriage did not make me respectable. My vagina does not make me more of a woman. My tits eliminate the questioning of my gender and I show as much or as little of them as I want. I'm educated but not elitist. I'm fat, sexy, beautiful, and ugly. I listen to whatever fucking music I want. I'm visibly unseen. I wear my hair curly, wavy, straight, blond, blue, orange and it doesn't make me unprofessional, ghetto, anti-Black, an oreo, or whatever other derogatory thing people want to call Black women with non-traditional hair styles and colors. I work for "the man" and I'm married to "the man" neither of which make me any less invested in the fight against oppression.

We live in a racist, patriarchal society[81] so the fight is always there. If you are a heterosexual woman, it is impossible to avoid dating and marrying sexists. It's a little easier to avoid marrying racists - don't marry a white person. It's almost impossible to avoid anti-Blackness though. That's as prevalent as sexism and everyone learns that shit in America, regardless of color.

My husband is sexist and racist because he was born into it. He fights it now and sees it's unjust. He didn't always think this way and his change is one of the things I love about him. As hard as it is, he now owns his racism and sexism. We no longer call it unconscious because it wasn't. It was unacknowledged.

And as much as white people hate hearing this, you are all racist. There is no opting-out of it. It's part of the society that's been built, a society where white people control the resources and the access to those resources. One where the laws are written to deny access to those resources for people of color. All the information given to us in school, media, and law serves to solidify the message that white equals normal and brown is less than that. Until the way this system operates is torn apart, white people are born racist.

---

[81] Hess, Amanda. "Sexists Don't Hate Women. They Just Prefer Men." Slate, 22 May 2014. Web. 20 July 2016.

Throughout your life, you learn bias, prejudice and how to support and enforce racist policies and ideologies. You learn how to oppress. You learn the rules – who is "good" who is "bad" and how to treat people based on the color of their skin. You learn the unwritten rules of racism – how to undermine, discredit or ignore Black people. You learn how to cater to and promote whiteness. You learn how to view Black people as less, and then you teach it to your children. Racism means you accept the system and promote is as just. Racism is assuming that Black people have criminal records or are inherently violent -or, even better, inherently more violent than white people. Racism is talking about the health problems of Black people without discussing the structural and legal inequities that create these conditions. Racism is feeling comfortable with the status quo because it doesn't affect people who look like you. Racism is choosing not to change it.

The only way to be less racist is to actively fight it. As long as you deny your racism, you aren't fighting it; you are protecting your feelings. Are your feelings more important than human lives? If you can't admit your racism, then that's exactly what you are saying. It's the same with men and sexism. It's the same with able-bodied people and ableism. We are the problem and have to keep owning that we are the problem in order to move forward in solving the problem.

Please note, Black people and people of color learn bias, prejudice, and how to enact and enforce racist policies, too. It's a survival technique that we are taught young and rewarded for as we get older. I've had to own the anti-Blackness, anti-womanism, and anti-feminism I've enacted. Now I work to recognize it and try to be better. I am able bodied person who struggle to overcome her ableism. I am a fat person who works to overcome her sizeism. These things are pervasive and constantly reinforced by everything around us. I continuously inhale the poison of America and exhale its tyranny. None of us is exempt and it is an ongoing struggle to push back against it.

And we need to push back against it. Our world will not improve if we continue to say that oppression and the violence it wreaks is acceptable. It was never acceptable; American history is a centuries long spin-doctoring designed to convince future generations that they aren't the descendants of monsters. Happy to break it to you, but you are. Modern day Americans are descended from some of the most brutal and savage people in history.

We are the offspring of violent tyrants, but we don't have to stay that way. Break the norm. Fight the power. Walk the path of liberation.

Oppression has too long been the song of American patriotism and it's time for that song to be unsung.

I am a Black woman because that's what the world tells me I am but I break that mold daily to create who I want to be.

— TaLynn Kel, It's Time to Own Our Shit and Change Everything

I'm Not Here to Make Men Feel Good About Themselves

I hate chivalry. Like, seriously hate it.

I didn't have to deal with it too much when I was in the northeast. Not that it wasn't there, I just didn't date much so my interactions with men were limited. I started dating in the south, after I moved to Georgia, and in the south, men believe in being *men*, whatever that means.

Actually, I soon learned what it meant, in little, annoying ways. It meant making myself vulnerable in ways I never needed to in the past. It meant letting strange men walk behind me because I was supposed to get off the elevator first. It meant being forced to acknowledge unknown men because they opened a door for me. It meant constantly having "help" forced on me despite my assurances that I could manage. It meant stepping back and letting a man handle things that I'd handled just fine before they appeared in my life.

It meant being called "mannish" for beating them at games. It meant being unfeminine for opening my own doors. It meant being mocked for splitting the check. It meant being constantly shamed for handling my business and living my life without centering the man in closest proximity to me.

And, frankly, I'm not here for that shit.

Just last week, I was in a work meeting with a woman who informed me that she was allowing incompetent white man number 1* to lead the meeting so that "he would feel important."

Wait, what? First, why would anyone do that and second, why would you tell me that? Not to mention that this man is demonstrably not good at his job, yet she wants him to feel "important." It's been days and I'm still struggling to wrap my head around that. Why are we catering to that fuckery? Why does he need to feel important, especially as he's not good at his job? It doesn't make him better at it. In fact, I'd wager it makes him worse because we keep rewarding him for subpar work. I am really not a fan of rewarding mediocrity, yet here I am, contributing to that bullshit because I like getting paid.

This is a man who inserts himself as an authority about things he doesn't understand. He provides input on projects where he lacks not just the background but any information in that subject area. He actively tries to silence people who disagree with him. He tries to belittle and undermine other people in the room. He projects himself as knowledgeable when he's really an embarrassment. And then we reward that shit by making him feel good about it.

He's subpar and needs to know it. But nobody will tell him because he's a white man and in America, that means more than competence or skills.

Mind you, this is in addition to the boss who admittedly has no experience in his current role but somehow has had it for several months, learning it on the fly. The boss passed over two Black women who'd been working in that department and doing that work for five years, in favor of a man who'd never done that type of work, ever. It is believed that these white men will excel at these jobs, despite all evidence to the contrary, including current performance. But, you know, they always get the job done if given a fair shake, right? Fuck hiring someone qualified; they can learn it fast enough. That's sarcasm, by the way cuz this is some straight up white male patriarchal bullshit.

Fast forward a few days to when I was carrying some boxes to my car and a male friend offered to help. I told him I was fine and thanked him for the offer. He asked again. I refused again. Third time is the shaming of why won't I just take help when I need it.

I didn't need it, though. Not only didn't I need it, I also didn't want it.

And this is the shit that really irritates me. I was minding my own business, and here comes some guy offering help. Ok, cool. I get it. You want to be helpful. No, thank you. Now go away.

But they don't go away. They usually ask a second time and sometimes they linger around to ask a third time, each time being more insistent. It doesn't matter that I said no. It doesn't matter that I want to do it myself. It doesn't matter that I am taking care of it. I am supposed to stop what I'm doing and focus my attention on some guy who is inserting himself in my life repeatedly, and then thank him for the intrusion. I'm supposed to be grateful for it. I'm supposed to want this kind of attention and I'm being hostile when I refuse it.

I can't stop men from offering help. In fact, I don't care the first time. It's when they assume I don't mean it when I say no and they keep trying to impose their will on me.

Fuck the fact that I *like* doing things for myself. Fuck the sense of accomplishment I feel when I figure some shit out and make it happen. Fuck what I want in this situation. It's all about some guy and his need to feel powerful around some woman.

I don't care about you, your need to feel helpful, or you fucking fragile ego.

I am not interested in letting a "man be a man." That's not my fucking job. I don't even know what that bullshit means. No, motherfucker. This is not your show.

If you need my helplessness to feel strong, you're not strong.

If you need my weakness to feel masculine, you're not masculine.

If you need me to submit to feel dominant, you're not dominant.

If your sense of self is in any way tied to my actions, you don't know who or what you are.

And I'm not here to help you figure that shit out. Your fragile male ego means nothing to me.

The thing that really pisses me off is how quickly I become the enemy when I don't cosign on this shit. I mean, I get it. Oppressors need buy-in. They create legal and social structures to reinforce their "dominance" and empower enforcers of that dominance. That's how you get women who endorse sexism – they are accepted as an honorary member and encouraged to enforce their sexist agenda. They are lauded as the women who "get it," who prove the system works. They gain superficial benefits to demonstrate to other women the rewards they can receive if they "get it" too. Many women are complicit in oppressive patriarchy, with some women becoming its most powerful supporters.

"It's not that big a deal. It makes them feel good about themselves. Men like being heroes; just let them rescue you every once in a while. It makes them feel strong."

Ignore your needs to appease theirs.

And that's just the American way, isn't it? I do it for white people. I do it for men. I do it for white women. I do it for cops. I do it for anyone who thinks they have some authority over me.

And me? I just disappear under the illusion of agreeableness because sometimes it's better to be invisible than it is to be a target.

If you need my helplessness to feel strong, you're not strong.

If you need my weakness to feel masculine, you're not masculine.

If you need me to submit to feel dominant, you're not dominant.

If your sense of self is in any way tied to my actions, you don't know who or what you are.

And I'm not here to help you figure that shit out.

— TaLynn Kel, I'm Not Here to Make Men Feel Good About Themselves

The Complexities of Racism and Identity

I had the weirdest conversation with a friend last week.

We were talking about my statement of all white Americans being racist. Like most people, she had a knee-jerk negative reaction to the statement—and I get it. "Racist" has been made into a loaded word that people equate with evil. But while being a racist is obviously bad, like with many things, there are shades of grey.

You have your overt, angry, openly hateful, violent racists. These are the white people who openly attack Black people in the name of white supremacy and ethnic cleansing. Then you have your "play nice" racists, who pretend that everything is okay when they are around Black people, but quickly descend into denigrating and derogatory comments about us in all-white spaces. After that you have the people who don't practice overt hate speech, but instead refer to us as "those people" or use euphemisms like "urban youth" and refer to themselves as conservatives.

Then you cross into the liberal side, where racism is especially coded. These are the people who easily live, work, and play around a certain type of Black people (i.e. college-educated, professional), but can't understand why those other Black people can't straighten themselves out. Next are the ones who "don't see color" and say they treat everyone equally...that is, until you point out some racist subtext to what they said and then it's "You're the one being racist, you close-minded asshole. Maybe if you stopped treating everything as a nail, you wouldn't have these problems. Only racists point out racism! My ex-boyfriend is Black!"—as if riding some Black man absolves you of white privilege and all the institutional benefits you and your family have received for being white.

Then there's the performative allies[82] (god I wish I'd developed this term) who stand in solidarity with you until you challenge their privilege in a way that makes them uncomfortable. And finally, you have the white people who know they are racist and challenge the racism of the white people in their lives while also using their privilege to assist Black people on Black people's terms. I include women like Jane Elliott[83] in that category. She goes all in.

All this is to say that yes, in America, all white people are racist, but the degree to which they are varies. Just like Black people can't opt out of experiencing racism, white people can't opt out of participating in it. What they can do is challenge it and contribute to the work to dismantle it.

[82] McKenzie, Mia. "How to Tell the Difference Between Real Solidarity and 'Ally Theater.'" Black Girl Dangerous, 04 Nov. 2015.

[83] Amen, Rael. "Jane Elliott speaks on racism white supremacy." YouTube, 01 July. 2016. Web. 20 Aug. 2016.

This is a difficult concept for people to accept. Part of it is the way the word "racist" is processed by white people. I mentioned before that people equate it with evil, and racism itself is an evil practice, rooted in colonialism, exploitation, torture, treachery, and cruelty so abhorrent that more than 100 years later, white people still can't come to grips with the evil their ancestors did. The actions that still happen in the name of racism are horrible crimes against humanity. They need to be ended right now. But racism is also a system that was created around these crimes against humanity and designed to keep power and autonomy away from Black people. This system is maintained on every level and in every public and private system. Racism and white supremacy are in the laws, rules, education, media. We are all taught through books, music, television that white always trumps black. Light always defeats darkness. White is purity while black is evil. Light is truth and dark is treachery. Bad things happen in the dark, but the light protects you.

Ironically, a lot of evil happened in the light by the white, and it was the lightness of skin that justified their evil.

White people rewrote history, scrubbed it of many of the abuses and horrors they inflicted on Black people, and called the lies "truth." They conducted studies[84] with the intent to prove that Black people were somehow more than superficially different from white people and called the lies "science." They stole land[85] and instituted laws that forbade Black people from purchasing land, or getting credit for their inventions. They lied on everything about Black people and then convinced themselves that Black people were the liars. That dark skin can't be trusted.

---

[84] Mo. "On the peculiarities of the Negro brain." Science Blogs, 29 July 2007. Web. 20 Aug 2016. Web. 20 August 2016.

[85] Moore, A. "8 Heartbreaking Cases Where Land Was Stolen from Black Americans Through Racism, Violence and Murder." Atlanta Black Star, 09 Oct. 2014. Web. 20 July 2016.

Which brings me back to the conversation with my friend. She asserted that people can be racist against their own race. That, I said, is not possible.

***

It's important to understand that racism is about more than the individual. A "racist Black person" may attempt to inflict racism, but the system won't protect them from that same treatment. As such, it's impossible to equate their participation in racist systems with those who always benefit from it.

Take, for example, the Black police officer who enforces "stop and frisk" policies on Black men, but still finds himself subjected to being stopped and frisked when off-duty. Despite his individual complicity within the system, he is still subjected to racist practices, and this increases based on his proximity to white people.

After discussing this with my friend, she asked about multi-racial children, the ones who could pass for white--and that is where things became really interesting.

I hesitate to comment on this because I am unquestioningly, unequivocally Black. I initially learned about the concept of "passing" as white from *Nella Larson's book, Passing*[86]; prior to that, I had no idea that this was something Black people could do, because race was based on how you looked and choice wasn't a factor. People who "pass" can move between the Black and white racial identities; they are not limited to one by their appearance. That double consciousness that Dubois talks about can take on a different meaning: It can be the consciousness of your Blackness masked behind your white presentation. It can be the rejection of your Blackness under that white presentation. It can be the projection of your Blackness through your white presentation. It can be the accepting of that whiteness and Blackness.

In truth, if someone does not look Black, people will assume they are not Black and treat them accordingly. Someone who does not look Black can, though, choose to opt in to a racial identity and to experience the racism that comes with that. They still, though, won't have the same experience, because that person will need to inform others of their chosen identity and may not receive the same treatment as people easily identified as Black.

---

[86] Larsen, Nella, Deborah E. McDowell, and Nella Larsen. Quicksand ; And, Passing. New Brunswick, N.J: Rutgers University Press, 1986. Print.

Multi-racial people who pass for white have privilege that can shift in ways that mine cannot. I sometimes wonder what identity I would choose if I had a choice. I can't fault anyone for either not disclosing or choosing the white identity; it provides access to spaces that are otherwise off-limits. It also seems like a lot of work to get people to recognize one's identity. While they get to navigate the world able to avoid many of the microaggressions and overt aggressions targeting Black people, they also are subject to myriad other anti-Black rhetoric and commentary that I wouldn't experience. They get to experience white people who believe they are in an all-white space and the complicated interactions that come with that. I cannot begin to imagine what that would be like.

I do know that to embrace whiteness, is to embrace the lie of white supremacy. It is to willfully ignore deceptions, diversions[87], and accept the many ways white America silences its bloody past. You would need to silence the part of yourself and your heritage that survived that despite overwhelming odds. It would mean embracing the racial violence your family both suffered and performed.

That's a rough road to walk.

---

[87] Diaz, Natasha. "My Multiracial Identity Isn't A Party Trick." The Establishment, 10 July 2016. Web. 20 July 2016.

So, to address the question of whether it's possible to be racist against your own race? From my limited perspective, if you've embraced the lie of whiteness, you've rejected Blackness as your identifier and decided that you are not Black. You have made the choice to access all the privileges granted to white people, and to fully participate in racism. You have spliced aspects of your behavior to conform with what you think makes you acceptable to white people. You've rejected behaviors and symbols that have been identified as "Black" and continue to modify yourself to be different. In your head, you aren't like those Black people. You're different. Better. You've assimilated and every symbol of approval you achieve in white America is considered to be success.

But while that may work for you now, there may come a point where you won't be able to choose your identity; because as much as identity can be a choice, more often than not, that choice is made for us. We see it with gender, size, sexuality . . . we are informed of who we are expected to be and are often required to conform to that expectation.

It's important to note that while Black people cannot technically be racist, we can be complicit. People like Clarence Thomas and Ben Carson, while they technically cannot be racist, deny their Black identity enough to set themselves up as exceptions to a system designed to work against them. That is, they aggressively support and enforce racist practices to gain white approval. They are the faces of performative anti-Blackness, hence their popularity among conservative, conventionally racist crowds. These men are the "Black friends" who don't have a problem with the racist shit white people do because they don't see themselves as those Black people who are still fighting for justice in an unjust country.

Racism is complicated. It stays complicated. It's a web of man-made bullshit designed to empower one group of people over others. Because the differences between people are superficial, the web keeps changing and all of it is to protect the lie that is white supremacy. Until racism is unraveled and destroyed, it will continue to destroy humanity through its oppression and cruelty. It will continue to dehumanize Black and brown people in order to maintain its façade. It is corruption, and until white people can own their shame and their pain, it will continue to spread and destroy.

The time has come for us to break the lie and let us, *all* of us, heal.

This story first appeared at TheEstablishment.co, a multimedia site entirely run and funded by women, on August 18, 2016 and was titled "Can People Be Racist Against Their Own Race?"[88]

---

[88] Kel, TaLynn. "Can People Be Racist Against Their Own Race?." The Establishment, 18 Aug. 2016. Web. 20 August 2016.

It's important to note that while Black people cannot technically be racist, we can be complicit. People like Clarence Thomas and Ben Carson, while they technically cannot be racist, deny their Black identity enough to set themselves up as exceptions to a system designed to work against them.

— TaLynn Kel, The Complexities of Racism and Identity

Question the Narrative

I spent the last week on an unintentional break from the news, writing, media, etc. and spent the week streaming movies. I looked for various titles, but many times just looked through the visual catalog Netflix provided. Nothing demonstrates how inclusive the movie industry is like seeing white face after white face on your screen as you try to decide what to watch. But I didn't let that bother me, I was sick and I wanted to feel comforted so I chose movies that made me feel nostalgic.

Now that I am more critical of what I consume, watching movies I previously enjoyed is challenging. I don't see tropes as harmless anymore. Every single image, every choice, every character is a message. It is a way to influence our thoughts. So when I watch movies, I pay more attention to the messages being promoted. I am not the best at it. There are tons of nuance that I still miss, but it still makes a huge difference in how I see things that I once viewed as mere entertainment, and that scares and saddens me.

I watched Small Soldiers, a movie whose message I thought, in addition to being anti-war, was "just because something looks monstrous, doesn't mean it is." And while that message was still a big take away, there were even bigger messages about white saviorism and tolerating toxic masculinity that I'd missed. And I missed then because of how we are programmed to watch movies – the protagonist is sympathetic. They deserve our empathy. We should always seek to understand their motives unless we are explicitly told that they are evil. In Small Soldiers, the protagonist is a white teenager who'd been expelled from two high schools for illegal activities (downplayed as pranks) who cannot take "no" for an answer from a girl that he likes. The entire movie, he repeatedly asks his neighbor out despite her many refusals because who cares what she wants. He wants her to go out with him and he's not going to give up.

This kid is a resentful teen, angry that his parents don't trust him, despite his violating that trust at every turn. He lies to his parents. He convinces a delivery man to "lose" a shipment of toys that he plans to sell while his father is away on business – toys that violate his father's deeply held belief against promoting violence. This kid, this criminal, who cannot abide simple rules and laws is the hero, and at one point I found myself actually sympathizing with this degenerate.

Movies are fucking insidious.

This movie presented the soldier toys as extreme examples of hyper-masculinity and then bombarded us with a less extreme version of toxic masculinity, masked as the hero, to soften our perspective. We see his persistence with the girl as a heroic quality – look at how he doesn't give up. Why don't his parents believe him about the toys? Sure, he's lied in the past, but they should trust him! Why can't they trust him? Look at him try to save his family from the problem that he created with his lies and machinations? He's a hero!

Fuckery.

And then there's the peaceful toys that the degenerate works to save…the peaceful Gorgonites who he has to pressure into saving themselves. Toys who "sacrifice" themselves to save the humans. It's pretty easy to see this storyline in so many narratives about people of color – that we appear dangerous, need to be contained and destroyed, cannot save ourselves and that in order to be redeemable, we must offer to sacrifice our very beings. Blah, blah, blah. It's fucking gross.

So yeah, Small Soldiers sucked.

A couple days later I followed that shit up with Good Will Hunting and OH MY GOD that movie made me so angry!

That movie, which put the poster boys for white liberal Hollywood bullshit on the national radar, is the epitome of white male privilege. It is the magnum opus of forgiveness of toxic masculinity. It is the fuckshittiest of fuckshit when it comes to the hypocrisy of how people are treated in this country. We spend an entire movie learning to empathize with a man who is willfully violent, angry, dangerous, and destructive. We are taught to afford him opportunity after opportunity, to bend over backwards to help accommodate this white man who consistently rejected every overture. Yes, he'd been abused. Yes, he had a hard life. This man transformed himself from a victim to a predator. He picked fights. He treated people like shit. He lied, repeatedly. And yet, we were supposed to empathize, sympathize, understand, and forgive.

Bullshit.

They talked to women like shit, treated them like shit, and fought over them like prizes to be won. And the entire movie, this grown ass man who made shitty, dangerous, violent decisions was referred to as a boy and forgiven his transgressions. And the take away? He's just misunderstood. So when your boyfriend screams at you and beats on the wall when you confront him about his lies, when that man spits on the job interviews you set up for him and mocks you incessantly, just remember that he may be a misunderstood boy who always deserves the benefit of the doubt.

This type of messaging is why the Charleston shooter got a bulletproof vest and McDonald's when he was taken alive after murdering 9 innocent people.

This type of messaging is why white men shoot at cops and are talked down.

This type of messaging is why people blame women for their abuse.

This type of messaging is why people blame Black people for racism.

We are continually bombarded with the message that white men deserve our trust, our forgiveness, our leniency, and our support and anyone who denies them these things is the enemy. White men feel entitled to these things, and when they are denied, the outcry reverberates throughout the land. This is white supremacist, patriarchal conditioning. And we are its victims.

Every time we turn on a television, watch a movie, and read a book, we are taught how to forgive white men and then men like GW Bush Jr, a man who was mediocre at best, become president for 8 years. Men like Bill Clinton fuck their interns and stay in power. Men like Trump lie, cheat, and steal but become viable presidential candidates. They are flawed. They made mistakes. They deserve our respect.

Except they don't and that we give it to them is disgusting.

So, next time you find yourself watching a movie with a white, male protagonist, assess their actions. Take a long, hard look at the main character and ask yourself if what they are doing is legal and moral. Ask yourself if you empathize with them. Ask yourself if they earned the benefit of the doubt. Ask yourself whether you'd like this person in real life.

Ask yourself, does this person deserve your regard and respect, or are you entitling them to something they haven't earned...and ask yourself why.

Always question the narrative.

I'm out.

We are continually bombarded with the message that white men deserve our trust, our forgiveness, our leniency, and our support and anyone who denies them these things is the enemy.

— TaLynn Kel, Question the Narrative

The Danger of Unchallenged Racism in Interracial Relationships

It shouldn't surprise me that interracial relationships are here to stay, considering that I'm in one. Still, I worry about the people in them. When I started dating "Kevin," I was concerned about the demographics of the relationship. I worried about how it would play out with our families and friends, the rest of the world.

The one thing I didn't really understand was how it would play out between us.

So I wrote about it. I wrote about how I'd desensitized myself to a lot of casual racism[89] in my life as a survival tactic. I wrote about how I'd internalized anti-Blackness. Then I wrote about retuning myself to hear the anti-Blackness in my relationship, and subsequently having to address it with my white spouse[90] before we ruined our marriage.

My husband was willing to change. He continues to change and address his racism. Because he's willing to do this work, we work.

I am one of the lucky ones.

---

[89] Kel, TaLynn. "Othering the Self – Learning to Recognize My Anti-Blackness." Black Girl Nerds, 02 March 2016. Web. 20 July 2016.

[90] Kel, TaLynn. "My Husband's Unconscious Racism Nearly Destroyed Our Marriage." The Establishment, 05 May. 2016. Web. 20 August 2016.

I'm lucky because even though it's hard for him, he admits his racism and actively works to dismantle it. He'll have the hard conversations. He accepts that there were things he supported in the past that were disgusting. He unmasks his lies and owns his mistakes. We both do. That we don't have children helps. We don't have the additional stress of inadvertently encoding any children with racism or self-hate. It is a humbling way to live, but it's real, raw, and truthful. We don't mask our ugly. We sit it right beside the pretty and figure out how we're going to live with it.

When I read the blogs of other interracial couples, I rarely hear about the ugly. I don't hear about how those couples confront the elephant in the room and fight to keep it from trampling everything. Instead, I hear odes to colorblind love and admiration for the white people who dared the ostracization of their white families and friends—something you don't hear about the Black partner because it's presumed that dating a white person is a come-up, not a downgrade. I read about the white person's bravery and their struggle.

What I see, though, is their internalized racism.

Just yesterday I read a blog about an interracial family[91]. The woman has a white son from a previous relationship and is currently married to a Black man, with whom she has a two-year-old son. In this essay, she reflects on her relationship as she has had to admit to herself the racism her husband experiences, and realize the future her toddler son faces. They have been together for years and now she is beginning to understand the inherent danger this country presents for people with brown skin. Now she sees that minor things like spending time alone with their white child or driving with a broken tail light are potentially lethal for her Black spouse. Finally, she is starting to see what's been in front of her all of her life. Finally.

---

[91] Chelsie. "When Suddenly No Lives Matter." 2 boys 1 blog and me, 09 July 2016. Web. 20 August 2016.

Her response? To tell her two-year-old Black child this: "You better make smart decisions. Safe decisions. No robbing a gas station. No walking down the street swinging a sword around. No rioting. You are to be respectful. You are to be a member of society that contributes to the world. You are to be proud of who you are and your heritage. If you are anything less than these things, you might not come home to me one day."

There was so much in that one quote that I wished I still smoked. I love how she made it all about her potential loss. Not fear about the life he may have to live, but her fear that he may not come home . . . to her. She told her child, "Don't be a kid. Grow up. Don't make mistakes. Don't confront the system. Don't rebel. Be quiet. Be still. Be invisible. Do what people say, but be proud of who you are, as long as it doesn't look like any kind of protest or disobedience."

On top of that, she threw in a few gems about only doing legal things because robbing a gas station is every Black person's aspiration unless they fight *really* hard not to. I also liked the shout out to Darrien Hunt[92], the young Black man who was murdered for cosplaying with an ornamental sword. They sell those swords at the mall, you know. I have six of them.

---

[92] Broadnax, Jamie. "Cosplay or No Cosplay: The Homicide of Darrien Hunt." Black Girl Nerds, 17 Sept. 2014. Web. 20 August 2016.

What she forgot to mention, however, was how being respectful, productive, proud, and lawful can still get Black people "legally" murdered by police and scared white people. How it can get you lynched in police custody[93]. How Black people are refused medical care by the police[94] until they die in custody. How scared white people kill Black people[95] asking for help. How Black people are killed by police for sleeping in their cars[96]. Did she forget this? Or has she just not acknowledged it yet? I wonder . . .

I wonder if she tells her white son these things. Does she think he'll be killed for being disrespectful?

I wonder how her husband responds to her casual racist attitude towards their child. I wonder how he feels when she dismisses his fears as "crazy paranoia." I wonder if it bothers him that it took another Black man being murdered for her to begin to understand his legitimate concerns.

---

[93] Graham, David A. "Sandra Bland and the Long History of Racism in Waller County, Texas." The Atlantic, 21 June 2015. Web. 20 Aug. 2016.

[94] Neyfakh, Leon. "50-Year-Old Black Woman Who Died in Jail Was Denied Water and Medication, Court Filings Allege." Slate, 25 Feb. 2016. Web. 20 Aug. 2016.

[95] Manuel-Logan, Ruth. "Police: Man Says He Killed Teen Seeking Help After Crash 'Accidentally.'" NewsOne, 2014. Web. 20 Aug. 2016.

[96] Agorist,Matt. "Parents on a Date Were Asleep in Car When Cops Arrived and Killed Them Both." The Free Thought Project, 25. Feb 2016. Web. 20 Aug. 2016.

I wonder how he feels when he reads her statement that everyone has the same opportunities and choices, completely ignoring the hundreds of years that many choices were illegal for Black people. I wonder if he questions himself when he hears her dismiss the hundreds of laws that explicitly forbade Black people from accessing the same benefits as white people. I know I questioned myself when Kevin did it. I questioned him, myself, and our relationship. I asked myself how much work was I willing to do to stay and how much I was willing to compromise for him. It was more than I would do now; my patience was in a different place then, but it's less than other people think it should be, as evidenced by every person asking if Kevin is okay with my essays.

For the record, Kevin is okay with my essays. He supports what I do and accepts that sometimes my writing will be about our relationship. He listens and learns and he calls out my hypocrisy—not to silence me, but to remind me of who I want to see in the mirror.

And I hold a mirror so he can see himself and ask if he's being the person he wants to be.

Then we hold up a mirror so that we can see ourselves, together, because honesty and accountability are everything.

I wonder who holds up the mirrors for the couple from the blog post, if they even have mirrors at all.

***

As hard as everything is right now, this social environment is an improvement. No longer are Black people silenced as easily as they were during my childhood. More Black people have voices than ever before. Injustice is called out, spread, the veil of American freedom lifted, our bullshit now visible to the rest of the world. It is both glorious and heartbreaking to see the volume of injustices across the country. It isn't surprising, though. Black people have been discussing this for decades.

For a long time, I gave white people the benefit of the doubt. I told myself that they didn't know what they were doing. They were ignorant. If only we explained it to them, helped them relate, then they'd understand. Over the past three years I've seen explanation after explanation and still people deny racism. They deny profiling. They deny persecution of Black people. They deny and when they can't deny, they lie. It was in the past six months that I finally accepted that all of this is 100% deliberate, including the "ignorance." It is willful. It is a choice.

My denial of this was the only thing that made me feel slightly safe in this world. It was what helped me stay optimistic about the future and aided me in giving white people the benefit of the doubt. I don't give them the benefit of the doubt anymore. Now I just understand that if they aren't challenging racism, they support it. I can no longer call my husband's racism unconscious. It was unchallenged. Now we both live with the challenge of what that means and how he needs to continue to change and grow.

Interracial couples are going to need to challenge the racism in their relationships. If you haven't yet, you will. Some of your relationships will end. Others will grow. Regardless, you need to unbury the lie. It is toxic to both you and your partner, but especially to your children. Don't raise them to hide and hate themselves.

I hope this woman's racism is challenged before she does more harm to her family. I get that this is her experience and she is doing her best.

But her best isn't good enough.

This story first appeared at TheEstablishment.co, a multimedia site entirely run and funded by women, on July 18, 2016.

I questioned him, myself, and our relationship. I asked myself how much work was I willing to do to stay and how much I was willing to compromise for him.

— TaLynn Kel, The Danger of Unchallenged Racism in Interracial Relationships

Tired of Whiteness

I have some white people in my life I still call friends. I call them that, but as I am less silent about the lies this country loves to propagate about people who look like me, Black people, I find myself being more honest about my relationships with white people. That honesty is hard because it tells me that I don't think of these people as my friends anymore. I'm scared to talk to them. I'm scared to be alone with them because I don't trust their perceptions of Blackness. And I don't trust them to understand the fear and horror of my reality.

They don't know how I struggle to face the day filled with casual slights about the skills, ethics, and morality of Black people. They don't know how I have to comport myself in an environment that actively denigrates and oppresses me. They don't know what it's like to work in a sea of brown faces that are intentionally excluded from protections they take for granted. I work in an organization that uses consistently uses contractors but only hires the non-Black ones, regardless of tenure. It is common to see a Black person stay in a contract position for years while white contractors hired years after them become employees. This one act keeps Black people in a positon of job insecurity as they wonder whether the contract will be renewed, and it keeps us unprotected from discrimination and racism, as the contracting company will keep the client happy at your expense. Imagine having a team who, should you push back against any violations, will have you removed and labeled a "problem employee" barring you from future roles. This is everyday reality because it's inconvenient for white people to admit, acknowledge, or combat racism.

Inconvenient.

And that's if they believe me or support me. It's a lot of work to support Black equality and slavery shows how this country felt about hard work.

I no longer have the patience to understand how white people don't understand racism. I no longer have the fortitude to listen to lazy excuses for why they don't get it. I know why. They don't care. It's not a problem for them. This isn't the life they know and as long as they limit their exposure to Black people, they never have to discuss it or deal with any of the ramifications of their indifference.

If they live their white lie lives, they never need to address the harm they do.

I am so fucking tired of complacent white people who think the status quo is fine. I am so tired of trying to figure out how to dismantle the current system while surviving in it. I am tired of trying to figure out how to escape...cuz I only see one way and it's not one you live through.

Every time a Black person is attacked, harassed, shot, or murdered by white people, I have to talk myself back from a ledge. My rage is burning out, and so is my will.

And I live a soft life. I have an office job, a home...all my basic and material needs are met. I have free time and I have options about what I do with that time. I am fortunate and privileged. And yet, I am still undone when I see Black people murdered for existing. Black men. Black women. Black children. Black transgender people. Black humans who are doing routine things are murdered for living their lives. Murdered by the police because cops are barely punished[97] for killing Black people. In fact, they are actively rewarded

---

[97] Ferner, Matt. "Here's How Many Cops Got Convicted Of Murder Last Year For On-Duty Shootings." Huffington Post, 13 Jan. 2016. Web. 21 Sept. 2016.

with monetary compensation[98] and paid leave[99] after murdering Black people.

And to have any person, especially any white person, try to justify that shit makes me hate them. It makes me look at them and hate who they are because their compassion is broken. Their empathy is warped. They will not admit that some part of them believe in the lie of some inherent danger of Blackness. That some part of them does not think I'm as human as they are.

The moment they say, "They should have complied."

The moment they ask, "Did they do what the cops said?" or "What did they do?"

In that moment, I'm put on notice that they are looking for a reason to blame someone for their own murder. And that means that I can't trust them.

If there is one thing I've had to accept, it's that white people protect white people. They protect them when they lie (see Donald Trump[100]). They protect them when they rape women (see David Becker[101] and Brock Turner[102]). They protect them

---

[98] Swaine, Jon. "GoFundMe defends Darren Wilson fundraising page despite racist postings." The Guardian, 22 Aug. 2014. Web. 21 Sept 2016.

[99] Pyke, Alan. "The People Stopping Police Departments From Addressing Colin Kaepernick's Protest." Think Progress, 30 Aug. 2016. Web. 21 Sept. 2016.

[100] Rich, Frank. "Matt Lauer's Gift to Donald Trump." New York Mag, 08 Sept. 2016. Web. 21 Sept. 2016.

[101] Johnson, Kimberley. "No Jail Time For Rapist So He Can Enjoy The 'College Experience'." Liberals Unite, 22 Aug. 2016. Web. 21 Sept. 2016.

[102] Grinberg, Emanuella; Shoichet, Catherine. "Brock Turner released from jail after serving 3 months for sexual assault." CNN, 03 Sept. 2016. Web. 21 Sept. 2016.

when they sexually abuse children (see Kraigen Grooms[103]). They protect them when they enable abuse (see Joe Paterno[104]). They protect them when they murder (see murderers of John Crawford[105], Michael Brown[106], Sandra Bland[107], Tamir Rice[108], Freddie Grey[109], Rekia Boyd[110], and on[111] and on[112] and on[113]).

In the meantime, we see news report[114] after news report[115] of white men shooting at police and being taken

---

[103] Guerra, Kristine. "Teen pleads guilty to sexual abuse of a 1-year-old girl, then a judge gives him no prison time." The Washington Post, 19 Sept. 2016. Web. 21 Sept. 2016.

[104] Bazelon, Emily; Levin, Josh. "The Most Damning Verdict." Slate, 12 July 2012. Web. 21 Sept 2016.

[105] Democracy Now! "No Charges in Ohio Police Killing of John Crawford as Wal-Mart Video Contradicts 911 Caller Account." Democracy Now! 25 Sept. 2014. Web. 21 Sept. 2016.

[106] Bouie, Jamelle. "Michael Brown Wasn't a Superhuman Demon." Slate, 26 Nov. 2014. Web. 21 Sept. 2016.

[107] Graham, David A. "Sandra Bland and the Long History of Racism in Waller County, Texas." The Atlantic, 21 June 2015. Web. 20 Aug. 2016.

[108] Flynn, Sean. "The Tamir Rice Story: How to Make a Police Shooting Disappear." GQ, 14 July 2016. Web. 21 Sept. 2016.

[109] McLaughlin, Eliot C. "Freddie Gray verdict: Officer Edward Nero not guilty." CNN, 24 May 2016. Web. 21 Sept. 2016.

[110] Bellware, Kim. "Chicago Cop Who Killed Rekia Boyd Quits, Preserving His Cushy Retirement." Huffington Post, 17 Sept. 2016. Web. 21 Sept. 2016.

[111] Stole, Bryn. "'Bad police work' in Alton Sterling death, but don't expect conviction." Sun Herald, 19 Sept. 2016. Web. 21 Sept. 2016.

[112] Ortiz, Erik. "Philando Castile and Cop Who Killed Him Crossed Paths Before, Records Show," NBC News, 22 July 2016. Web. 21 Sept. 2016.

[113] Felton, Ryan. "'Our kids can't play with toy guns': Tyre King police shooting a painful reminder." The Guardian, 20 Sept. 2016. Web. 21 Sept. 2016.

[114] King, Elizabeth. "White Man in California Shoots at Cops With Gun, Gets Shot With Beanbags and Arrested." Complex, 17 Aug. 2016. Web. 21 Sept. 2016.

alive. We hear about white men who killed innocent, unarmed people being taken alive (see Dylan Roof[116], Robert Dear[117], and James Holmes[118]). We see white people manage to engage in acts of unspeakable violence and still be considered worthy of our compassion and charity, while Black people murdered in the street somehow deserved it.

So, no. I don't trust white people with my Blackness and that makes me sad. It makes me especially sad because sometimes that includes my husband.

And it makes me wonder if this is any way to live.

[115] Jones, Jeremiah. "White Guy Shot TWO COPS. But Don't Worry He's Fine." Countercurrent News, 21 Aug. 2016. Web. 21 Sept. 2016.

[116] NBC News. "Charleston Church Shooting." NBC News, 2016-2017. Web. 21 Sept. 2016.

[117] Hughes, Trevor. "Planned Parenthood shooter 'happy' with his attack." USA Today, 11 April 2016. Web. 21 Sept. 2016.

[118] CBS News. "Colorado movie theater massacre." CBS News, 2016. Web. 21 Sept. 2016.

I no longer have the patience to understand how white people don't understand racism. I no longer have the fortitude to listen to lazy excuses for why they don't get it. I know why. They don't care. It's not a problem for them.

— TaLynn Kel, Tired of Whiteness

You Are Not My White Savior

Imagine what it's like to sit in a room being told that your existence is a burden on society. Imagine being the only one who looks like you while being told that. You, in your brown skin, hearing that specific characteristic be pathologized and dissected as though it is the problem - not the systems designed to oppress those with the characteristic, but you, specifically are the problem. You, who sits there surrounded by white peers who habitually congratulate themselves for sacrificing their potential earnings by dedicating themselves to public service as they work to eliminate the burden that you, Black person, place on society.

Imagine your pale skinned professors as they talk about how to solve the problem of Black people because it is their dream to save us from ourselves, since we have proven ourselves incapable of the task. Listen as they coordinate tours through urban neighborhoods to discuss the shitty conditions Black people live in. As they discuss everything from your body, homes, and retail options, they blame you. They blame you for the circumstances that created your health conditions. They blame you for living in a neighborhood without a supermarket. They blame you for using the bus. They blame you for having a low wage job. You see their pity, their disdain, their feelings of superiority. You feel their certainty in their actions and their pride that they are working so hard to make the world better by judging people who look like you. And you feel their expectations of approval for taking the time to care, because someone has to care about Black people who don't seem to care about themselves. They are our saviors and we better fucking appreciate it.

And not once does racism ever enter the conversation.

This was my experience in graduate school as I earned my degree in public health. It was white judgement, pity, and sacrifice wrapped in white fragility. It was constantly talking around the problem without ever acknowledging the actual problem. I remember having full class discussions about disparities in infant mortality[119] – how Black people still experience higher rates, even when income is less of a factor. We never talked about how white doctors see Black patients[120] as inferior, unintelligent, or less susceptible to pain[121]. We didn't talk about how racial biases affect patient treatment. We didn't talk about how funding and zoning impacts the distribution of services and that areas designated as "minority" were of lower priority[122]. We didn't talk about how living immersed in constant negative imagery and rhetoric psychologically affects Black people[123]. Instead we sat there and wondered why Black women struggled with pregnancy and tried to think of ways to give Black women access to pre-natal care. We didn't talk about the assumption they weren't receiving pre-natal care was also racist.

I listened to white professors blame people for their problems. I listened as they talked about the economic, societal, and social burden of Black people. I listened as they talked about people like me absorbing resources with no visible improvement in outcomes. I listened as they rationalized reducing those resources because the impact wasn't worthwhile.

---

[119] Florido, Adrian. "Why do black infants die so much more often than white infants?" 89.3 KPCC, 03 March 2014. Web. 25 Sept. 2016.

[120] Schroeder, Michael O. "Racial Bias in Medicine Leads to Worse Care for Minorities." U.S. News and World Reports, 11 Feb. 2016. Web. 25 Sept. 2016.

[121] Samarrai, Fariss. "Study Links Disparities in Pain Management to Racial Bias." University of Virginia, 04 April 2016. Web. 25 Sept. 2016.

[122] Bouie, Jamelle. "How We Built the Ghettos." The Daily Beast, 13 March 2014. Web. 25 Sept. 2016.

[123] Silverstein, Jason. "How Racism Is Bad for Our Bodies." The Atlantic, 12 March 2013. Web. 25 Sept. 2016.

I listened as public health educators taught the future public health workforce that they were justified in their superiority complex and how to rationalize continuing to marginalize people of color, and it was sold as societal morality.

I didn't confront it – at least, not often. I know how the system works. I get to stay if I don't rattle the cage. Once, I engaged in a spirited classroom debate which resulted in some people telling the professor they were afraid to express themselves in class. I got the message; it wasn't new. My entire life has been using my silence to keep white people comfortable with their oppression.

Should you speak to discuss the obvious, you are met with two forms of resistance. There is the white male denial – these are the white men who try to invalidate your experience. They tell you that you are exaggerating; that racism is over. Look at how we are all in class together. They deny, deny, deny until you are exhausted. The white women...they sympathized. They listened to your story then told you how bad it made them feel. They asked you to find ways to help them assuage their guilt while you still live under the boot of their privilege and in the shadow of their disregard. You don't seek their approval, but these are the disciples of the gatekeepers. You can see the future and hope that one day, when you are less frustrated into silence, you can plant a seed and one day change a mind. There are never enough people who look like you to mount a resistance. You are one of very few, surrounded on all sides by people who either work to discredit you or overshadow you with their feelings. And so you pay your silence, shore the defenses, and over time lose hope that anything will ever change.

It's an interesting thing, navigating white spaces. You learn to look away, to ignore, to silence your thoughts. You learn to be very still until you leave and cleanse yourself of the muck that is the big white lie. I'd forgotten what it was like to be taught that Black lives didn't matter. I'd forgotten what it was like to for all Blackness to be ignored until it was a problem. Working in public health constantly reminds me of that.

In grad school, I navigated this space. I didn't do it well. I cried a lot, internalized a lot, and really disliked a lot of my classmates. I struggled with the idea of removing race from surveys because of the bias it both generated and perpetuated. I finally understood that while race isn't real, racism is very real because white people created it, legalized it, socialized it, enforced it, and now pretend that it does not shape our society. I had to start erasing the decades of racist programming and see the world how it truly is. I still fuck up. I've made some decisions whose consequences I struggle with now, but more than anything, I keep finding my center and shoring it up to withstand the waves of marginalization that continue sweeping towards me.

It's funny. I've had white people try to silence me by saying that I was too invested in dismantling racisms for my opinion to be trusted. What they fail to acknowledge is that white people have too much invested in maintaining white supremacy for them to be trusted about dismantling racism. Are you going to work to dismantle something that has benefitted you? Does it matter that your benefits came at the expense of other people's human rights? It should. This is a question of conscience and after 400+ years of racially driven inhumanity, I have to ask - do white people have consciences? The quickness with which people dismiss the oppression of others makes me think they don't.

I never thought that embracing and acknowledging my humanity would be a form of protest. I never imagined that merely existing would bother groups of people so much that they would kill to silence me. I would never have anticipated that having the strength to stand in all my hubris and complexity and say, "I am here and I am staying" is revolutionary. That acknowledging my joy, my pleasure, my contradictions, my humanity is my resistance. I am enough.

I thrived in grad school, despite the bullshit. I came out with a stronger sense of self as I rejected the racist ideas they taught. I accepted my place on the outside, and while I'm still figuring out what that means, I refuse to be silent about it. I've found my voice and regardless of what any supposed "authority" says, it matters.

I matter. And I don't need to be saved by you.

I listened as public health educators taught the future public health workforce that they were justified in their superiority complex and how to rationalize continuing to marginalize people of color, and it was sold as societal morality.

— TaLynn Kel, You Are Not My White Savior

Leslie Jones is the Least Protected Blackness of Us All

This essay originally published on the week that she was viciously and relentlessly attacked by racists on Twitter. It was so cruel and dehumanizing, yet unsurprising because white men on the internet seem to relish being bottom feeders.

This was my response.

*****

It all started with the idea to remake a classic and beloved movie—*Ghostbusters*.

And, as it's 2016, why not make the cast all women? Shouldn't be a big deal, right? Women are equal—we can vote, have jobs, own property...it really *shouldn't* have mattered. But it did. It mattered so much that sexists led a charge to tank the movie[124], simply for starring women.

After its release, the movie got middle of the road reviews[125] and did okay financially[126]. But that wasn't enough[127] for all the anti-Ghostbuster trolls. Nope. They needed to punish someone for the film being made. And the target they chose was Leslie Jones.

---

[124] Cox, Carolyn. "The Ghostbusters Trailer Backlash Shows Men Believe in the Power of Representation (But Only When It Applies to Them)." The Mary Sue, 01 May 2016. Web. 23 Aug. 2016.

[125] Ghostbusters (2016). Rotten Tomatoes, 2016. Web. 23 Aug. 2016.

[126] Ghostbusters (2016). Box Office Mojo, 2016. Web. 23 Aug. 2016.

[127] Riedel, Sam. "Why Busting 'Ghostbusters' Reboot Myths May No Longer Matter." The Establishment, 19 Aug 2016. Web. 23 Aug. 2016.

They called her names, went on a now-infamous racist and sexist insult-spree that temporarily drove her from Twitter[128], and yesterday we found out that someone hacked her account and leaked nude photos of her (I refuse to link to any of that).

Do you know why they keep attacking Leslie? They keep attacking her because she's a Black woman and think this makes her a "safe" target. I mean, why *wouldn't* they think that? Historically, Black women have been cruelly and viciously attacked by white people. We have been victimized, brutalized, and vehemently attacked by men of *every* race. We have been belittled, ridiculed, and mocked at every turn.

And historically, we haven't been defended, protected, or appreciated. These attacks happen and the only people who demand justice are Black women. Not Black men, not white anyone. Not any other group. We stand up for ourselves and are consumed and regurgitated as stereotypes in the process: Angry Black woman. Belligerent Black woman. Loud Black woman. Sassy Black woman. Strong Black woman. Invulnerable Black woman. Tired Black woman.

This angry, belligerent, loud, sassy, strong, invulnerable, tired Black woman faces constant and consistent misogynoir[129]. Like my peers, we are always fighting against physical and emotional abuse dealt to us by a culture that tells us that we are nothing. That we are not privy to the rights of white people or men. That we are not loved. That we are not equal. That the only protection we have is in the community we build for ourselves.

---

[128] For Harriet. "Leslie Jones Quits Twitter After Spending a Day Battling Racist Twitter." For Harriet, 19, July 2016. Web. 23 Aug. 2016.

[129] Bristol, Keir. "On Moya Bailey, Misogynoir, and Why Both Are Important." The Visibility Project, 27 May, 2014. Web. 23 Aug. 2016.

And even within that community there is internalized racism in the form of colorism[130]. There is this idea that only the lightest of us deserve humanity and empathy. The darkest of us are treated as an embarrassment, as someone who shouldn't be seen. The darkest of us are treated as an embarrassment, as people who shouldn't be seen. Even when Black people are front and center, we are the ones who remain hidden.

Leslie, in all her beauty and strength, embodies the least protected Blackness of all.

Her pain is our pain when our nudes are leaked and people pretend it's a fucking compliment that anyone wants to see us naked[131].

It is our pain when we are physically assaulted and raped[132] and people assume we invited it either with our aggressive personalities or hypersexual bodies.

It is our pain when we are misgendered as an insult[133] and that misgendering permits people to ignore our abuse[134].

---

[130] LaSha. "We Need to Talk About Leslie Jones and Colorism in Our Community." Ebony, 12 Aug 2016. Web. 23 Aug. 2016.

[131] Lennard, Natasha. "'Why are black women less attractive?' asks Psychology Today." Salon, 17 May 2011. Web. 23 Aug. 2016.

[132] Leicht, Angelica. "Suspects Arrested, Charged in #Jadapose Rape Case." Houston Press, 17 Oct. 2014. Web. 23 Aug. 2016.

[133] Roberts, Monica. "Misgendering Attacks On A Black Woman's Femininity Aren't Funny." TransGriot, 02 June 2015. Web. 23 Aug. 2016.

[134] Cooper, Brittney. "The world only has ugliness for black women. That's why Serena Williams is so important." Salon, 15 July 2015. Web. 23 Aug. 2016.

It is our pain when we are taught that calling the police on a Black male abuser is a bigger sin than being abused[135].

It is our pain when a Black man harasses or rapes a Black woman[136] and moves on with minimal impact to his career[137] while we are attacked for speaking out against the rapist[138].

It is our pain that survives in a world designed to beat us down—and it is our resilience that demands that we still rise.

---

[135] Azalia, Loy. "My struggle to protect black men when they've been my abuser." Blavity, August 2016. Web. 23 Aug. 2016.

[136] Blay, Zeba. "'Confirmation' And The Silencing Of Black Women To Shield Black Men." Huffington Post, 15 April 2016. Web. 23 Aug. 2016.

[137] Drayton, Tiffanie. "On Nate Parker's College Rape Case & Why Black Women Should Not Watch 'Birth of a Nation.'" Clutch, Aug. 2016. Web. 23 Aug. 2016.

[138] Shackelford, Ashleigh. "Stop Excusing Black Men's Violence – Like Nate Parker's – for the Sake of Black Liberation." Wear Your Voice Magazine, 16 Aug. 2016. Web. 23 Aug. 2016.

We are the fastest growing group of entrepreneurs[139] and are earning degrees at a higher rate[140] than any other group in the United States. We are beacons of style and innovation. From our hairstyles[141], to our bodies[142], from our original content[143] to our political movements[144], white people revisit their colonialist roots by appropriating every fucking thing we do[145] and then trying to destroy us when we fight back.

And still we fight. And still we shine. Black Girl Magic[146] is real.

This shit that's happening to Leslie Jones is yet another manifestation of white supremacy and its utter disregard and disrespect for Black women. It is a travesty of the highest order.

If I could say anything to Leslie Jones, it would be this:

Dear Leslie,

---

[139] Haimerl, Amy. "The fastest-growing group of entrepreneurs in America." Fortune, 29 June 2015. Web. 23 Aug. 2016.

[140] Davis, Rachaell. "New Study Shows Black Women Are Among The Most Educated Group In The United States." Essence, 07 June 2016. Web. 23 Aug. 2016.

[141] Kinks, Klassy. "White Hair Blog Claims Bantu Knots Were "Inspired" By Marc Jacobs, Black Twitter Goes Nuts." Black Girl Long Hair, 27 May 2015. Web. 23 Aug. 2016.

[142] Wellington, Elizabeth. "When Black Girls Get Criticized and White Girls Get Celebrated." For Harriet, Oct. 2014. Web. 23 Aug. 2016.

[143] Phillips, Kady. "Blavity Exclusive: Akilah Obviously on BuzzFeed and #StopBuzzThieves." Blavity, Aug. 2016. Web. 23 Aug. 2016.

[144] Bowerman, Mary. "Is White Lives Matter a movement or white supremacist group?" USAToday, 22 Aug. 2016. Web. 23 Aug. 2016.

[145] Kel, TaLynn. "When White People Consume Blackness For Personal Gain." The Establishment, 29 June 2016. Web. 23 Aug. 2016.

[146] Wilson, Julee. "The Meaning Of #BlackGirlMagic, And How You Can Get Some of It." Huffington Post, 12 Jan. 2016. Web. 23 Aug. 2016.

I'm sorry that you are experiencing this. I am enraged on your behalf. All you did was your job and as a result, you are facing outrageous and illegal attacks upon your person, your privacy, and your wellbeing. I'm not going to bullshit you by saying that this is going to be easy. It's not. It's fucking horrendous and I hope you are able to find these criminals and fuck their lives up. This will not make you stronger. It will make you acutely aware of just how vulnerable you are, but your vulnerability is not the problem. The problem is these entitled fucks who feel like they have the right to abuse anyone they choose. I hope they pay with everything they are because they have revoked their humanity.

You did not deserve this and they deserve to suffer.

Let me know how I can help.

TaLynn

This story first appeared at TheEstablishment.co, a multimedia site entirely run and funded by women, on August 25, 2016.

These attacks happen and the only people who demand justice are Black women. Not Black men, not white anyone. Not any other group. We stand up for ourselves and are consumed and regurgitated as stereotypes in the process: Angry Black woman. Belligerent Black woman. Loud Black woman. Sassy Black woman. Strong Black woman. Invulnerable Black woman. Tired Black woman.

– TaLynn Kel, Leslie Jones is the Least Protected Blackness of Us All

Dear People Who Comment on My Facebook Posts to Silence Me

To the people in my life who only comment on my Facebook posts to defend white supremacist bullshit:

Fuck all the way off.

You know who you are. You are the people who tell me to be less negative when I share how something is racist. You say I'm choosing to see the world through a racist lens instead of recognizing teachable moments. You say that my refusal to teach means I have a bad attitude. You say that calling anything racist or sexist or ableist is just me choosing to *think* our society has serious systemic issues. You say that I am treating everything as though it is a personal attack against me. You say that I am the problem.

You tell me that I have closed myself off to people and that maybe, just maybe, if I were a little more open, a bit less judgmental, maybe I'd realize that the world isn't out to get me.

Well, maybe the *world* isn't out to get me—but the United States is and has been for years. This is why Black people are policed more. It's why we are suspended from school for minor infractions more[147]. It's why average human behavior is criminalized[148] and our mere presence is a threat. It's why it's okay to murder us during "routine" traffic stops[149] or because we asked the police questions[150], while white people can use drugs[151], rape[152], murder[153], engage in gang shoot outs[154], shoot at police[155], and still be seen as people deserving forgiveness and second chances. From redlining[156], to inflated loan rates[157], to mass poisonings while those responsible stay

[147] Gomez, Amanda. "Study finds higher expulsion rates for black students in South." PBS, 25 Aug. 2015. Web. 05 Sept. 2016.

[148] Countercurrent News. "Police Admit They're 'Racist' During Arrest of Black Walmart Shoppers Who Were 'Walking Too Slow.'" Countercurrent News. 14 June 2015. Web. 05 Sept. 2016.

[149] Allen, Nick. "Fatal shooting of black man Philando Castile by police during traffic stop in Minneapolis caught on video by girlfriend." The Telegraph, 07 July 2016. Web. 05 Sept. 2016.

[150] The Grio. "Cops Taser black man mistaken for suspect, arrest him for asking questions." The Grio, 16 July 2016. Web. 05 Sept. 2016.

[151] Vanity Fair. "Robert Downey Jr. Speaks About His Addictions." Vanity Fair, Oct. 2014. Web. 05 Sept. 2016.

[152] Gauthier, Brendan. "Stanford rapist Brock Turner released from jail after serving just three months." Salon, 02 Sept. 2016. Web. 05 Sept. 2016.

[153] McCormack, Simon. "White Ex-Police Chief Who Killed Unarmed Black Man Avoids Jail Time." Huffington Post, 01 Sept. 2016. Web. 05 Sept. 2016.

[154] Morton, Clay. "Of 170 held after Waco biker shooting, all are now out of jail, with none charged in killings." Dallas News, 04 Oct. 2015. Web. 05 Sept. 2016.

[155] Cahill, Tom. "Heavily Armed White Man Arrested Alive After Shooting at Police Officer." US Uncut, 07 July 2016. Web. 05 Sept. 2016.

[156] Madrigal, Alexis. "The Racist Housing Policy That Made Your Neighborhood." The Atlantic, 22 May 2014. Web. 05 Sept. 2016.

[157] King, Shaun. "King: It's payback time for Toyota, other lenders who charged blacks, Asians and Latinos higher interest rates." New York Daily News, 04 Feb. 2016. Web. 05 Sept. 2016.

in their seats of power[158] (I'm looking at you, Governor Snyder), America continues to wage war on Black people.

And according to you, my so-called Facebook "friends," we are just supposed to continue enduring it?

Years ago, your shitty gaslighting tactics would have worked, just as they continue to work on so many. I would have been on the defensive, wondering if I was being too sensitive and picking up nuance that wasn't there. I would've quietly wondered what was so wrong with me, and why I was bothered by stuff that didn't seem to bother anyone else. I would've spent time explaining my feelings and apologizing for calling out your racism, and I would have felt ashamed for holding you accountable for your words.

There was a time when I assumed that your anti-Black responses to my posts were an indication that you simply didn't understand what you were saying. There was a time when I'd spend days figuring out how to explain why your comments were so fucked up, all the while making sure I didn't say anything too confrontational. Because you'd accuse me of pulling the "race card" (no such thing) and of getting too emotional, and then refuse to listen until I "calmed down," I'd put extra effort into projecting civility and calm, hoping you'd understand the rationality and legitimacy of what I had to say. I'd call your words "insensitive" instead of racist, because using the r-word is an automatic eject from a conversation.

Meanwhile, under the continued threat of disengagement, you, with your casual rudeness and convenient ignorance, would claim to be unbiased and "fair."

You'd dehumanize and dismiss me and then have the audacity to expect me to thank you for it.

---

[158] Ganim, Sara; Sanchez, Ray. "Flint water crisis: New criminal charges are brought." CNN, 03 Aug. 2016. Web. 05 Sept 2016.

Over and over, I engaged in this dialogue—until, finally, I realized that there aren't two sides to my humanity, racism doesn't go both ways, and it's emotionally dangerous to fuck with people who think that shit.

And they don't just *think* it. They enforce it via threats involving employment, housing, incarceration, and death. And while this is a reality I navigate in many other aspects of my life, I will no longer do it in my personal relationships, including online.

I have spent too much of my life and energy learning how to tap dance around protecting whiteness and its defenders. I have sacrificed too much of myself to the altar of white feelings. I've lived with severe depression, isolation, marginalization, and daily insults from people who lack the ability to comprehend simple ideas, routines and work processes. I've worked for white mediocrity and had every single idea and innovation suppressed until I funneled it through white-acceptable bodies, i.e. coworkers who didn't look like me. I've sat in rooms with white people justifying immoral and criminal behavior of white people who moments later accuse Black people of looking criminal for standing somewhere. Hypocrites and liars, the whole lot of them, and I'm not kowtowing to that bullshit anymore.

When you, Facebook "friend," only speak to me when you think I'm being...

...Too harsh about racism...

...Too mean to Trump supporters...

...Too unforgiving about white people's racism...

...Too harsh to people of color who co-sign white people's racism...

...Too mean for cutting racist people from my life...

...Too hard on my husband for demanding he start acknowledging his racism...

...Too honest with the world for expressing how damaging and dangerous white lies are...

What you are actually saying is stop being an uppity negro and get back in my place. But I have no place and fuck you for trying to convince me I do. Fuck you for being a complacent asshole who'd rather be a cowardly bigot than a human being. Fuck you for insisting I ignore problems with the people in this country, and fuck you for trying to silence me.

Fuck you for who you are, which is beneath me.

You think you can tell me how to feel; who to fight for; that I'm worthless, voiceless, powerless; that I am not worth fighting for. You say you're helping me by blaming me for hundreds of years of racially inflicted violence and violation, and then you dare to call me a friend while trying to convince me that *my* voice is the problem.

And the worst part is that you think you're being a good person, that you are helping me live a better life, a happier life, with your unsolicited advice. You pat yourself on the back while you twist a knife in mine.

You aren't my friend. In truth, you are my enemy. You try to weaken me with your complicity and your advice on being a better Black person in a racist society that "isn't *really* racist" seeks to undermine my self-worth.

Your anti-Blackness is showing and I don't have room for your lies in my life anymore. As it's been years and you still only speak up to defend white supremacist bullshit and, by association, the genocide of Black people, you've chosen your place and it's not with me.

Consider us "unfriended." Goodbye.

This story first appeared at TheEstablishment.co, a multimedia site entirely run and funded by women, on September 7, 2016.

You say that calling anything racist or sexist or ableist is just me choosing to think our society has serious systemic issues.

— TaLynn Kel, Dear People Who Comment on My Facebook Posts to Silence Me

Demanding Black Forgiveness Is Just Another Way to Control Us

When I was six, my favorite uncle came by to visit. I loved spending time with him; He was always playful and fun. On this day for some reason I didn't want to hang out with him. When he called me to him, I refused. A few minutes later he offered me a dollar, and being six with no allowance, I went. That was when he pocketed the dollar, grabbed my wrist, and spanked me in front of my entire family while laughing at my humiliation. Afterward, he demanded I apologize for making him spank me. I refused, ran off, and never spoke to him again.

I was fortunate that my parents didn't undermine my will by insisting I forgive someone who'd overstepped my boundaries. I wasn't forced to be polite or acknowledge him ever again and I didn't. I mourned his death when he passed, but 35 years later, I still haven't forgiven him.

I've always been perplexed by the obligation to forgive. For my family, forgiveness was part of Christian belief, but I've never been able to accept church teachings without asking questions. When I think of forgiving my uncle, I'm confused; while a part of me feels like I missed out on our relationship, the rest of me thinks about a grown man who tried to control me and punished me for demonstrating my autonomy. Why would I forgive that person? What good could it possibly do?

I feel the same when I see demands, carefully designed to appear as requests, for forgiveness from grieving Black families who have lost loved ones to racial violence. We see this asked for, implicitly and sometimes explicitly, every time there's a new tragedy. We've seen Black people punished[159] for refusing to grant it, for exposing their pain and expressing their rage; we've seen their forgiveness made into a public show for white America's consumption[160]. We've seen people forced to apologize[161] for daring to be human. We've seen this message twisted every possible way, from those saying it's the Christian thing to do[162] to others saying it's a way to help you move forward[163].

On a societal level, this public spectacle of forgiveness is complete and utter bullshit. But white people eat it up. Our forgiveness reassures them that Black people still know their place in this country; it eases their minds, reassures them that nothing has to change, that they don't have to upset their carefully crafted, artfully curated, violently maintained societal advantages. Black forgiveness sends the message that white people are still on top.

---

[159] Bacon, John. "Police consider charges against Michael Brown's stepdad." USA Today, 02 Dec. 2014. Web. 08 Aug. 2016.

[160] Berman, Mark. "'I forgive you.' Relatives of Charleston church shooting victims address Dylann Roof." The Washington Post, 19 June 2015. Web. 08 Aug. 2016.

[161] ABC News Staff. "Michael Brown's Stepfather Apologizes for 'Burn' Outburst in Ferguson." ABC News, 03 Dec. 2014. Web. 08 Aug. 2016.

[162] Relevant Staff. "Trayvon Martin's Parents: 'As Christians We Must Forgive Zimmerman.'" Relevant, 27 Aug. 2013. Web. 08 Aug. 2016.

[163] Ortberg, Mallory; Wallace, Carvell. "You're Not Off The Hook: The White Myth Of Black Forgiveness." The Toast, 23 June 2015. Web. 08 Aug. 2016.

On a personal level, we are told that forgiveness is a tool for healing—that it will help us through our pain. That is a confusing message to me. Forgiveness, to me, means recognizing that the pain has dissipated. I can't recognize that when the wound is still fresh, and being reopened all the time.

We are told that forgiveness will help us with our anger, that it will keep our rage from destroying us. This doesn't make sense to me either. My anger fuels me. Almost every positive change I've made in my life has been because something bothered me enough to want to do something about it. If I forgave the people and situations that outraged me, I am not sure I'd be motivated enough to change it. Change often means destroying the old, and I wouldn't destroy something I found acceptable.

We are told that forgiveness allows us to move forward. This, too, is not true. One of the few constants is that life goes on, regardless of what tragedies we face. Time is what allows us to move forward—indeed, it means that moving forward is something we can't avoid. Forgiveness is not required for progress.

We are told that forgiveness is personal. If the act of forgiveness is personal, why does it need to be shared publicly? People ask for forgiveness. They demand forgiveness. If forgiveness is personal, something I should do for myself, then you don't need it and you don't get to ask for it. That you are seeking it tells me that it's a tool for you, not me.

We are told that forgiveness and anger aren't mutually exclusive, that we can be angry and still forgive someone. I don't know what definition of "forgiveness" people are using for that one, but for me, anger is something that demands change, while forgiveness means accepting things as they are. Forgiveness is complacency. I cannot be outraged by you and forgiving of you at the same time. Either I'm angry and we're going to work on improving the situation or I've decided to accept your bullshit. It's not both. It's never both.

Forgiveness requires that I lie to myself; I choose to live my truth. It demands I rot inside; I opt to continue my growth. It expects me to swallow my anger and suppress my pain; I express my rage and refine my voice. It requires that I choke on my discomfort to appease you; I allow you to choke on your discomfort and exit, unappeased.

I do not forgive—and please, if I wrong you, I don't want you to forgive me either. I want nothing to do with a tool designed to quiet the mistreated, to manipulate them, to deny them humanity.

I do not seek your complacency. I do not want you to tell me shit is fine when it isn't. I do not want you to hide yourself, lie to yourself, deny yourself. I do not want you to cull your emotions, quell your anger, or gut your pain to meet forgiveness' demands. I do not want to keep you still, silent, and part of the status quo.

I want us to be free.

In the beginning of our relationship[164], when my S.O. said racist shit, I explained how he messed up and forgave him. I was hurt. I was angry. It hadn't been resolved, but I forgave him. Then he did it again and I went through all the forgiveness narrative a second time.

Then he did it again and that time I did not forgive him.

I let my rage fly and let my pain show through. I stopped trying to be stoic and understanding and told him that he was a shitty human being who was fucking up. I let him know that he did not make me happy and I wrestled with whether I would stay in this relationship. I did not forgive him. I do not forgive him. When he fucks up, I express my anger and demand better. And he works to be better. I'll admit, both of us live with the fear that we will say or do something that the other cannot live with, but we accept that as a part of our relationship. This is what it means to be in an interracial relationship where racism is the norm. This is the burden we carry and work to unpack in a white supremacist world.

This is what it means to destroy the lie that is forgiveness.

Be angry. Be outraged. Feel what you feel. Do not pretend to be something you aren't. Do not pretend to be calm when you are enraged. Do not pretend to be fine when you are hurting. Do not pretend you don't care when you do. Do not suppress your emotions with those who help or harm you. Stop lying about how you fucking feel and just FEEL.

---

[164] Kel, TaLynn. "My Husband's Unconscious Racism Nearly Destroyed Our Marriage." The Establishment, 26 May 2016. Web. 20 Aug. 2016.

What is guiding me if not my emotions? The law? That's often wrong. Morality? That shit is fluid at the best of times. My joy and pain tell me what is happening around me. My fear and disgust protect me. My love shields me and my anger motivates me. Forgiveness sacrifices my anger, and that is too high a price to pay. There are too many people shaming others into being what they want instead of letting them be who they are. It's ugly and oppressive, all to the benefit of those controlling the narrative.

Don't let that bullshit control you anymore. Recognize, acknowledge, grieve, target, destroy, and change everything.

We all deserve to be free.

This story first appeared at TheEstablishment.co, a multimedia site entirely run and funded by women, on August 10, 2016.

I do not forgive—and please, if I wrong you, I don't want you to forgive me either. I want nothing to do with a tool designed to quiet the mistreated, to manipulate them, to deny them humanity.

– TaLynn Kel, Demanding Black Forgiveness Is Just Another Way to Control Us

White People, You Have a Lying Problem

White people, you have a motherfucking problem.

You lie too goddamn much.

You teach your kids to lie too goddamn much. You tell your families to lie too goddamn much. All you fucking do is lie and lie and lie about lying to the point that you are killing everyone, including yourselves.

You lie at the highest levels, so much so that we expect it from our elected officials. Our presidents have told lies[165] that resulted in the death of more than 50,000 American soldiers[166].

You lie about civilian massacres[167]. You lie about terrorist attacks against Black Americans[168].

You lie about sex education[169] and risk the health of your children.

---

[165] Schwartz, Larry. "The 7 Biggest Liars in Presidential History." Alternet, 07 Feb. 2016. Web. 08 July 2016.

[166] National Archives. "Statistical information about casualties of the Vietnam War." National Archives, August 2013. Web. 08 July 2016.

[167] History.com Staff. "My Lai Massacre." History.com, 2009. Web. 08 July 2016.

[168] Moore, A. "8 Successful and Aspiring Black Communities Destroyed by White Neighbors." Atlanta Black Star, 04 Dec. 2013. Web. 09 July. 2016.

[169] Advocates for Youth Staff. "The Truth About Abstinence-Only Programs." Advocates for Youth, 2008. Web. 08 July 2016.

You lie about your friends' qualifications to run national agencies[170], which results in unnecessary deaths.

You lie about your experiences while reporting[171]. You lie about American history[172]. You lie about historical heroes[173]. You lie about slavery[174].

You lie and lie and lie on a massive scale and cover up the lies, protect the liars, rehire the liars[175], and elect the liars because *shrug* everybody lies.

You lie about the littlest things, like if you ate the last cookie.

You lie to your spouse about their annoying habits.

You lie to your kids about how to make babies.

You lie to your neighbors about your debt.

You lie to your boss about sleeping in.

You lie to your co-workers about your weekend.

---

[170] Myers, Lisa; NBC Investigative Unit. "Critics Question FEMA Director's Qualifications." MSNBC, 13 Sept. 2005. Web. 08 July 2016.

[171] McCormack, Simon. "Brian Williams Investigation Uncovers More Alleged Lies." Huffington Post, 25 April 2015. Web. 08 July 2016.

[172] Raphael, Ray. "Are U.S. History Textbooks Still Full of Lies and Half-Truths?" History News Network, 19 Sept. 2004. Web. 08 July 2016.

[173] Blitz, Matt. "The Truth about Christopher Columbus." Today I Found Out, 26 Jan. 2016. Web. 08 July 2016.

[174] Bouie Jamelle; Onion, Rebecca. "Slavery Myths Debunked." Slate, 29 Sept. 2015. Web. 08 July 2016.

[175] Poniewozik, James "Why Brian Williams Lost His Job, and Why He Has a New One." Time, 10 June 2015. Web. 08 July 2016.

You lie to your doctor about your body.

You lie to everyone and say you are fine. And you lie to yourself about how wonderful and *nice* a human being you are.

But you aren't nice. You wear a veneer of nice. You are a rotten tooth in the mouth of the world. Instead of taking care of yourself and preventing decay, you feed on the power of your whiteness like candy. When you start to smell, you use mouthwash and mints to hide it. When you start to visibly decay, you try to hide it with whitening gel. When you start to hurt, you take pain medication. When the pain becomes too great, you finally seek help—and that help is to numb yourself, pull out the nerve, then slap a crown on it so that no one can see your empty core. Instead they see a perfect veneer passing for a healthy tooth. But it is a tooth that feels no pain and only emulates the others.

In case you didn't know, that ability to feel is called empathy. And as far as I can see, white America has none.

Or maybe you do. Maybe you have empathy, but it's overshadowed by the centuries of stinky, infected rot left by your presidents, your congressmen, your police, your lawyers, your corporations, your lobbyists, your business leaders, your forefathers, and your motherland, all in the name of colonialism. Maybe you don't know what empathy even feels like anymore.

Human rights violations are so interwoven with American history that you can no longer tell what's right...if indeed you ever could.

I know, I know, not all white people. My husband is white. Except I wrote an entire fucking essay[176] about how I needed to put his ass in check for his lack of empathy. Except that I spent years tuning him into what the fuck is going on with the huge swath of the population that doesn't look like him. And I still deal with the empathy-less white people he's brought into my life. Not often, because I love myself too much to deal with that weird combination of superficiality and toxicity that permeates white society and dictates their interactions, but still. They are in my life, kind of.

And at work? The fact that these people categorize murder by cop as politics makes me want to throw a goddamn table. *"I don't talk politics at work."* People were murdered and you liken it to the ego-stroking and ass-kissing office bullshit that I put up with for my check? Get the fuck outta here!

Seriously, get the fuck outta here.

Can you really not see the difference? Does this really not resonate with you? Does the constant replaying of the murder of Black people really not matter?

You don't have to answer that. I already know. We aren't human to you. We never have been.

But you won't admit that because it means telling the truth. And if there is one thing white people have taught me, it's that you cannot stand the truth in any of its forms.

---

[176] Kel, TaLynn. "My Husband's Unconscious Racism Nearly Destroyed Our Marriage." The Establishment, 26 May 2016. Web. 08 July 2016.

I keep asking myself—when will they see the monster in the mirror? When will they see who they really are? What they do? How they destroy the world with their endless quest for power and the tireless subjugation of others to do it? When will they admit their fucking inability to see the humanity in difference?

Honestly, I wouldn't care if so many white people didn't have so much fucking power. But y'all do, and your consistent abuse of that power has destroyed countless lives and continues to do so. From your rapist sons[177], to your murdering daughters[178], you continue to destroy everything you touch.

But I have hope for you.

My hope is that one day, enough of you will stop lying to yourselves and heal. That one day you will stop lying to yourself and admit that you are an empty shell, existing on the continued pain of others as you beg, borrow, and steal from EVERYONE else to feel relevant.

One day you will stop killing everyone who doesn't fit your image.

One day you will stop attacking anyone who questions your decayed foundation.

One day you will actually love instead of trying to destroy people who live, love, and somehow thrive despite your oppression.

---

[177] Stack, Liam. "Light Sentence for Brock Turner in Stanford Rape Case Draws Outrage." The New York Times, 06 June 2016. Web. 08 July 2016.

[178] Apel, Therese. "2 Women in Truck That Ran Down Black Man Get Max Terms." USA Today, 10 April 2015. Web. 08 July 2016.

In these times of tragedy, we talk about Black healing. It's a necessary conversation about something we have a lot of practice doing. Hundreds of years' worth, actually.

What we need is white accountability. Are you strong enough to do it?

I'll wait.

This story first appeared at TheEstablishment.co, a multimedia site entirely run and funded by women, on July 8, 2016.

Maybe you have empathy, but it's overshadowed by the centuries of stinky, infected rot left by your presidents, your congressmen, your police, your lawyers, your corporations, your lobbyists, your business leaders, your forefathers, and your motherland, all in the name of colonialism. Maybe you don't know what empathy even feels like anymore.

– TaLynn Kel, White People, You Have a Lying Problem

Why I Cut My Racist In-Laws Out of My Life

I won't lie and say that I never had issues with the demographics of my mixed-race marriage. I definitely did. I worried about what my mom would think, and what my dad would say were he alive. I worried about what his parents thought. I worried about how the world would treat us.

I still worry.

After all, 2016 has all the hallmarks of an impending racial schism, and interracial couples are straddling a fence that may not be tenable.

When I entered my own relationship, I told myself that my significant other (S.O.) was different. That he wasn't with me because of some fetish. That he loved me, all of me. That my brown skin didn't matter to him. Over time came the revelations of his racism. I shouldn't actually call them revelations, as they were more a matter of me acknowledging the truth. I repeatedly pulled the veil over my eyes and told myself that love was enough. Over and over again, I'd feel this buildup of dread as time would reveal some other facet of his racism. Then we'd talk. Then we'd fight. Then we'd talk some more. It is painful and confusing to have someone love you, cherish you, support you, and then wound you with their inability to accept the whole of you. But how our love and communication about racism evolved[179] is another story.

This is the story of the kind of love I have with my in-laws.

***

---

[179] Kel, TaLynn. "My Husband's Unconscious Racism Nearly Destroyed Our Marriage." The Establishment, 26 May 2016. Web. 31 July 2016.

You know the expression about how you don't just marry the person, you marry their entire family? This is both true and false, as it depends on how close your partner is with them. I am close with some members of my immediate family, but not others, and I have no relationship with my brother at all. My S.O. has a superficial relationship with his immediate family. We say hi and occasionally spend holidays together, but for the most part, we live in different parts of the country and rarely interact. We are casual Facebook friends, but have limited face-to-face time. When my S.O. goes to visit them, I go with him for support, but truly, these people are still kind of strangers to me.

I know that he has some resentment toward his family, which is something I've tried to help him work through. I'd just lost my father when I met my S.O., and while I was close with my dad, I still felt guilt about the many ways I wasn't there for him. I don't want my S.O. to experience that, so I encourage his relationship with his family as much as I can without forcing him into it. All I can do is champion and love him as he figures it out.

Yet even though I want him and his family to be closer, there is a part of me that is comfortable with the emotional and physical distance.

When I married my S.O., I married into whiteness and the bullshit that comes with it[180]. He doesn't remember this, but when he told his parents my name, there was a moment of pause from his mother. He mentioned that she expressed some concern about my being Black, but as he isn't invested in her opinion, he didn't pursue it. I, of course, was ravenous for information and completely unaware of how non-confrontational his family is. This family is comprised of passive aggressive people who will never confront you with their feelings and will visibly back away from you if you try to confront them. If you've read any of my other essays, you know that I am the complete opposite of that; if you are bothering me, chances are I'm just going to tell you. Not his family, though. If you bother someone, rather than tell you, they will tell another family member, and then another family member until everyone knows there's a problem except you. They will make snide remarks, but the moment you try to talk about it, they will retreat behind the wall of, "Oh, I meant nothing by it. It's not a big deal. Sorry."

Habitual liars, the whole lot of them. And in fact, this was a habit I had to help my S.O. break. He would agree to things just to make me go away. One time he replied with something that was so obviously a lie that I had to ask, "Why'd you lie about that?" He replied, "I don't know. It just...I don't know." Now he's more honest about such things, and I love watching him assert himself and break away from that toxic dynamic he grew up in.

---

[180] Kel, TaLynn. "White People, You Have A Lying Problem." The Establishment. 07 July 2016. Web. 31 July. 2016.

Old habits die hard, though, and when he and his family get together, I see him revert back to the passive-aggressive liar I once knew. He changed because it was damaging our relationship. Suppressing his needs to avoid conflict isn't healthy, and because this is how his family operates, our relationship with them is not healthy.

I didn't want it to be this way, a relationship full of meaningless lies and petty obfuscations. Yet, any opportunity we had to improve our relationship was met with banality and superficial happiness. We talk about the weather and good restaurants. When the conversation finally begins to attain some depth, it's about work and people who don't matter. The dance to avoid any topic that may contain meaning is intricate and empty. I do not like socializing with people who are afraid of themselves, afraid of making mistakes, afraid of being wrong. I do not like people lying to me and avoiding important topics because they make them uncomfortable. As much as they think they are hiding behind the curtain, it's transparent and nothing is unseen. It's just ignored.

A part of me feels guilty about not pushing to change our relationship, but the rest of me is glad that I can recognize emotional danger when I see it. They are dangerous in their deceptions. The honesty my S.O. and I share is too much for them. His mom was constantly taken aback at holidays when I would speak my mind. They worked so hard to maintain a veneer of civility and calm, but the veneer is thin. Easy to break. Just a little nudge and they are frantic in their attempts to mask the hole. I struggled to tiptoe through their world—it is ugly to me, and I want as little contact as possible. I often laugh to cover my distaste, but my laughter is often filled with bitterness and my disgust is apparent.

Because we had such little contact with them, there were few opportunities for their casual racism to show. But every opportunity they had, they took. Each and every visit there was one moment when my friends would be referred to as a gang, or there would be mention of some lack of Black something, be it angels, ornaments, cards . . . with no acknowledgement as to why that is. There would be a question asking how Black people did some common thing, as though there was some mystical secret passed down orally from mother to daughter, carefully hidden from prying white eyes. There would be some reference to pretty, interracial babies with lovely skin or an inquiry about the best plantations to visit while in Georgia. For the limited exposure I had to them, his family managed to slip in some amazingly racist comments. And out of a mistaken sense of duty, I ate the pain and let many of them pass.

The first time I truly learned what I was dealing with was when I confronted his sister for asking me about plantations to visit. She asked via Facebook, so she did not see me visibly recoil from the question. When I told my S.O. about his sister's question, his response was, "She thinks of plantations like vineyards. She doesn't know what she's asking."

I thought about that for several minutes. I know American history has been whitewashed into complete fiction in order to protect white people from the atrocities of their ancestors, but *that* level of ignorance was shocking to me. What I didn't understand at the time was that white people care so little about the wrongs they've done to Black people throughout history that they don't bother to get educated about the people they've wronged. I'd married into the intersection of intentional ignorance, casual disregard, and the mistaken perception of supremacy—what I like to call the white bubble of bullshit that continues to poison this country.

I took the time to craft a polite, but clear explanation about why this was not just an insensitive question, but fucking shitty as hell. Her response was to blow it off—she didn't mean to upset me; no harm, no foul. Her casual dismissal and closing of the conversation sent me into a whole other level of rage. Between her dismissal and my S.O.'s defense of her fuckery, I was done.

That day, I told him that he was responsible for his family's ignorance. No longer could he avoid addressing the shit they said. No longer could he defend them or their whiteness. We'd already addressed this with his friends, but now it applied to family, too. The one pass I gave him was his delayed recognition of racist shit, because for him it just sounds like everyday conversation. But once that shit was identified, it was his job to confront it.

For a while, this worked. Then his mother posted some video of a Black man co-signing on America's racism and police brutality by asking for patience in collecting the evidence in the murders of Alton Sterling and Philando Castile[181]. She captioned it with, "If only we could get everyone to understand this."

Have I mentioned that his parents remain silent about anything having to do with racism? They avoid the topic like the plague. Then, when she finally says *anything*, it's about waiting to find some reason to validate the murders of these two men who were visibly unarmed and shot by government-approved murderers. This post was so vile that I decided to remove her from my life.

Her replies to my telling her I no longer wanted her toxicity in my life?

---

[181] Wright, Kai. " Why Alton Sterling and Philando Castile Are Dead." The Nation, 07 July 2016. Web. 31 July 2016.

"No matter what I say it's going to be wrong."

"I have friends that are black."

"Shootings, no matter who does them are not always justified."

"I love you both. I don't understand. I am NOT for any group (BLM) or whatever."

It's times like this that I am grateful and sad for the internet. Grateful because I now recognize her responses for what they are—intentional blindness. This is someone who chooses to ignore and acknowledge the wrongness of this country because it makes her feel bad. Instead she chooses to pretend that she's neutral, something I recognize better because, thanks to the internet, I see it more often. The downside is that thanks to the internet, I see white people ducking and weaving the truth on a national scale. It is a hard thing to witness. It feels impossible to fight.

She is not neutral. A part of me wonders if one of her Black friends got shot, would she wait for all the evidence? Actually, I don't wonder. They aren't really her friends and I don't believe she is capable of having a discussion about racism with a Black person. I don't think she's brave enough to try. And her husband stands by her. They are a team and she is their representative, a person who cannot be honest about the country we live in.

That day I accepted that my S.O. cannot protect me from his family's racism. That day I decided to be my own hero and remove them from my sphere of influence. I won't make him choose between us; I know he needs his parents. I just won't let them in my home or my life. Their values are incompatible with mine.

Some people will say that I should give them a chance. That I should keep working to meet them halfway. To them I say that while I chose to attach whiteness to my personal life through my significant other, I also choose to set limits on the amount of damage I will allow it to wreak upon my life. I will not tolerate being tolerated. I will not tolerate liars. I will not cuddle you in your white fragility and co-sign on your racist bullshit so that you can feel good about yourself. If you lack the humanity to see that my skin, my body, my mind is human just like you, then you are not deserving of me, my time, or my energy. I will not continue to prove my worth to people who are not worthy, even if I am legally bound to you. That brown skin is such a goddamn deal breaker for white people makes me vacillate between rage and despair for this country, for this world.

Releasing people from your life isn't easy, and I don't expect this to be easy. It's only been a couple of weeks, so we'll see how this eventually plays out. 2016 has been a shitty year for a lot of reasons. I stopped speaking to people I've known for years, and I'm watching many friends struggle with doing the same. This is the year of cutting ties and closing doors.

But let's hope that this is also lighting the path to a better future.

This story first appeared at TheEstablishment.co, a multimedia site entirely run and funded by women, on August 2, 2016.

*That day I accepted that my
S.O. cannot protect me from
his family's racism. That day I
decided to be my own hero and
remove them from my sphere
of influence. I won't make him
choose between us; I know he
needs his parents. I just won't
let them in my home or my life.
Their values are incompatible
with mine.*

*– TaLynn Kel, Why I Cut My
Racist In-Laws Out of My Life*

As a Fat, Black Woman, Cosplay Has Tried to Make Me Invisible

I never considered myself a geek until I picked up a new hobby: costume play, aka cosplay. It's one of those things that happened organically. Someone took me to a geek convention, I saw people in costume, and not once did it occur to me *not* to dress up like them. Before I'd been there an hour, I had plans, ideas, hopes, and dreams for how to become a part of this world.

In short: I love cosplay. It is one of the highlights of my life, providing an outlet for my creativity, my problem-solving, my mild exhibitionism, and my need for expression.

I often try to capture my joy for cosplay through photos, of which I have many. And recently, when I did a cosplay photo shoot in my Asgardian Storm costume, I asked my significant other (S.O.) what he thought of one of my pictures. His response: "There's a little too much boob."

A little too much boob.

I looked at him, angry and offended, and said, "This is my body. That's just how it looks."

"I just think it detracts from the costume," he responded.

My S.O. loves my body. I know this. But for him to say that my body was a problem in the costume was *shaming*. It was judgment. It was him expressing that somehow my body was the problem in this costume that was designed with a top that is open-laced to the navel.

His comment brought back all the ways I'd experienced body criticism throughout my life. And it reminded me how, even in the cosplay community that has allowed me to be so free, I am still not immune from body shaming.

***

Growing up, I was taught to be ashamed of my size and my breasts. I remember being in grade school, and my teacher loudly whispering during attendance that I needed a bra—and then my classmates talking behind my back when the molded-cup bra my mom then bought me made me look even more developed than I was. I remember being teased during gym class for how much my breasts bounced when I ran; I wore two bras to compensate and still faced comments like "you're going to give yourself a black eye" or "try not to get a concussion."

At the same time, I was told my body excited men. They felt entitled to inform me how I should dress, when I should smile, and how I should always try to make myself appealing for them. When I wore fitted clothes, people would tell me I looked "fuckable." When I wore baggy clothes to make my fuckability less pronounced, people told me I looked sloppy and should dress better.

My clothing was monitored and criticized by both men *and* women. I was told to look available, but not *too* available; approachable but not *too* comfortable . . . because comfortable meant I wasn't trying hard enough. I needed to show my body but not my skin; skin invited trouble.

I was shamed and policed for more than just the shape of my body. Because I am brown, I was told to stay indoors and avoid the sun because *heaven forbid* I get darker. I was told most sports weren't feminine and the ones on the approved list were subject to rules that moderated and tempered girls' aggression. I was taught that my bigger, browner body scared white women and that it was my responsibility to manage my effect on them.

I hated this. I still hate it. I've been groomed all my life to seek this body-related attention as an affirmation of my womanly worth—despite its apparent simultaneous lack of appeal.

Cosplay is ostensibly a community that accepts those, like me, who exist outside mainstream normative ideals. But in this community, I've simply found another arena where I need to manage body commodification and shaming, and in ways I didn't anticipate.

As a cosplayer, your audience, the people who enjoy cosplay, don't always see you as a person. They often see you as the embodiment of the fictional character you're portraying, and sometimes they impose their standards, their desires, and their interpretation of that character onto you. The cosplay stops being about you and instead becomes about you fitting into someone else's narrative about a character.

But I often *don't* fit that narrative. I don't/can't/won't physically resemble the character enough to satisfy a fan's embodiment of a beloved character—and so, I'm often rendered invisible.

This wasn't true when I first started. There were so few people dressing up that people were excited to see *anyone* adorned as their favorite character. As cosplay got more popular, though, there was an increasing number of people who actually looked like the characters—or who were willing to change their bodies enough to get as close to looking like the characters as humanly possible. And suddenly, *that* became the ideal.

Because I am a fat Black woman, I have worn costumes that are 95% accurate to the screen or comic book version of the character, but been dismissed and ridiculed. When I dressed as Cable, an X-Men character, people couldn't tell who I was because I was brown and obviously a woman. Because people associate brown skin and white hair with Storm, people kept asking if that's who I was; never mind my silver arm, illuminated eye, and extraneous yellow pouches, all characteristics of classic Cable.

At the same time, I've seen people who are slim or muscular or whatever the current illusion of attractive is wear a scaled-back version of the costume and be adored. They look "right" even if they aren't trying to be "right."

Since people like me don't really exist in comics, I can get a little closer if the character is masculine or an inhuman skin color. I recognize that this is both funny and fucked up—that my cosplay becomes more realistic for people the farther I step away from my identity.

This isn't to say marginalized people are never accepted in the cosplay world, but even this acceptance isn't what it should be. Just like the broader body positivity movement endorses certain bodies over others—the hourglass curvy, not the round curvy; the white bodies, not the brown ones; the cellulite-free bodies, not the ones with visible cellulite—true acceptance is modified.

When you look up Black women cosplayers, when you think about those you know, they are usually light-skinned and not fat. If they are darker skinned, they are thin and curvy. If they are fat, they are lighter skinned. I very rarely see dark-skinned, fat women cosplayers, and while I cannot say why that is, I can guess: Even in this community that built itself to accept the socially unaccepted, there remains misfit toys.

It's also worth noting that the cosplay community is hardly immune from the objectification of female bodies. I've experienced what it's like to have men try to make me responsible for their sexual desire, where I've been accused of teasing them and enticing them because of what I chose to wear. I know what it feels like to have strangers project their sexual fantasies onto me, to have them overwrite my humanity with their lust as they try to shape me into that fantasy. I've had them turn our interactions into the verbal equivalent of those fantasies, until they are not talking with me anymore and I'm just a placeholder for future jack-off material.

***

I've always been aware that there are approved looks—socially approved beauty. And I've always known that I do not represent this. My brown skin alone rules me out of acceptability, but my broad nose, my full lips, my dark brown eyes, my fat body . . . all these things together firmly place me into the unapproved category. I see how some people are treated in the cosplay community, and as inclusive as it is, not everyone is visible. People like me are not visible.

Cosplay culture mimics societal "norms" in virtually every way, including body shaming and celebrating certain body types. And just like in "mainstream" culture, there are people who exist outside the accepted norm and who push back—and are still marginalized. Those of us who keep doing what we're doing, who keep occupying space in this hobby that actively tries to ignore us are pushing back. Every race, body, or gender nonconforming person who refuses to step aside is pushing back. Every person who has been told that they don't fit but they stay anyway is pushing back. We are making spaces for ourselves and when doors are shut in our faces, we cut another hole in the wall to make a new one.

Our bodies don't need to be tamed. They can be loved, cherished, and appreciated regardless of how they look or what they are capable of doing . . . including when they're dressed in a cosplay costume.

This story first appeared at TheEstablishment.co, a multimedia site entirely run and funded by women, on September 20, 2016.

I know what it feels like to have strangers project their sexual fantasies onto me, to have them overwrite my humanity with their lust as they try to shape me into that fantasy. I've had them turn our interactions into the verbal equivalent of those fantasies, until they are not talking with me anymore and I'm just a placeholder for future jack-off material.

– TaLynn Kel, As a Fat, Black Woman, Cosplay Has Tried to Make Me Invisible

America, Stop Protecting Your Monsters

Hey America: I know it's close to Halloween and you're all psyched to pull out your scary masks and get off on scaring the shit out of each other. But instead of embracing this romanticized idea of monsters as red/green/blue-faced creatures from some otherworld darkness or abyss, it's time we realized that most of our monsters can be found by looking in the mirror.

I need you to stop pretending that we don't create a slew of new monsters every damn day. It's like we have a damn kit.

You know the kit I'm talking about. The one that convinces little white boys that their opinion is fact. The one that teaches little white girls to accept bullying and controlling from white boys because submission is feminine. The kit that makes heroes of murderers, gives them holidays, and puts their faces on money. The kit that demonizes people for the color of their skin and then bends over backwards to protect white men from being punished for their crimes. Even when they are caught in the act[182]. Even when they planned, committed, and admitted[183] to it. Even when they are proud of what they've done[184].

You know that kit.

---

[182] Kingkade, Tyler. "If Not For 2 Strangers, Brock Turner May Have Never Been Arrested." Huffington Post, 06 June 2016. Web. 14 Oct. 2016.

[183] CBS News Staff. "Colorado Theater Massacre." CBS News, 2016. Web. 14 Oct. 2016.

[184] Hughes, Trevor. "Planned Parenthood Shooter 'happy' with his attack." USA Today, 11 April 2016. Web. 21 Sept. 2016.

It's the Brock Turner "prison would ruin his life but to hell with that woman he was caught raping[185]" kit.

It's the Martin Blake "yeah he raped his 12-year old daughter but all he deserves is probation[186]" kit.

It's the Dylan Roof "deserves our sympathy instead of being labeled a terrorist[187]" kit.

It's the Donald Trump "grab them by the pussy doesn't eliminate him as a presidential candidate[188]" kit.

It's the Nate Parker "he was acquitted of rape and his writing partner's case was dismissed[189]" kit.

It's the men who protect each other, the women who protect men, and the way both groups directly take a shit on anyone who tries to make the criminal justice system address criminals, instead of those who just look like they might be up to something.

It's the rabid protection of patriarchy, folks. And it's killing us.

---

[185] Schwartz, Gadi; Ortiz, Erik. "Brock Turner, Convicted Sexual Assault Offender, Released From Jail After 3 Months." NBC News, 02 Sept. 2016. Web. 14 Oct. 2016.

[186] Cahill, Tom. "Montana father gets probation after he admits to raping 12-year-old daughter." US Uncut, 13 Oct. 2016. Web. 14 Oct. 2016.

[187] Robles, Frances; Stewart, Nikita. "Dylann Roof's Past Reveals Trouble at Home and School." The New York Times, 16 July 2015. Web. 14 Oct. 2016.

[188] Smith, Candace. "Trump's Female Supporters Back Him Despite Sexual Assault Accusations." ABC News, 15 Oct. 2016. Web. 14 Oct. 2016.

[189] Shackelford, Ashleigh. "Stop Excusing Black Men's Violence – Like Nate Parker's – for the Sake of Black Liberation." Wear Your Voice Magazine, 16 Aug. 2016. Web. 14 Oct. 2016.

Let's be real. We have sexual predators in Congress[190], law enforcement[191], and the judicial system[192]. We have sexual predators in the church[193]. New stories about pastors[194] and priests[195] who have molested and raped children come out all the time. Known abusers like Roman Polanski[196] and Woody Allen[197] still haven't been punished for their crimes.

[190] Raymond, Laurel. "Longest-Serving GOP Speaker In History Is A Liar And Serial Child Molester, Federal Judge Says." Think Progress, 27 April 2016. Web. 14 Oct. 2016.

[191] Queally, James. "Oakland police to fire 4 officers, suspend 7 others, in sexual misconduct scandal." Los Angeles Times, 07 Sept. 2016, Web. 14 Oct, 2016.

[192] Washington Blade Staff. "Arkansas Judge Resigns Amid Sex Scandal." Washington Blade, 11 May 2016. Web. 14 Oct. 2016.

[193] Evans, Robert. "Why I Kept My Rape by A Priest A Secret (And Can't Anymore)." Cracked, 25 July 2016. Web. 14 Oct. 2016.

[194] Fox 5 News Staff. "Pastor Charged with Rape of 10-Year Old Girl." Fox 5, 16 Sept. 2016. Web. 14 Oct. 2016.

[195] ABC News Staff. "Priest Arrested for Child Rape." ABC News, 02 May 2016. Web. 14 Oct. 2016.

[196] Lewis, Andy. "Roman Polanski Rape Victim Unveils Startling, Disturbing Photo for Book Cover (Exclusive)" The Hollywood Reporter, 24 July 2013. Web. 14 Oct. 2016.

[197] Orth, Maureen. "10 Undeniable Facts about the Woody Allen Sexual Abuse Allegation." Vanity Fair, 07 Feb. 2014. Web. 14 Oct. 2016.

We see patriarchy being protected with the long-ass list of men who are barely punished when they are convicted of rape, like Martin Blake[198], Brock Turner[199], David Becker[200], and Kraigen Grooms[201]. We see it with physical[202] and sexual abusers, the men who enable abuse[203], and the enforcers who refuse to enforce the laws[204].

We saw the affluenza teen's mother get arrested to protect her murderous son from prison. Then, in a classic example of white privilege, we saw her released on house arrest[205], after fleeing the country with her criminal kid, who is now seeking early release[206]—because white male privilege knows no limits.

---

[198] Cahill, Tom. "Montana father gets probation after he admits to raping 12-year-old daughter." US Uncut, 13 Oct. 2016. Web. 14 Oct. 2016.

[199] Grinberg, Emanuella; Shoichet, Catherine E. "Brock Turner Released from Jail after Serving 3 Months for Sexual Assault." CNN, 02 Sept. 2016. Web. 14 Oct. 2016.

[200] Johnson, Kimberley. "No Jail Time for Rapist So He Can Enjoy 'The College Experience." Liberals Unite, 22 Aug. 2016. Web. 14 Oct. 2016.

[201] Guerra, Kristine. "Teen pleads guilty to sexual abuse of a 1-year-old girl, then a judge gives him no prison time." The Washington Post, 19 Sept. 2016. Web. 14 Oct. 2016.

[202] Agorist, Matt. "Cops Beat Their Wives and Girlfriends at Double the National Rate, Still Receive Promotions." The Free Thought Project, 07 May 2014. Web. 14 Oct. 2016.

[203] Bazelon, Emily; Levin, Josh. "The Most Damning Verdict." Slate, 12 July 2012. Web. 14 Oct. 2016.

[204] Cohen, Sarah; Ruiz, Rebecca; Childress, Sarah. "Departments Are Slow to Police Their Own Abusers." The New York Times, 23 Nov. 2013. Web. 14 Oct. 2016.

[205] Crimesider Staff. "New Charge for Tonya Couch, 'Affluenza' Teen's Mom." CBS News, 26 May 2016. Web. 14 Oct, 2016.

[206] Frazier, Charise. "'Affluenza' Teen's Attorney Seeks Early Release." NewsOne, Sept. 2016. Web. 14 Oct. 2016.

Like Frankenstein's monster, patriarchy, white lies[207], and white privilege have been sutured together, helping America reach peak fuckery with this election. We have women defending Donald Trump's[208] horrific campaign built on racism, xenophobia, white supremacy, and lies. His lies are so numerous that we can't even keep track anymore[209].

And still this corrupt, immoral piece of shit is considered a better candidate than Hillary Clinton, who is guilty of being a politician, just like every other person who has run in the past 20 years. She's problematic and dangerous, especially to Black Americans[210] and brown people in other countries, but she hasn't threatened[211] more than half the population with deportation, groping, and prison.

[207] Kel, TaLynn. "White People, You Have A Lying Problem." The Establishment. 07 July 2016. Web. 14 Sept. 2016.

[208] CNN. "Trump Supporters Standing by Their Man." CNN, 11 Oct. 2016. Web. 14 Oct. 2016.

[209] Politifact Editors. "Donald Trump's File." Politifact, 2016. Web. 14 Oct. 2016.

[210] Alexander, Michelle. "Why Hillary Clinton Doesn't Deserve the Black Vote." The Nation, 10 Feb. 2016. Web. 14 Oct. 2016.

[211] Timm, Trevor. "Trumps Many Many Threats to Sue the Press Since Launching His Campaign." Columbia Journalism Review, 03 Oct. 2016. Web. 14 Oct. 2016.

And I get it—the bar feels pretty fucking low. The reason for that is that America has been lowering the bar since its inception. From founding fathers condemning slavery while owning slaves[212], to doctors performing non-consensual experiments on Black people[213] and prisoners[214], America has a shitty track record on human rights[215]. From old Jim Crow to new Jim Crow[216], from women's rights[217] and reproductive rights[218] to police reform[219], America is in the red. Time and time again, we prioritize profits over people, to the point that our health system is driven solely by profit and tied to our employment, making it extremely difficult for those who are unemployed or self-employed to get health care. We see the prices of medications manipulated by shareholders, adjusted by health systems, and ultimately harming people in need[220]. Companies poison entire communities[221] and

---

[212] Iaccarino, Anthony. "The Founding Fathers and Slavery." Encyclopedia Britannica, 28 July 2016. Web. 14 Oct. 2016.

[213] Ojanuga, Durrenda. "The Medical Ethics of the 'Father of Gynaecology', Dr. Marion Sims." Journal of Medical Ethics, 1993 vol 19: 28-31. Web. 14 Oct. 2016.

[214] Goodman, Howard. "Studying prison experiments Research: For 20 years, a dermatologist used the inmates of a Philadelphia prison as the willing subjects of tests on shampoo, foot powder, deodorant, and later, mind-altering drugs and dioxin." The Baltimore Sun, 21 June 1998. Web. 14 Oct. 2016.

[215] Human Rights Watch. "World Report: United States - Events of 2015." HRW.org, 2015. Web. 14 Oct. 2016.

[216] Thirteen Media with Impact – WNET. "The Rise and Fall of Jim Crow." PBS Educational Broadcasting Corporation, 2002. Web. 14 Oct. 2016.

[217] ACLU.com Editors. "Women's Rights." ACLU.com, 2016. Web. 14 Oct. 2016.

[218] ACLU.com Editors. "Reproductive Freedom." ACLU.com, 2016. Web. 14 Oct. 2016.

[219] ACLU.com Editors. "Reforming Police Practices." ACLU.com, 2016. Web. 14 Oct. 2016.

[220] Thomas, Katie. "The Complex Math Behind Spiraling Prescription Drug Prices." The New York Times, 24 Aug. 2016. Web. 14 Oct. 2016.

governments scramble to protect themselves[222] from fixing their damage.

We are a country that looks at its neighbors, neighbors whose lawns we've poisoned, and say, "at least we're better than that." Then we pat ourselves on the back, lower the bar, and spend untold amounts of time and money hiding the damage we're doing to ourselves and everyone else.

We are a country filled with monsters who ravage and kill the vulnerable among us, but who are enabled to prowl unseen in the darkness of America.

And here's the thing: We don't have to be this way. We *can* be good and human. We can relocate residents of Flint. Buy their homes and offer them the option of moving, either temporarily or permanently as we fix the infrastructure. But will we? Nope. Instead we'll start a bureaucratic process to talk about where the funds will come from and start making excuses as to why this is too expensive an endeavor to undertake. In the meantime, people continue to live with a poisoned water supply, owing money on a home they can't sell, and facing legal repercussions for abandoning the area, not to mention ruining their credit and fucking up their financial prospects—also known as modern-day shackles.

We have homes sitting empty and food rotting in dumpsters every day because giving any of this away undermines our capitalist system.

We have avenues for police reform, but that would mean enforcing the laws on the enforcers who have always held themselves above the law.

---

[221] Moore, Michael. "10 Things They Won't Tell You about the Flint Water Tragedy. But I Will." MichaelMoore.com, 29 Jan. 2016. Web. 14 Oct. 2016.

[222] Judge, Monique. "State of Michigan Removes Flint's Ability to Sue Over Water Crisis." The Root, 20 Sept. 2016. Web. 14 Oct. 2016.

And so we leave people to be poisoned, starve, freeze, and die because it's just too hard.

No. It's not that it's too hard. It's that our system is designed to keep everything as it is and to protect monstrous people from their own monstrosity. Every single time we manipulate the truth, i.e. lie, we make it easier for the next person to get away with being deplorable. When you protect your fucked-up kid, brother, uncle, husband, you make it possible for the next person to use that same convoluted logic to protect themselves. We are empowering them and eventually that monster runs for president.

When your teenage son has sex with a 7-year-old, he's a pedophile. There is no defense for that.

When your grown son has sex with someone without consent, he is a rapist. There is no defense for that.

When your kid kills anyone who isn't attacking him, he's a murderer. When he kills many people, he's a mass murderer. I don't care how many family trips he took or how loving he was before he decided to shoot up a school, theater, club, park, or church. He's a mass murderer. There is no defense for that.

I'm not blaming parents for giving birth to people who do terrible things. It happens all the time. Every asshole you meet has parents. Every liar, every murderer, every rapist, every abuser. They also have extended family, friends, teachers, schools, jobs, and a slew of other people who opt out of calling people on their shit and decide to let it slide.

As a country, we spend a lot of time and energy trying to make our murderers, rapists, and abusers look like they were created in isolation instead of flourishing in the society we created. We try real hard to separate them from the rest of us, because who wants to feel like they are responsible for the horrific decisions of others? Who wants that guilt? Who wants that blood on their hands?

But we have to ask the question—how much of their monstrousness is a result of America's teachings?

Because a lot of times they learned to be better monsters by watching other monsters. They learned it by watching you.

Did you protect them from their lies? Their thefts? Their abuses? Their crimes?

Did you lie for them? Did you enable them? Did you help them inflict damage on more and more people?

Were you silent when you could have spoken? Did you cause someone else harm with your silence?

Are you complicit in the damage being done in our country? In the world?

I have been, and now I'm working to change that shit.

There comes a point when you have to accept your responsibility in unleashing American monstrosity—when you must pull it from the shadows, and drag it into the light.

Every time you do, you are saving someone—including yourself.

This story first appeared at TheEstablishment.co, a multimedia site entirely run and funded by women, on October 18, 2016.

We are a country that looks at its neighbors, neighbors whose lawns we've poisoned, and say, "at least we're better than that." Then we pat ourselves on the back, lower the bar, and spend untold amounts of time and money hiding the damage we're doing to ourselves and everyone else.

– TaLynn Kel, America, Stop Protecting Your Monsters

Blackface Isn't a Compliment

Be it Halloween or a convention, anytime there is an opportunity to costume or cosplay, the issue of skin color arises—specifically, the brown skin of Black people. White people believe that they can paint it on and wash it off with impunity. I've heard every excuse possible, from the "it's harmless" to "my Black friend is okay with it" to "it's a sign of how much I love the character."

But regardless of how you wrap it in your head, blackface is not a compliment. It's a dehumanizing insult that people literally paint themselves in and try to hustle other people into believing. That anyone can look at the history of Black people in America—hell, the world[223]—and think that this is some kind of tribute only reflects how completely divorced they are from reality.

You see it in the cosplay community, any time a new brown-skinned character appears on the scene. White people and non-Black people of color promote the lie that skin-darkening is an attempt at authenticity. "It's an inherent part of the character," they say. "You should feel honored," they say.

Why? Why should I feel honored? Do you think that you are doing me or any other Black person a favor? Why would you think that? What is it about wearing my skin color that makes you think you are doing something nice? Especially when so many Black people have spoken about how fucking insulting it is? Every year there are posts, essays, videos, podcasts talking about how terrible blackface is, and every year there's a new crop of costumers crying victim when Black people tell them it's wrong.

---

[223] Blaque, Kat. "Are Zwarte Pieten Racist?" YouTube, 19 Oct. 2014. Web. 27 Sept. 2016.

If you really want to honor me or any Black person, how about listening when we say that culture isn't a costume[224], blackface isn't okay[225], and it certainly isn't a compliment. And then how about you stop doing that shit.

When you take a person's characteristics and shrink them down to their skin color, you are promoting a dangerous way of thinking about people. This is a technique that has been used to dehumanize and destroy Black people for hundreds of years. You may claim to associate brown skin with strength of character, but historically it's been used to say Black people are animals, criminals, primitive, and in need of strong discipline. To this day, white people interpret brown skin as dangerous and threatening. That is one of the reasons why police are so quick to use excessive violence to "subdue" us instead of just talking to us. Any movement we make is deemed threatening and they feel justified in using physical force to suppress it. This is a very real interpretation of my skin color, something over which I had no control.

---

[224] Blaque, Kat. "Cultures are Not Costumes" YouTube, 08 Oct. 2014. Web. 27 Sept. 2016.

[225] Blaque, Kat. "Veds 28: What Is Blackface?" YouTube, 29 Sept. 2014. Web. 27 Sept. 2016.

It doesn't matter that you see my brown skin as strength. It doesn't matter if you see it as resilience. Strength and resilience are indeed traits I possess, but they're traits that I've had to develop to compensate for the racist environment I live in. It doesn't matter that you think my skin is beautiful. It doesn't matter how many positive descriptors you load onto my Blackness—it doesn't validate the dehumanizing aspect of it. This act of reducing my worth to my skin color is how stereotypes are made and doing it erases the complexity of human identity. It limits me to some finite list of characteristics that in many cases I've had to protect myself from—like the oversexed Jezebel stereotype that follows Black girls and women around, coloring their friendships and relationships throughout life and the angry Black woman stereotype that negatively affects how I'm regarded in the workplace[226].

Assigning specific behaviors and characteristics to skin color makes it easy for people to project their idea of what they think I am on me. They create the me they think I should be instead of actually getting to know who I am. I've gone to clubs and had white people approach me demanding that I show them how to dance because "everybody knows Black people can dance." (For the record, I love dancing, but I'm terrible at it.) I've had men assume I was available because I was at the bar having drinks. I've had co-workers assume I'm violent because I was angry about something.

---

[226] Kel, Talynn. "The Face that Paused a Thousand Meetings." Breaking Normal, 28 April 2016. Web. 27 Sept. 2016.

It is annoying and aggravating to constantly inform people to squash their assumptions. I've lost the expectation that new people will actually try to know me instead of projecting whatever their expectations of Black women are onto me. I'm not a caricature, and I'm not a costume to be put on—or a voice to be affected, so please don't yell "yaaaaass girlfriend!" and then make strong eye contact for some affirmation that we are in the secret Black girl club. I don't fucking talk like that and I sure as hell don't appreciate either the projection or the mimicry.

These stereotypes are boring and trite, but more than that, they're dangerous. Just ask 17- year old Trayvon Martin[227], 13-year old Tyre King[228], and 12-year old Tamir Rice[229]—all murdered because of the assumptions someone's overactive imagination projected on their skin.

This is what we Black people live with. We live with the knowledge that our skin, a superficial physical characteristic we were born with, has been tainted by white people. Marred by white people with power. Disparaged by white people who work to punish us for existing. Growing up, we learn that the people around us, the pale ones who burn in the sun, actively and passively suppress us, oppress us, and benefit from mistreating us. We learn that you lie in your heads and hearts about us, and then lie to our faces[230] when you say we're all human and equal.

---

[227] Biography.com Editors. "Trayvon Martin Biography." The Biography.com Website, 09 Feb. 2016. Web. 27 Sept. 2016.

[228] Josefczyk, Aaron. "Community Gathers to Mourn 13-Year-Ole Tyre King Who Was Killed by Cops." The Huffington Post, 26 Sept. 2016. Web. 27 Sept. 2016.

[229] Williams, Joseph P. "Tamir Rice Shooting: Not Just a Tragedy." U.S. News and World Reports, 29 Dec. 2015. Web. 27 Sept. 2016.

[230] Kel, TaLynn. "White People, You Have A Lying Problem." The Establishment. 07 July 2016. Web. 27 Sept. 2016.

American history does not agree with you and we are living in its toxic present. A present where white people continue to make dehumanization a social norm.

You wouldn't skin someone and wear their skin. So ask yourself, what are you actually trying to do when you feel the need to darken your skin in order to costume as your favorite Black person or character? What are you saying when you claim that darkening your skin makes you feel closer to them, like you are embodying them? It's like you're trying to symbolically absorb them into you and replace them. You are trying to be them and that isn't admiration. It's psychological cannibalism and it's sickening.

Is this type of behavior the modern-day descendant of colonialism? Is this constant cannibalism[231] of other people, other cultures, until you absorb them at every level and become them feeding the inherited need to conquer, consume, and destroy?

I don't know. What I do know is that absorbing us won't make you into a better person. It doesn't imbue you with the strengths you admire. It just feeds your sickness and masks your rot a little longer.

This story first appeared at TheEstablishment.co, a multimedia site entirely run and funded by women, on October 24, 2016.

---

[231] Kel, TaLynn. "When White People Consume Blackness for Personal Gain." The Establishment. 29 June 2016. Web. 27 Sept. 2016.

You may claim to associate brown skin with strength of character, but historically it's been used to say Black people are animals, criminals, primitive, and in need of strong discipline.

– TaLynn Kel, Blackface Isn't a Compliment

White People: Shut the Fuck Up About Black Voters

Repeat after me:

WHITE VOTERS NOMINATED TRUMP!

WHITE VOTERS ARE ELECTING TRUMP!

WHITE VOTERS ARE ELECTING TRUMP!!!!

That's right. White voters. Your friends. Your family. Your neighbors. The polite, friendly white communities in your life who don't think they have anything to lose by electing him. The people who think that Clinton is worse than a racist, misogynistic, sexist, ableist, violent, pro-corporation, anti-climate change, pro-war, xenophobic, anti-education idiot who lies about shit he said last week - shit that's on video, who the media coddled until they created a monster who speaks to the dark heart of this country.

The dark, silent heart of this country that has always been here, quietly lurking, strengthening, and enforcing America's racist origins through legislation, redlining, policing, and entertainment.

In case you didn't realize, which apparently, a bunch of you fucking didn't, America's always been racist, sexist, and xenophobic. ALWAYS. When overt racism, sexism, and xenophobia became less popular, this country got better at talking around it and people got better at lying about it being gone. This country consistently used exceptions to the norm to lie about what the norm actually is.

"Look, we have a Black man as president! Racism is gone!"

"Women work in all kinds of jobs. I have a woman boss. Sexism is gone!"

"I have Black coworkers. My boss is a Black person. I had sex with a Black person once. I'm not racist."

"My wife/daughter/sister can work, own property, vote. If she doesn't act like a slut, she's great. Sexism is gone!"

Are you fucking kidding me? The norm is Donald Trump and white people are proving it.

I'm so angry right now. I'm fucking mad at the media for their stories about threats of violence at polling places. I'm angry at all the reports of voter suppression that people are conveniently ignoring. I'm mad at SCOTUS for gutting the biting rights act that Republicans leaped on to start changing voting laws and access to polls. I'm mad at President Obama for not fighting more for Black people in this country.

I'm mad at all the threats being made by racist shit bags who are angry that they can't unilaterally decide to only do what's best for white men. Did you know there are reports of armed white men standing at polling places, like that's not fucking frightening as hell. And law enforcement is apparently okay with it because it's in open carry states like Georgia, where I live. Fuck, we have media reporting on a militia "preparing" for post-election fallout[232] cuz I wasn't already scared enough.

---

[232] Eldridge, Ellen. "Georgia Militia Prepares for 'Fallout' After Election." Atlanta Journal Constitution, 04 Nov. 2016. Web. 08 Nov. 2016.

I'm mad at the self-righteous third party voters who think they have nothing to lose. I'm mad at my significant other's parents who fucking out right said, "I was raised white. This is the only thing I know to do," when talking about voting for Trump. I'm mad at the U.S. government for being dominated by out of touch, amoral, rich white people and sheltering the abundance of racists currently in law enforcement and government. I'm mad that running for public office is so expensive that only the rich can do it.

I'm mad at the fucking plethora of lies we choke down and call democracy.

And I'm scared. I'm scared for my friends, my family, myself. I'm terrified of what's next because no matter which was this goes, violence is in our future.

The past year has been nothing but psychological warfare and trauma for me and people who look like me as we watched the pile of bodies grow at the hands of police violence and then watched most of its perpetrators walk away with their jobs and crowdsourced funds for their murders. We have had to adapt to seeing brutality enacted on people who protest the wrongdoings of our police and criminal justice system over and over again.

We have had to learn what our parents and grandparents experienced first-hand as we struggle for equality and safe spaces in America. And America keeps showing us that we are lying to ourselves if we think that's possible. That shit isn't for Black Americans, Native Americans, Asian Americans, Muslim Americans, any non-white Americans, apparently. Nope. The message to us is shut up, get out, or die. And every single day I have to pretend that isn't the message I continue to receive loud and clear while I go through the motions of living. Each day it's a struggle to wake up because I am horribly depressed and anxious and scared every damn day and my body is responding as bodies do to extreme stress – by breaking down.

So, congratulations white America. You might get your fucking country back for racist, sexist, xenophobic, islamophobic, anti-human rights, anti-civil rights, pro-militarized police, pro-corporation, pro-pollution, homophobic, transphobic, ableist white people. Just remember, the straight, cisgender men get first pickings and the rest of you can fight it out for what's left. That's what's known as making America great again.

And any of you white people asking about Black voter turnout? Y'all need to take a long hard look in the mirror when you're looking for someone to blame for this fuckery called the 2016 presidential election and its after-effects. It's your fucking friends and family who nominated that shitbag. It's your friends and family voting for him. What the fuck did you do to try to keep this from happening, huh?

I'll wait.

When overt racism, sexism, and xenophobia became less popular, this country got better at talking around it and people got better at lying about it being gone. This country consistently used exceptions to the norm to lie about what the norm actually is.

– TaLynn Kel, White People: Shut the Fuck Up About Black Voters

Reflections on the 2016 Election – Election Day

From the moment Trump started gaining traction with his hate speech, I knew we were in a shitload of trouble. The GOP has always been racist, sexist, ableist, homophobic, transphobic and all that bullshit. Always. So has the Democratic party. So has America. This is America. Every single person who pushes back on it by existing, living out loud, mobilizing, informing is pushing back on the lie America calls normalcy. Our existence and refusal to be invisible shows everyone who's never felt or considered themselves normal that there is no normal. There is only us and we all belong here. There is room for all of us here. And that is the fight that I fight.

The violence, the bigotry, the hate has always been there, especially in group think situations. It's always been there and hidden because we had no way to push it out. No way to get eyes, ears, and minds on the myriad of injustices we face daily. Until the past few years. And the thing that scared me the most about all of it was the number of people who chose not to listen. These were people I grew up with. People I found myself related to. One I'd even married. When I married my significant other (S.O.), I gained a front row seat to white denial, intentional ignorance, callous indifference, and the pathological lies they tell themselves about it.

It was shocking for me.

It was in this relationship that I found the voice to speak about things I'd been conditioned never to speak about. My generation grew up after the Civil Rights Act was passed. I grew up hearing that we'd come a long way and to work hard, twice as hard to prove we deserved to be here. I was taught that I would be looked down upon, underestimated because I'm Black and to quietly prove I deserved all the rights and privileges white people took as their rote. I was taught never to trust white people because when the time came to choose, they would always choose other white people over me.

This is why I won't force my S.O. to abandon his family. I don't trust that he will choose me. Regardless of how many times he does choose me, and he has, multiple times, I still don't trust him to do it. I hope he will and so far, he has. But I'm still scared and I continue to be wary. I'm also transparent with him about this because he needs to know how I feel and why I sometimes pull away when things get tense. That fear and hope...they make for a complicated relationship.

We know that there may come a time when sides must be chosen. And the thing is, it's not a race issue, although race is at the core of it. It's a human rights issue, and the fact that there is a large segment of the American population that believes they should be able to deny human rights to anyone they don't like. Shit, they believe that they should ALWAYS have more human rights than people who are brown and Black. The GOP has always softly whispered this and encouraged oppression in their base. They did it in a way that they felt comfortable, and could deny as racism because they weren't specifying People of Color (POCs); they were targeting social issues around locations, diseases, illnesses, educational systems...They were working to "fix" a pathology they created around race and using the systems that segmented people to hide the inherent racism of their rhetoric.

And it worked. How often did we hear about the inner cities during this election cycle? Or entitlements? Or "that dangerous element" that needs to be addressed? Whenever the issue of gun violence arose, it wasn't to talk about white gun owners; it was to talk about Chicago and gangs and getting the guns out of the hands of those we suspected were criminals (they mean Black people). Stop and frisk is a code word for searching any Black person because they feel like it. All of this is code for Black people are dangerous and need to be treated as such at all times. And all of this is oppression.

And you see how white people will support stop and frisk[233] but then say they aren't racist. They will say they want to clean up neighborhoods, but won't admit that what they mean is displace the Black populations and replace them with white ones[234]. That when they want to privatize schools, that it's to destroy the public school systems[235] that they've diverted money out of for years until they began to collapse under the strain and then blame the Black families for their demise. There is a huge swath of the population that believes that supporting this doesn't make them racist, when actually this is the definition of racism.

What's funny is the number of republican women who didn't think the party was sexist and their surprise at it now. This is how ensconced they are in the bullshit and the lies. A bunch of women supported GOP sexists until the sexism became so overtly violent, they couldn't lie to themselves anymore. "Grab them by the pussy" has become the white woman's "n***er." And still a bunch of women support the GOP because...because...fuck if I know. I want to call them names but all the names I want to call them are ableist and I'm trying to do better so I won't. But damn.

We got fucking white people supporting white supremacy and then saying they aren't racist[236]. What the fuck kind of cognitive disconnect do you have going on to believe that shit?

---

[233] Fagan, Jeffrey; Braga, Anthony A.; Brunson, Rod K.; Pattavina, April. "An Analysis of Race and Ethnicity Patterns in Boston Police Department Field Interrogation, Observation, Frisk, and/or Search Reports." Raceandpolicing.issuelab.org, 15 June 2015. Web. 08 Nov. 2016.

[234] Brown, Kara. "How Racism is Driving New York City's Gentrification." Jezebel, 12 May 2015. Web. 08 Nov. 2016.

[235] Comissiong, Solomon. "Public Education in America: A Pillar of Institutional Racism." Black Agenda Report. 21 July 2009. Web. 08 Nov. 2016.

[236] Hughes, Martin. "The Amazing Atheist Denies He's Racist...By Being Racist." Patheos, 30 June 2016. 08 Nov. 2016.

That is how illogical so much of this country is and it's terrifying.

The thing is, this election gave racists a leader[237]. It gave them a banner to unite under. It gave them a feeling of legitimacy. It gave them hope that they could enact the oppressions that they'd been raised to believe were the natural order of things. And they plan to enforce that natural order, with violence if necessary.

This is where I'm supposed to say "not all Trump supporters" but fuck that. Silence is violence and all you silent mofos are complicit[238] as hell. You are the problem and your denial means exactly nothing. Stop fucking lying about the role you've chosen to play. It's embarrassing.

For all you former racism deniers – I'm glad you see it now. I'm glad you can now see the systems you've maintained and the actively fed through your insistence that racism was over. I hope you keep working within your communities to shine the light on racist practices and then start dismantling them. I hope you speak up when you see it, hear it. I hope you intervene. Because to start fixing what's wrong, you need to intervene with your friends, families, co-workers, neighborhoods, local governments...everywhere. You need to step in and say, "No. We're not doing this. Not anymore."

Oppression happens in silence and violence. It's in the background of everything we do in this country. You see it. Now fight it. Don't leave this country broken. Fix your people because it's dangerous for ALL of us.

---

[237] Holston, Paul. "Experts say white supremacists see Trump as 'last stand.'" PBS, 11 Aug. 2016. Web. 08 Nov. 2016.

[238] Brown, Yawo. "The Subtle Linguistics of Polite White Supremacy." The Magical Negro.net, 14 Aug. 2015. Web. 08 Nov. 2016.

I'll leave you with this quote from my estranged mother-in-law on why she's voting for the GOP candidate:

"I was raised white. This is the only thing I know to do."

That is America. Home of the free and the slave.

The GOP has always softly whispered this and encouraged oppression in their base. They did it in a way that they felt comfortable, and could deny as racism because they weren't specifying People of Color (POCs); they were targeting social issues around locations, diseases, illnesses, educational systems...They were working to "fix" a pathology they created around race and using the systems that segmented people to hide the inherent racism of their rhetoric.

– TaLynn Kel, Reflections on the 2016 Election – Election Day

Keeping It Real About Interracial Relationships as a Person of Color

I will admit, I'm super annoyed that it took the election of Donald Trump as our next president to make white people admit to racism. And while I'm sad and worried about the coming days, I'm not surprised by this outcome. This was not a shock for me, or any Black people I know. It was just the confirmation of everything we'd been saying, our parents said, our great grandparents said, etc. Racism has always been a part of America.

White people just can't hide it as well anymore.

And they are still trying. The rhetoric around Trump's rise and his supporters is being downplayed. Revisionist history is taking place before our eyes. The main stream media is pretending that he's not racist and everyone from President Obama to Oprah is begging us to forgive his racist as fuck supporters and work with that dusty Cheeto.

I think I'm going to pass on that hypocritical bullshit.

Despite that, there are a lot of us people of color (POCs) who have white people in our lives. Some of us have friends who are white. In my case, my spouse is white and we had to do a shit ton of work to get us to a decent place. But that work wasn't soft shoeing around the issues. It was both of us coming to some hard truths and admitting some shit that was painful as hell. And once we understood who we were, we could work on being better for each other. I learned a lot from that experience and thought I'd share some things I applied to all my interracial relationships.

Reality #1 – If your white friend/lover was raised in America, that person is racist.

There are no exceptions to this. The very best version is the white person who knows and understands they were raised this way. They understand that they still live in a white supremacist environment and benefits from systemic racism. They also understand that they will need to challenge this in themselves for the rest of their lives.

The issue I've had is that white people refuse to admit they are racist. They will flat out deny it without the hint of reflection. To them, racist is a slur, not a set of actions, attitudes, beliefs, and assumptions that can be challenged and changed. Instead they get defensive and upset. Then, in many cases, they lash out at you. Many times, they will call you a racist, and at that point you know that this person does not understand what racism is or how it works. They haven't done the work and that makes them untrustworthy. Hell, it makes them dangerous.

Reality #2 – Call out culture will be a part of your relationship.

This is the part that kind of sucks because it requires that you constantly confront the white people in your life about their racism. You will be the one to challenge their assertions. You will be the one to point out that they are fucking up. It's uncomfortable and a buzzkill for them but then again, their racist comment was a buzzkill for you. Then again, why should you be the only one on the shitty experience train?

When I do this, it's not fun for me. But it's necessary. I don't want to be in a room with a bunch of people saying derogatory things about POCs. I don't want to entertain it in my life and I definitely don't want them to feel comfortable doing it around me. I know for a fact that it has made me persona non-grata in many white spaces but it's also made my social events more relaxed and fun. The thing to remember is that racism is abuse. It can be psychological or physical, but it's abuse and your relationship is toxic. You will need to decide how to address that toxicity but you don't have to live with it. It's not healthy for you.

Reality #3 – Anti-Blackness transcends race and you need to learn about yours.

To have a real conversation with white people about race, you are going to have to examine your anti-Blackness. Otherwise, you won't have honest conversations. While Black people cannot be racist, they can believe and do racist things, also known as practicing anti-Blackness. This is a very nuanced view because it means looking at a system verses individual actions. As an individual, I can discriminate against other Black people, but this is within a system that was designed to exploit and exclude Black people. As such, it can benefit Black people to harm other Black people.

If you've spent a lot of time in white spaces, you see the subtle approval you receive when you don't confront someone's racism. You see how popular media is that portrays Black people as drug addicts, prostitutes, violent criminals, and such. You've probably also seen how trying to advance or protect Black people can result in negative criticism from your employer. Over time you learn to choose when you will challenge people's assumptions and depending on how hostile your work environment, you may learn to never challenge it. You learn to join in on the jokes about Black people's names and how Black people speak. You learn that you'll receive subtle approval for making disparaging remarks about certain neighborhoods or certain behaviors associated with Black people. You learn to hate the things associated with being Black.

This is a tough one because it is a behavior rooted in self-preservation but it's dangerous and damaging. It's self-hate, which Black people learn in childhood that must be unlearned constantly. I still find myself questioning some of the things I say and having to self-correct. But I learn and I improve and I fight when it creeps back up on me.

And the thing with anti-Blackness is that anyone can practice it. When Peter Liang murdered Akai Gurley[239] in New York, Chinese people protested his arrest because white people got away with murdering Black people, so he should too. And while he was convicted, he got no jail time. I've seen Asian blackface[240], seen racist commercials, and they use racist depictions of Black people in anime[241]. Anti-Blackness is real and it is practiced by all.

Reality #4 – You can't lie to yourself about reality.

The hardest thing I had to face in my relationship was being honest about the fact that I'd married a racist. Sure, he wasn't an angry, violent racist, but he was a product of his environment. America is a terribly racist, violent, and hypocritical country. It is a country that constantly and consistently lies to itself about how great it is. Then it tells that lie to the world despite the overwhelming evidence to the contrary. The lie of American exceptionalism has eroded this country into a massive human rights violation with leaders who lack the ability to address its problems because they can't stop lying long enough. We elected a racist, sexist, ableist, xenophobic, pro-corporation, anti-environment, anti-LGBTQIA, unqualified man for president because people in this country cannot admit to their fucking biases. White people were surprised that their friends and neighbors supported Trump because they spent too much time trying to convince Black

---

[239] "No Prison Time for Ex-NYPD Officer Peter Liang in Fatal Shooting of Akai Gurley." Los Angeles Times, 19, April 2916. Web. 15 Nov. 2016.

[240] Winn, Patrick. "Asia Embraces Blackface-Style Ads. Get Ready to Cringe." PRI, 01 July 2014. Web. 15 Nov. 2016.

[241] Kel, Talynn. "One Punch Man." Breaking Normal, 22 Dec. 2015. Web. 15 Nov. 2016.

people that we were misinterpreting racist situations instead of listening and recognizing racism in their white circles.

It is this lying, this self-deception, and this ridiculous need to control how people see you instead of doing the work to be better human beings that leads to fucked up, life changing, toxic situations. If you can't admit your biases and limitations to yourself, they will damage your relationships. If you can't admit that you are a product of your environment and figure out how that harms you, it will harm your relationship. There's a reason why Black people must confront their own anti-Blackness – it is to see the ways you harm yourself so that you fix it before you harm others. And white people need to take a long hard look at themselves and accept that they were raised immersed in racism and white supremacy. Only then can they begin to dismantle it.

You can't be honest with others if you can't be honest with yourself. You also can't fix shit if you won't admit it's broken. Be honest with yourself and then fix your shit.

Reality #5 – They won't always understand.

The thing is, these experiences are personal and are rooted in how we interact with the world and the way the world interacts with us. While there are some similarities, no white person can truly understand how racism affects me. And that's ok.

What I needed was support and caring. I need my white friends to believe me and accept my truth, regardless of how it differs from theirs. For any relationship to work, there must be trust and if they are denying my reality, we aren't friends. They are allowed not to understand but they cannot dismiss or deny. That is bullshit.

Reality #6 – The work to confront racism doesn't stop.

It's constant. It's necessary and makes self-care[242] hella important. Please remember to take care of yourself and to put yourself first. You don't have to do maintain your interracial relationships. They are optional. In fact, if it's harming you, it's okay to break up. Hell, I encourage it. This is a deal-breaker issue. The work that you need to do will always exist and it is exhausting. The people with whom I've been successful did a lot of work to prove to me that they were worth the effort and I've embraced that this might change. They may still cross a line that will destroy our relationship because this is too important to treat casually. I'd be lying if I didn't share that there were days I'd cry and ask why I chose this path for myself. It hurt and it took a long time to get to a place of healing. We know that we still have work to do and we accept that it will never stop.

***

This concludes the six hard realities I faced in my interracial relationships. They are not the only truths, but they are the ones I needed to understand to manage my relationships.

If you are a person of color and plan to have close relationships with white people you need to understand that it's work. It's constant, messy work. It's work that makes you feel vulnerable. It's work that will empower you. It's work that will hurt and heal you. And, if that person isn't worthy, it's work that's optional. I chose to do this work in some of my relationships and while I have been successful in some, I've failed in others and I can't count the number of people with whom I didn't bother to try. In many cases, they weren't worth the effort and frankly, everyone isn't capable or willing to have real dialogue about racism.

_____

[242] Pérez, Miriam Zoila. "4 Self-Care Resources for Days When the World is Terrible." Colorlines, 07 July 2016. Web. 09 Dec. 2016.

Maybe it's time for white people to get out of their feelings and fucking accept what they are. It won't kill them. In fact, it'll heal a bunch of shit that's wrong with this country and eventually make it a better place for everyone.

Or we'll burn it to the ground. I don't know what to expect anymore.

The hardest thing I had to face in my relationship was being honest about the fact that I'd married a racist. Sure, he wasn't an angry, violent racist, but he was a product of his environment. America is a terribly racist, violent, and hypocritical country.

— TaLynn Kel, Keeping It Real About Interracial Relationships as a Person of Color

When White People Are Too Hateful to Realize They Screwed Up

You ever have that shitty boss who likes to micromanage you? They want you to check in when you get to work, check out before you leave. They make random walks through the office to see if you are at your desk and challenge everything you're working on. They insert themselves into your projects, make changes that are often incorrect, blame you for the fuck-up, and then try to force you to apologize so that you can keep coming back for that same bullshit. They are petty tyrants and they get a kick out of lording their tiny bit of power over you. And you keep coming back because you need income and this is better than homelessness and starvation.

For Black people, that petty tyrant is white Amerikkka, and in 2016 they elected someone who promised to let them keep their petty tyrant title.

That's right. America elected a thoughtless, entitled, ignorant, racist, sexist, anti-LGBTQIA, ableist jerk as the next president of Amerikkka because he promised that they could keep their mediocre status over people of color. They elected a man who ruined his businesses, threatened and assaulted many people, lied repeatedly, kept secrets, and has no plan for the country. He openly promised segregation, mass deportation, and a wall to keep brown people from the south from crossing the imaginary border around the U.S. And they did it because they believe they will be able to actively oppress other people who they don't consider human.

They did it to feel powerful.

Many of them voted against their best interests because they think this will put white people at the top of the pecking order in America. Like they ever weren't. They voted to keep the illusion of power. The thing is, unless they have money, Trump doesn't give a shit about them. All the things they think Trump will do, he can't actually do—except continue to oppress marginalized populations. He can continue doing that because if Amerikkka has proven one thing, it's that it doesn't care about People of Color and that feeds into the superiority complex of mediocre white Amerikkka. Terrorizing people who are perceived as lesser is what bullies need to feel strong.

And terrorizing is what will happen. It's already started, but once Trump's changes illuminate how everything they *thought* they voted for actually brought them nothing? When they realize the shell game Trump played with their emotions? When they realize that the shit they fought to repeal will actually hurt them? These people, the fucking poorest of the white people who thought being racist would solve their problems, will seek out those they think are weaker than them and do everything in their power to scare, threaten, and terrorize them.

They will lose their insurance. The jobs won't come back. Their towns will continue to die. People will die because they can't afford medication or treatment. There will be more pollution as the environmental protection laws are gutted and they will have no legal recourse when fully mechanized manufacturing facilities pollute their land and water. And as they suffer, they will turn to Black people and blame us for their fuck-up, and then try to punish us for the future they chose.

Because white supremacy is the lie that leaves white people wallowing in their mediocrity. It is the pathway to their demise. I'm just fighting not to go down with them, which is basically, it's business as usual but with a lot more white supremacist rage, entitlement, and empowerment.

And white people, y'all gotta own that shit—especially white women. I can't even begin to understand how sexual assault is okay with you, except, apparently, racism overrules everything. Even your own safety. Even your self-worth. Even your right to your body. Fuck all that, gotta have that white supremacy. Cuz Amerikkka's always been great for women, especially back in the olden days. Y'all fucked this up and you're going to feel it. Your fuckery would be impressive if so many people weren't about to suffer because of it.

The future is bleak and I am horrified by half the people in this country. Amerikkka is a bunch of impotent petty tyrants willing to burn it all down rather than reflect, learn, grow, and collaborate. It is full of silent racists who think they have nothing to lose and while I'd love to watch you burn in the fire of your hateful rage, I gotta save myself and others from your ignorance and selfishness.

May your self-righteous ignorance render you sterile as you are crushed by the rocks from your fucking wall.

This story first appeared at TheEstablishment.co, a multimedia site entirely run and funded by women, on November 10, 2016.

Because white supremacy is the lie that leaves white people wallowing in their mediocrity. It is the pathway to their demise. I'm just fighting not to go down with them, which is basically, it's business as usual but with a lot more white supremacist rage, entitlement, and empowerment.

– TaLynn Kel, When White People Are Too Hateful to Realize They Screwed Up

White People, You've Broken My Trust

Since the 2016 election, I've had to let go of many assumptions about white people. I've had to truly accept that white people mean me harm.

Not explicitly. Not directly. Not in a way that soils their hands and makes them realize the depth of their hatred. They want to harm me in the same way that meat ends up in the grocery store: far away where someone else does the dirty work for them. En masse so that it seems impersonal. On such a large scale that it feels as though it was out of their control. Fueled by lies so they can claim its justified.

They want me under their foot or out of the way so that they can feel dominant and in control. But they don't want the guilt and shame that comes with direct engagement from those they seek to oppress.

AmeriKKKa will die on its inability to be honest with itself. And since I'm going down anyway, I want to watch.

I've grown up knowing that white people don't think shit about Black people. I've been taught, encouraged, conditioned, trained, forced into centering whiteness in many of my conversations if white people are present. It's a difficult conditioning to break, especially as my significant other (S.O.) is white. I didn't understand these dynamics before our relationship. I didn't understand these dynamics before this year. I sort of understood that I had a kind of freedom with Black people that I didn't have in racially diverse groups and definitely didn't have in predominantly white groups. I knew there were "safe" topics I could discuss around white people, and they usually did not include politics or social justice. I knew that many times I didn't feel safe around white people, and this was something I experienced in my relationship with my S.O. And because I didn't want to deal with the conflicting emotions it caused, I sometimes pushed it to the side to deal with later. Later became years of unpleasant social interactions with people I felt I needed to hide myself from. I still feel that way, which is why I do not interact with them much.

Their coded language. Their not so hidden racism and misogynoir. It was there. It is always there. I just needed to re-tune myself to its melody and cadence, both a self-protective and self-harming act. My continued proximity to whiteness, both through my marriage and my employment, demands I hear the violence of their soft words. Exposing me to their thinly veiled hostility, their muted hatred. I bleed from cuts made by verbal knives, designed to pierce Black bodies. I field multiple attacks through shifting context, morphing intent, modified and commodified rage and dismissal. Gentrification. Redlining. Political discourse. Health concerns. Freedom of speech. Freedom of expression. Their hate, constantly protected from scrutiny, protest, rebuttal, dismissal and woven into every inch of the fabric of America...while those who resist, push-back, criticize, protest, and reveal the incessant inconsistencies, lies, hidden truths, and fabrications are attacked more for daring to speak truth.

Oh, the many ways I've experienced racism from my peers. The many ways oppression has manifested itself in language. It is varied and ever-changing, while its damage it consistent. See the list. Learn the code.

- Annoyed: I mean I get that they have been disenfranchised, attacked, and murdered but do they have to be so loud about it?

- Benevolent: "we're all the same and I'm good to everyone regardless of color."

- Condescending: We will go save all the brown skinned people from their ignorance. White people can help EVERYONE!

- Conditional: See, if you had been nicer and maybe less angry, I would have been on your side but since you weren't, I can't support you.

- Denial: I am not racist. It's not my fault that Black people didn't understand what I meant!

- Dismissive: You definitely misunderstood. You need to stop being so sensitive. Everything isn't about race.

- Doubting: Are you sure that what they said was racist? Maybe you misunderstood.

- Economic: The Civil War was about the economy, not slavery.

- Educational: They just can't learn the way white people learn. Their brains don't work the same way.

- Insistent: Racism isn't real. It's just something Black people say to get special treatment.

- Judgmental: Prove that you deserve a chance. That you're better than the others.

- Murderous: Kill the n*ggers!

- Passive Aggressive: I understand your concerns about all the new hires being white. Let's schedule a conversation to talk about this.

- Patronizing: Nobody's going to listen to you if you keep whining like spoiled brats.

- Ridiculous: Even if human life did originate in Africa, all it means is that Black people are less evolved than white people.

- Sanctimonious: We must forgive the Black people for they know not what they do.

- Scientific: You know the brains of children raised with food insecurity develop differently. A lot of Black people are raised in poverty, so...

- Sexualized: Black women are wild in bed. They just bring this primitive freakiness you just can't get in a white woman.

- Sexualized & Racially Violent: You know you want it. All you Black bitches stay in heat for this shit.

- Undermining: The job can't be that hard if she can do it.

*****

Racism is the one area where white people are consistently creative, marketing geniuses. How now, instead of racist or nazi, they are the "alt-right." How lies are now "post-truths," protesters are rioters, anti-racists are bullies, Black people are racists, Black Lives Matter is a hate group and the KKK is not a terrorist organization. White people are the spin doctors of oppression and now we watch many of them continue to unify under a mountain of lies and a promise of racial violence. Why is this the norm?

Why is racism normal?

The depressing part is that it's always been normal in America. It is an intrinsic part of colonialism. Psychological and emotional violence are the ground we walk on, the church we pray in, the job we work for, and the bed we sleep in. This IS America. And, when I pay attention, it is always painful.

I've mentioned repeatedly that my father told me to never trust white people. That they would always fight for white supremacy and that I would always be to whom they felt superior. For most of my life, I told myself it wasn't true. I bet my marriage, and potentially my life on that. This election has shown me that my judgement is flawed and I'm not quite sure what to do with that.

My S.O. is pressured to constantly prove he's different. How long will my marriage last under that strain? The white people I call my friends, too, must prove they are different. How many friendships will collapse under that burden? And yet, this is what I need to feel comfortable keeping them in my life. This proof. This constant proof. Kinda like the proof I have to provide to show I deserve my degrees, my job, my home, my freedom. And when I think about it that way, I feel less bothered.

Welcome to the world of not being good enough because of your skin color. It's still not balanced. It's still not fair. And it's a pretty shitty place to live.

But this is AmeriKKKa, the country built on hundreds of years of POC corpses by beneficiaries who deny their racially violent history because it makes them feel bad.

Ugh.

Racism is the one area where white people are consistently creative, marketing geniuses. How now, instead of racist or nazi, they are the "alt-right." How lies are now "post-truths," protesters are rioters, anti-racists are bullies, Black people are racists, Black Lives Matter is a hate group and the KKK is not a terrorist organization.

— TaLynn Kel, White People, You've Broken My Trust4

I Learned It Was My Fault

Trigger Warning: This essay discusses sexual assault.

As a child, I remember being taught to never be alone with guys.

I was taught to expect violence from men, specifically sexual violence. I wasn't allowed to play with some kids. If I did and something happened, I understood that it was my fault because I should have known better. I am always expected to know better than the men in my life...than anybody else in my life.

And when I don't know better, my options are to live privately with the shame or live publicly with it. Like many people, I've chosen to live with my shame privately, which is why I've never spoken about how I was sexually assaulted by an older kid when I was six years old.

Even three decades later I'm embarrassed about it. I was supposed to know better. I wasn't supposed to wander off. I wasn't supposed to go into the neighbor's house. I was supposed to recognize a predator, even at six-years-old. I was supposed to know. And the kid who did it, who was years older, was known to be dangerous. I didn't know but other people in the neighborhood did. He was violent, a bully, known to be untrustworthy. He'd assaulted other children. People *knew* and did nothing because...I don't know. I guess because we protect our men at the expense of our women and children. Sometimes we do it because we financially cannot afford to live without them. Other times we do because it feels safer to go with the abuser you know.

I had classmates who were sexually abused by their fathers and punished for daring to fight back. I have friends who were raped by cousins, molested by uncles, assaulted by classmates, other neighborhood children and we were the ones labeled fast, easy, asking for it. I was six. How did I ask for sexual attention when I didn't even understand what it was?

But somehow, I did.

I learned the lessons I was meant to learn – that abuse was my fault. That sexual assault was my fault for having the audacity to be female. Regardless of how I shucked the trappings of femininity, I was still the problem. This was the message from my father, my mother, and every other authority in my life. I was the problem. I blamed the breasts my body had the gall to develop. I blamed my uterus for daring to make me vulnerable to pregnancy.

And I blamed the boys club that all men seem to be a part of. The club that perpetuates physical and emotional violations against those perceived as less – women, children, LGBTQIA, people of color. The club that protects its enactors and protects them from the consequences of their actions.

In many ways, I blame my dad. His hypocrisy in how he treated me compared to my older brother was obvious and when confronted about it, he didn't lie. He told me I had different rules just because I was a girl and he was okay with that. I loved him, but I hated this about him – not the honesty, but the sexism. I hated that he sometimes tried to groom me into the type of woman he thought was attractive. I hated that he encouraged me to suppress myself to attract men. He believed that I needed to be married with children. He believed I should not show my strength and intelligence to men. He believed that I was less than, while simultaneously demanding more of me.

He protected my brother from the consequences of his actions, to the point that sometimes I was punished for my older brother's mistakes. And when it was clear I had nothing to do with his infractions, my dad was always there to fix it for him. If my brother got a ticket, Dad paid it. When my brother got in trouble with any authority, my father stepped in to sort it out. To be fair, my brother is a Black man living in America with an intellectual disability and mental health issues. We have no relationship because he we don't trust each other and I don't like the person he's become. My father treated us differently because we were different, but his rationale was rooted in sexism. My brother was granted more freedom for being male and I was watched and guarded more closely for being female. Freedom vs control. My brother was free to find himself, fuck up, and my dad would fix it. I was groomed, protected, and expected to be perfect. When I fucked up, Dad would protect me, but he made sure I knew he wouldn't have needed to if I'd just stayed under his control.

Now that he's gone, I find myself wanting to protect my dad. He was wrong. How he tried to groom me was wrong. The way he promoted the "boys will be boys so protect yourself" rhetoric was wrong. I don't know if he did any work to help women. I don't know if he understood his complicity in this fucked up society but I do know that I find myself wanting to defend him when I shouldn't. He didn't always treat women well. And he struggled with accepting my independence and wanting me to be self-sufficient because it somewhat conflicted with how he thought women should be. He was the problem. He was my first patriarchal problem.

He spent my childhood molding me into the woman he thought I should be, while trying to accept the person I was. I was not silly or ignorant. I was not fragile or afraid. I was smart, opinionated, assertive, unafraid, determined, inquisitive, and strong-willed. I was everything he thought was unfeminine but everything he respected in another person.

I don't think he resolved that conflict in himself, that conflict about me. Or maybe he did. As I got older, I felt less pressure from him to be a feminine ideal and more acceptance for who I was. It didn't undo any of the psychological damage he did. That other fathers did. That their sons, brothers, uncles, cousins, friends did and continue to do as they continue the cycles of abuse and absolution on and for one another.

I have seen so many shitty as boys grow up into shitty ass men: former friends, family, classmates... Men who cannot admit to their vulnerability or ignorance. Men who have been conditioned to deny their emotions, to suppress everything until they are incapable of empathy. Until they are unrecognizable to themselves.

I've seen women grow up afraid of the men they were supposed to seek as partners. I've watched them twist themselves into who they thought they should be and demand the same behavior from other women. I've watched them punish them for not conforming as I have been punished and excluded for not conforming.

It's a travesty that this is the norm. That we promote this perversion of the human condition and call it correct and proper. This a frightening and horrific practice that we enforce on babies and violently reinforce throughout their whole lives. We protect it and defend it. We hire it. Promote it. Elect it.

When, really, the humane thing would be to destroy it.

We need to learn and believe and enforce that these acts are not normal. Assault is not normal – not even when president-elect cheeto does it. We need to stop protecting men from their violence and make a stand for its victims. All its victims, like the six-year-old child who just wanted to play a game.

We need to stop making the violence we experience our fault and lay the blame squarely on its perpetrators.

Let's stop protecting the monsters and create a society of which we can be proud.

I have seen so many shitty as boys grow up into shitty ass men: former friends, family, classmates... Men who cannot admit to their vulnerability or ignorance. Men who have been conditioned to deny their emotions, to suppress everything until they are incapable of empathy. Until they are unrecognizable to themselves.

– TaLynn Kel, I Learned It Was My Fault

Becoming an Agent of Whiteness

Do you know what white supremacy is? It's the doubt you have about your safety in predominantly Black neighborhoods. It's that skepticism you feel when your doctor isn't white. It's the hesitation you have when you question a Black person's abilities. It's the surprise you have that a Black person is good at something . . . anything. It's the devaluing you do when someone like me accomplishes something a white person cannot. It's the excuses you make to explain why and how I outperformed white people.

If you are a person of color (POC) in this white supremacist society, you are taught to hate yourself before you know what hate is. You are trained to prioritize white people at all costs. Self-destructive behaviors, like silencing yourself, are normalized, while protective behaviors, like self-respect, are weaponized against you.

You spend your life being conditioned into thinking you are less than white people—less intelligent, less capable, less trustworthy. You learn that no matter what you do, you are a problem. You find ways to survive, muting and hiding yourself as much as possible. Accepting verbal abuse and ridicule for things out of your control. You suppress, suppress, suppress, and prove, prove, prove, until that is all you know. Or you lash out and find your completely understandable and protective behavior deemed illegal and regulated at the potential cost of your life.

You learn that approval is gained from self-deprecating behaviors. That diminishing yourself and those who look like you can provide growing returns. You learn that your proximity to whiteness, while painful, allows you access to things you've been taught to desire. Money. Status. Power. You learn that little pieces of your dignity, pride, and self-respect hold value on the white open market.

The thing that you don't learn is that this is a form of self-abuse.

It is complicated navigating white spaces as a person of color. Your appearance plays a huge role in how much or little you will be accepted. The less you resemble a POC, the easier time you will have navigating whiteness. Provided you ritually sacrifice aspects of your identity for white acceptance, you will be allowed on the fringe of these groups. You learn to hear, see, and say no to Otherness, to embrace whiteness in all its false glory. You are told that if you are Black, you should renounce your Blackness. Remove all its trappings from your life. Embrace the light that is white Jesus, white pride, white supremacy, and know your true worth—as a footstool upon which whiteness rests. Learn your place and you shall be held high, a lord among peasants—the price being all that makes you...you.

So, you eat the apple, gain the access, and allow the insidious, sleeping protector of whiteness into your body, because survival requires it, success dictates it, and you, on some level, want it. It is, superficially, an easier path to walk. That protector, be it large or small, is poison to you, incompatible with who and what you are, ingesting you from the inside out. White supremacy is poison to all who touch it, and is currently engineering the global destruction of humanity through methods like global warming, continued consumption of fossil fuels, and unending genocide.

"Consume, consume, consume," it chants, normalizing the cannibalization of others. Normalizing the cannibalization of self. Nestled inside you, aware, awake, guiding your every decision. Shadowing your every move. It is the echo chamber in your head, confusing your need to survive with the need to absorb and ingest the otherness of yourself and the otherness of others. Repackage yourself, your friends, your lovers. Soften your edges to appeal to more palates. Strip yourself of your history, individuality, nuance just enough to intrigue without overwhelming. Hide, dissect, and serve yourself to whiteness in small, manageable pieces. Exotify your experiences. Be that delicious tidbit that whiteness loves to devour. Let it absorb, reshape, and regurgitate an empty version of yourself to continue the work of white consumption in its stead.

You become, in part, the poison of whiteness, wolf in sheep's clothing, infecting everyone you touch until they also become ever-consuming agents of destruction.

This is what whiteness is. This is what whiteness does. And when you defend those who promote it, when you rationalize their intentions, empathize with their motives, sympathize with their actions, defend their rhetoric, and support being open and understanding, you are its agent, corrupting from the inside out.

For white supremacy doesn't embrace the humanity of all. It embraces the humanity of whiteness. All others are sustenance for its insatiable hunger for domination and control.

This story first appeared at TheEstablishment.co, a multimedia site entirely run and funded by women, on December 5, 2016.

You learn that your proximity to whiteness, while painful, allows you access to things you've been taught to desire. Money. Status. Power. You learn that little pieces of your dignity, pride, and self-respect hold value on the white open market.

– TaLynn Kel, Becoming an Agent of Whiteness

When the Space You Promised Hurts Like Hell

Last night my significant other (S.O.) and I got into a discussion about the oppression-driven division in this country and it sucked. It sucked for so many reasons. It sucked because I promised him the space to be wrong as he learns more about racism and oppression. I promised him the space to fuck up and grow from his mistakes. I promised him that I would continue to help him address and dissect his cultivated white supremacist education...and it sucked. It sucked because he didn't see how he was wrong. It sucked because I thought we were past this bullshit where we gave any legitimacy to the "other side." The side that doesn't respect my humanity. The side that thinks I am subhuman. The side that is actively fighting to keep me in a space where white people can use, abuse, and discard me at their discretion. The side that is fighting to ensure their perceived superiority.

A side that he was raised to think is the way things are supposed to be.

But he's white and white people have controlled the narrative of who deserves equality and who doesn't for hundreds of years. Apparently, it takes more than seven years with me for him to understand that it's a lie. Not just a lie, but flat out wrong. And immoral. And dehumanizing. And a violation of my personhood; my humanity; my life.

He doesn't understand how dangerous all this is.

It all started with Trevor Noah and Charlamagne the Sucka's radio interview[243]. I've been irritated at Trevor for his New York Times op-ed since I read it on Monday and decided he wasn't about shit. In fact, I'd written an essay a couple of weeks ago[244] that went live the same day as his op-ed[245] about exactly what Trevor was doing – legitimizing and doing the work for white supremacy. This work was done by inviting Tomi Lahren, a known racist, on his platform and then going out of his way to be nice and accepting of her. He gave legitimacy to her brand and, with this interview, doubled down on his promotion of her as someone worth listening to - as though the shit she spews doesn't actively hurt people. It's almost like he's part of the racist Barbie promotional tour, complete with cupcakes. Thanks to this one act, that nasty little hatemonger gained access to an entirely new audience and he made that possible. His op-ed explains why he thought that bullshit was the right thing to do. For him to willingly share his following with an active and vocal, intentionally ill-informed white supremacist is baffling to me and I've be openly and actively vocal about what bullshit this was.

---

[243] The Breakfast Club Power 105.1 FM. "Trevor Noah Talks Tomi Lahren, Donald Trump, Racism in America & More." YouTube, 07 Dec. 2016. Web. 09 Dec. 2016.

[244] Kel, TaLynn. "Becoming an Agent of Whiteness." The Establishment, 05 Dec. 2016. Web. 09 Dec. 2016.

[245] Noah, Trevor. "Trevor Noah: Let's Not Be Divided. Divided People Are Easier to Rule." The New York Times, 05 Dec. 2016. Web. 09 Dec. 2016.

Then Charlamagne, a personality I've never paid any attention to, started being a Tomy-ite all while conveniently claiming on Twitter that Black women don't do exponentially better shit than that vapid, racist shit storm... It was just a week where Black women found themselves being attacked and de-legitimized by Black men claiming they were being fair. Isn't it interesting how fair is about letting someone who shouts ignorant, informed, racist shit access to your audience and elevating their media profile. Bene Viera said it best in her essay for The Frisky[246]:

"Thanks to black men, Tomi Lahren has been all the buzz in media for over a week. She didn't have to do anything but cozy up with black men and let her mediocrity and proximity to them do the work. The way she hustled these fools reminds me that 13% of black men voted for Trump. As much as things change they remain the same."

As much things change they remain the same.

My relationship with my significant other has changed a lot over the past seven years. From his complete avoidance of talking about racism to him becoming active and vocal in speaking against it. Then he posted that interview between two agents of whiteness as though it's totally fine to have two black men advocate for racists. His reason: nothing will get better if the two sides don't talk to each other and that's what they were talking about."

Long stare in frustrated and disappointed Black woman

---

[246] Viera, Bené. "Here's the problem with black men like Trevor Noah and Charlamagne Tha God." The Frisky, 07 Dec. 2016. Web. 09 Dec. 2016.

Two sides, he said. What two sides? The side that says "hey, we're all human and deserve equal rights and protections under the law" vs the side that says "White people have run this shit and if you don't like what we've allowed you to have you can leave...or we can kill you and understand that we'll do both."

Another long stare in frustrated disbelieving Black woman

The conversation started with why what these men, Trevor and Charlamagne, were doing was problematic. How they were promoting rhetoric that was damaging to Black people and operated under the assumption that this conversation, this resistance to the dehumanization of Black people hasn't been going on for hundreds of years. That their whole "nothing's going to change if both sides aren't talking" ignores the hundreds of years that Black people have fought to get this far. It ignores that many, many white people don't want to have these conversations at all. It ignores the propaganda machine that operates expressly to devalue the needs of Black people; the systems that exist to actively destroy any cohesion and make every day a fight for survival. It ignores the escapes[247], the hiding[248], the building[249], the destruction, the casual, unjustified murders of Black people[250]. It ignores the violent and murderous rampages enacted by white people[251] on Black people who were doing nothing more than living their lives. It ignores how every fucking way we push back against this is somehow a problem.

---

[247] History.com Staff. "Harriet Tubman." History.com. Web. 09 Dec. 2016.

[248] Loewen, James W.; Kaplan, Fran; Smith, Robert. "Sundown Towns: Racial Segregation Past and Present." America's Black Holocaust Museum. Web. 09 Dec. 2016.

[249] Sanders, Brandee. "History's Lost Black Towns." The Root, 27 Jan. 2016. Web. 09 Dec. 2016.

[250] The Establishment. "Every Day a Funeral." The Establishment, 20 Sept. 2016. Web. 09 Dec. 2016.

[251] Moore, A. "8 Successful and Aspiring Black Communities Destroyed by White Neighbors." Atlanta Black Star, 04 Dec. 2013. Web. 09 Dec. 2016.

It ignores the fact that many white people participate in the destruction of Black people, both explicitly and implicitly, including him. And yes, he needs to continue working on himself and the white people in his life to destroy this shit. And it's not going to happen in his lifetime, but he still fucking needs to work on it. Always. Just like I do. Like many Black people do. Like we *must* do because this is about the right to our humanity[252] and our survival.

I shared my personal experiences of racial discrimination with him and he said that there are white people who experience the same discrimination, bias, and threats of violence. Really? REALLY? Who? His response was that he could find someone online. Somebody online.

So, nobody he knows? Nobody he can call on the phone? Cuz I can invite 30 people over today who can tell him about the racist shit they've had to deal with. The threats. The discrimination. The inequities in the law and social imbalance.

And this is always my question for white people: who the fuck can you call who experienced racism from Black people? Who do you know? Who was assumed to be a bad influence and removed from classes as punishment? Who had their privileges revoked because they were NEAR an altercation? Who had their teachers, professors, counselors assume they didn't understand the lesson, accuse them of plagiarism, tell them not to aim high because that success wasn't meant for someone like them? Who do you personally know who lived on toxic land surrounded by white adults who would threaten to kill them for entering their neighborhood?

---

[252] Oluo, Ijeoma. "You Don't Have To Like Me—You Just Have To Believe I'm A Human Being." The Establishment, 29 Nov. 2016. Web. 09 Dec. 2016.

I don't need to read a fucking essay to understand what racism is and how it works. I live it. And I know I'm a goddamn privileged exception with my ivy league education and high paying job. I KNOW this. And despite all this fucking white approval, I still deal with racist co-workers and racist systems that explicitly deny me entry to certain circles. I still work for unqualified white men who somehow "earned" their place despite having zero experience in that field. I still know that an interaction with police or some angry white person with a gun can result in my death and my corpse will be blamed for its murder.

But you got a fucking YouTube video. Get the fuck outta here.

This is the shit people in interracial relationships skate past. These discussions where you have to look at the white person in your life and realize this motherfucker is a white supremacist in denial. My S.O. has on more than one occasion admitted that he thinks this way and he's trying not to. He's trying. But all the information he's getting from white sources are feeding that belief system and he's fucking up.

He's hit his white supremacy reset button and that is a motherfucking problem.

While he no longer says that racism isn't real and no longer claims that he doesn't benefit from racism, he still seems to think racism isn't as dangerous as it is. He seems to think the people on the "other side" have the right to fight to oppress Black people and other people of color without repercussions. He seems to think that their fight for dominance is not problematic. That it's ok for them to fight to keep Black people beneath them and under their control.

He doesn't accept that the white people fighting to maintain this oppression don't think I'm equal. He doesn't grasp that there is a large part of the country that thinks he married a beast and is dirtying himself by being with me.

He doesn't accept that these people do not want to be at a table talking to me. They don't think I have anything worthwhile to say.

And he believes that my I'm being mean when I acknowledge this. He's fucking trying to protect them and their hate that he doesn't quite interpret as hate. To him, it's just a difference of opinion.

How did we get back here? How does the man who is astounded at the recent mistrial in South Carolina despite video evidence, who donated and supported Standing Rock and was outraged by the media's silence about it, say these things to me? Believe these things?

Did he lie to me about knowing these things aren't real? Did he lie to me about understand how racism works one way? And why is he making my conversations about racism about his feelings? Why is he trying to tell me to soften my stance about the shitty things white people do?

The more things change, the more they stay the same.

Right now, in this moment, I feel like I've wasted years of my life. Do I hate myself? I must hate myself to put myself through this.

Can I trust him? I'm starting to wonder...again. I'm starting to wonder again.

Is this worth it? I honestly do not know and whether I love him is irrelevant. I'm aware enough to know that loving a person doesn't mean they are healthy for you.

Last night he told me that he's scared that I'm talking about him when I talk about white fuckery. Well, sometimes I am. He does fucked up shit that is endemic to white people because of the privilege and power they hold in this society. One of those things is telling himself that he can't be racist or do racist shit because he married a Black woman. Another is pretending that white supremacy isn't the heartbeat of this country. He does this shit and he needs to keep pushing to change it, both within himself and those around him.

White people, if you are truly in this shit, in this fight for equal rights, you got a lot of fucking work to do. You got a lot of self-reflection, analysis, and introspection ahead. It's going to hurt. It's going to reveal some very hurtful things about yourself, and you're going to backslide because it sucks feeling like a shitty human. But this is your chance to work on changing that about yourself.

If something I'm saying hurts you, fucking examine that shit. Ask yourself why. If something I say makes you feel defensive, stop and ask why that is. Take the time. Do the work. Understand your reactions to POCs when they talk about racism, white supremacy, and white privilege. Learn why you fight so hard to deny it.

If you are about anti-racism work, this is a huge part of it. Embrace the pain that is fighting for the rights of everyone. Do the self-care so that you can stay in the fight. This is your time to fight for the rights of everyone.

People of Color, this is the shitty ass work of being with a white partner. This is the knife's edge you will find yourself perched upon as we establish our equality.

They will try to make us doubt ourselves. Don't let them.

They will try to undermine us. Fight them.

They will try to dismiss us. Understand and believe that you are right and deserve to be here, fighting for your rights and that if they can't see that, they are the problem.

We will hold our ground and make them bend. Our humanity is not in question. Our self-worth is not conditional. Our rights are not up for fucking debate.

There are not two sides to establishing my goddamn humanity and I will under no circumstances pretend that there is. I will not have a fucking conversation to debate my rights. I will not remotely entertain the idea that you are worth listening to. I am human. White people, you either fucking work the rest out or go join your brethren who are working so diligently to deny that.

Either way, get the fuck away from me.

This story first appeared at TheEstablishment.co, a multimedia site entirely run and funded by women, on January 3, 2017.

He doesn't accept that the white people fighting to maintain this oppression don't think I'm equal. He doesn't grasp that there is a large part of the country that thinks he married a beast and is dirtying himself by being with me.

– TaLynn Kel, When the Space You Promised Hurts Like Hell

References

The Reimagining of Self: Why I Love Marvel's Typhoid Mary

Kel, TaLynn. "The Reimagining of Self: Why I Love Marvel's Typhoid Mary." Black Girl Nerds, 29 Jan. 2016. Web. 30 Dec. 2016.

Santora, Marc. "New York Police to Limit Seizing of Condoms in Prostitution Cases." The New York Times, 12 May 2014. Web. 05 January, 2017.

Allon, Janey. "Arrested for Having a Miscarriage? 7 Appalling Instances Where Pregnant Women Were Criminalized." Alternet, 12, November 2015. Web. 05 January 2017.

Culp-Ressler, Tara. "Woman Who Is Just 12 Weeks Pregnant Charged with Child Endangerment." ThinkProgress, 3 Sept. 2014. Web. 5 Jan. 2017.

Zoom, Doktor. "Miscarrying Lady Almost Dies at Catholic Hospital, But At Least She Didn't Get an Abortion." Wonkette, 2 June 2015. Web. 05 Jan. 2017.

Rape Disguised as Romance: Why I Stop Reading Most Romance Novels

Kel, TaLynn. "Rape Disguised as Romance: Why I Stop Reading Most Romance Novels." Black Girl Nerds, 10 Feb. 2016. Web. 30 Dec. 2016.

Romance Writers of America. "Romance Statistics." Web. . 05 Jan. 2017.

Lawlor, George. "Why I don't need consent lessons." 14 Oct. 2015. Web. 05 Jan 2017.

Baker, Katie. "Rapists Explain Themselves on Reddit, and We Should Listen." Jezebel. 27 July 2012. Web. 02 Feb. 2016.

Making Space

Humphrey, Bryan. Blade. 2011, Photograph. Atlanta, Georgia. *Bryan Humphrey*. Web. 04 Feb. 2016.

Living Online

Kel, TaLynn. "The Reimagining of Self: Why I Love Marvel's Typhoid Mary." Black Girl Nerds, 29 Jan. 2016. Web. 30 Dec. 2016.

Kel, TaLynn. "Rape Disguised as Romance: Why I Stop Reading Most Romance Novels." Black Girl Nerds, 10 Feb. 2016. Web. 30 Dec. 2016.

Kel, TaLynn. "So I Wrote About Rape and Romance Novels..." Storify, 10 Feb. 2016. Web. 05 Jan. 2017.

Othering the Self: Learning to Recognize My Anti-Blackness

Kel, TaLynn. "Othering the Self – Learning to Recognize My Anti-Blackness." Black Girl Nerds, 02 March 2016. Web. 30 Dec. 2016.

Moser, Laura. "Schools in the South Suspend and Expel Black Students Way More Than White Ones." Slate 25 Aug. 2015. Web. 20 Feb. 2016.

Hooks, bell. "Eating the Other: Desire and Resistance." 1992. Web. 21 Feb. 2016.

Zevallos, Zuleyka. "What is Otherness?" The Other Sociologist, 14 Oct. 2011 Web. 21 Feb. 2016.

Abbey-Lambertz, Kate. "These 15 Black Women Were Killed During Police Encounters. Their Lives Matter, Too." Huffington Post, 13 Feb. 2015. Web. 1 Feb 2016.

Swaine, Jon; Laughland, Oliver; Lartey; James; McCarthy, Ciara. "Young Black Men Killed by U.S. Police at Highest Rate in Year of 1,134 Deaths." Alternet 02 Jan. 2016. Web. 21 Feb. 2016.

Berman, Mark; Lowery, Wesley. "The 12 key highlights from the DOJ's scathing Ferguson report." The Washington Post 04 March 2015. Web. 21 Feb. 2016.

Boggioni, Tom. "New York City police union threatens to join Miami cops in Beyoncé boycott: 'Stop portraying us as bad guys'." Rawstory, 19 Feb. 2016. Web. 21 Feb. 2016.

Let's Talk Racism in Cosplay

World of Black Heroes. Web. 4 March 2016.

Nigatu, Heben. "21 Racial Microaggressions You Hear on A Daily Basis." BuzzFeed, 09 Dec. 2013. Web. 04 March 2016.

DixonFuller2011. "Doll Test." YouTube, 07 Feb. 2012. Web. 04 Mar. 2016.

Utt, Jamie. "'That's Racist Against White People!' A Discussion on Power and Privilege." 20 Aug. 2013. Web. 04 March 2016.

Bouie, Jamelle. "The Rising Tide of Anti-Black Racism." 07 Feb. 2013. Web. 04 March 2016.

Ortiz, E. "The Face of Cosplay: Racism & Cosplayers of Color." 28 Feb. 2012. Web. 04 March. 2016.

Eddy, Max. "Cosplayers Speak Out on Racism in the Fandom." 13 Oct. 2013. Web. 04 March 2016.

Blaque, Kat. "Cultures are Not Costumes." YouTube, 08 Oct. 2014. Web. 04 Mar. 2016.

My Cosplay is Intersectional

Tatum, Erin. "Think It's Creepy When Men Pursue Underage Girls? You'll Shudder When You Realize How Our Society Encourages It." Everyday Feminism, 11 May 2015. Web. 07 April, 2016.

Pappas, Stephanie. "30% of Girls' Clothing Is Sexualized in Major Sales Trend." LiveScience, 20 May 2011. Web. 07 April, 2016.

American Psychological Association. "Sexualization of Girls." American Psychology Association. Web. 07 April 2016.

Boguhn, Ally. "5 Alternatives to Taking Your Spouse's Last Name." Everyday Feminism, 30 Jan. 2015. Web. 07 April 2016.

Grigsby Bates, Karen. "Study: Black Girls Are Being Pushed Out of School." Code Switch, 13 Feb. 2015. Web. 07 April 2016.

Sargent, Antwaun. "7 Lies We Have to Stop Telling About Black Girls." Everyday Feminism, 06 Aug. 2014. Web. 07 April 2016.

Kite, Lindsay. "Beauty Whitewashed: How White Ideals Exclude Women of Color." Everyday Feminism, 24 Nov. 2012. Web. 07 April 2016.

Susan, Trudy. "The Sad Truth About Natural Hair Discrimination." Ebony, 21 May 2014. Web. 07 April 2016.

Nittle, Nadra Kareem. "What Is Colorism - Skin Tone Discrimination in America." About Race Relations, 2016. Web. 07 April 2016.

Hooks, bell. "Eating the Other: Desire and Resistance." 1992. Web. 07 April 2016.

Oppression: It's the American Way

Edwards, David. "Maine approves Christian ballot initiative to strip gay rights from Human Rights Act." Rawstory, 06 April 2016. Web. 13 April 2016.

WBTV. "NC professor explains implications of HB2." WNCN CBS North Carolina, 07 April 2016. Web. 13 April, 2016.

Fang, Marina. "Tennessee Passes Anti-LGBT Counseling Bill." Huffington Post, 11 April 2016. Web. 13 April 2016.

Stewart, Katherine. "Why Mississippi's New Anti-LGBT Law Is the Most Dangerous One To Be Passed Yet." The Nation, 08 April 2016. Web. 13 April 2016.

Fat Issues

Chastain, Ragan. "11 Reasons Why I Focus on Health and Not Weight." Dances with Fat, 29 February 2016. Web. 18 April 2016.

The Face That Paused a Thousand Meetings

Hobson, Janell. "Angry or Complicated? Misrecognizing Black Women." Ms. Blog, 22 Sept. 2014. Web. 28 April 2016.

Yancy, George. "Walking While Black in the 'White Gaze.'" The New York Times, 01 Sept. 2013. Web. 28 April 2016.

Conger, Cristen. "How the 'Angry Black Woman' Stereotype Tries to Control Black Women." Everyday Feminism, 03 March 2016. Web. 28 April 2016.

Boylorn, R. "Working While Black: 10 Racial Microaggressions Experienced in the Workplace." Crunk Feminist Collective, 11 Nov. 2014. Web. 28 April 2016.

Woodard, Monique. "The White Elephant in The Room." 13 April 2016. Web. 28 April 2016.

Johnson, Maisha Z. "6 Struggles of Being Unapologetically Black in a Professional Environment." Everyday Feminism, 04 Nov. 2014. Web. 28 April 2016.

My Husband's Unconscious Racism Nearly Destroyed Our Marriage

Clark-Flory, Tracy. "John Mayer's Johnson hates black women." Salon, 10 Feb. 2010. Web. 21 Feb. 2016.

Fear is the Mind Killer

Gardiner, Becky; Mansfield, Mahana; Anderson, Ian; Holder, Josh; Louter, Daan; Ulmanu, Monica. "The Dark Side of Guardian Comments." The Guardian, 12 April, 2016. Web. 06 June 2016.

Mansfield, Mahana. "How We analysed 70m Comments on the Guardian Website." The Guardian, 12 April, 2016. Web. 06 June 2016.

Starr, Terrell Jermaine. "The Unbelievable Harassment Black Women Face Daily on Twitter." Alternet, 16 Sept. 2014. Web. 06 June 2016.

Hunt, Elle. "Online Harassment of Women at Risk of Becoming 'Established Norm', Study Finds." The Guardian, 07 March 2016. Web. 06 June 2016.

Culp-Ressler. "All Of The Things Women Are Supposed To Do To Prevent Rape." Think Progress, 10 June 2014. Web 06 June 2016.

Kasperkevic, Jana. "Private Violence: Up to 75% of Abused Women Who are Murdered are Killed After They Leave Their Partners." The Guardian, 20 Oct. 2014. Web. 06 June 2016.

Peck, Adam. "Victim's House Burned Down After She Accuses Football Star Of Rape." Think Progress, 14 Oct. 2013. Web. 06 June 2016.

Wallace, Scott. "Why Do Environmentalists Keep Getting Killed Around the World?" Smithsonian Mag, February 2014. Web. 06 June 2016.

Kutner, Jenny. "This Woman Is Calling Out Facebook's Shameful Double Standard on Sexual Harassment." Mic, 28 March 2016. Web. 06 June 2016.

Hood, Carol. "Azealia Banks' Twitter Ban Reminds Us Freedom Of Speech Is For Whites Only." The Establishment, 13 May 2016. Web. 06 June 2016.

Caping for Cops

Gyamfi, Nana; Abdullah, Melina. "Black Lives Matter Activist Convicted of 'Felony Lynching": "It's More Than Ironic, It's Disgusting.'" Democracy Now! 02 June 2016. Web. 26 June 2016.

Agorist, Matt. "Disturbing Video Shows a Cop Brutally Beat a Child for Riding Her Bike, Charges HER with Assault." The Free Thought Project, 14 May 2016. Web. 26 June 2016.

Graham, David A. "Sandra Bland and the Long History of Racism in Waller County, Texas." The Atlantic, 21 June 2015. Web. 26 June 2016.

Sidner, Sara. "Sex, suicide and failure to report: How Oakland police scandal unfolded." CNN, 25 June 2016. Web. 26 June 2016.

Carroll, Jon. "Leaked documents reveal Dothan Police Department planted drugs on black men for years." The Henry Report, 01 Dec 2015. Web. 26 June 2016.

The Innocence Project. Web. 26 June 2016.

Pearl, Mike. "How Many People Die in Police Custody in America?" Vice, 30 June 2015. Web. 26 June 2016.

When White People Consume Blackness for Personal Gain

Carroll, Rebecca. "Justin Timberlake on Jesse Williams's BET speech wasn't woke, just white." The Guardian, 27 June 2016. Web. 28 June 2016.

Brown, Lauren. "Read the Full Transcript of Jesse Williams' Epically Inspiring BET Awards Speech." Glamour, 27 June 2016. Web. 28 June 2016.

Hooks, bell. "Eating the Other: Desire and Resistance." 1992. Web. 21 Feb. 2016.

Slavery and the Making of America. Georgia Public Broadcasting. Web. 27 June 2016.

Oscars. "Chris Rock's Opening Monologue." YouTube, 23 March. 2016. Web. 27 June 2016.

Campbell, Christopher. "Who Else is Upset About the Death in "X-Men: First Class"?" Indiewire, 07 June 2011. Web. 27 June 2016.

Shackelford, Ashleigh. "Orange is the New Black is Trauma Porn Written for White People [Spoilers]." Wear Your Voice, 20 June 2016. Web. 27 June 2016.

Howze, Thaddeus. "On the Death of James Rhodes — War Machine." Medium, 22 June 2016. Web. 27 June 2016.

Nededog, Jethro. "'Fear the Walking Dead' fans aren't happy about the amount of black deaths." Business Insider, 31 August 2015. Web. 27 June 2016.

Paschal, Jaylin. "Smarter Than That: On the Assumptions Made About Ebonics and Intelligence." For Harriett, May 2016. Web. 27 June 2016.

Mangum, Trey. "Hayes Grier's 'T-Rex' dance is cultural appropriation at its finest and Black Twitter is over it." Blavity, 15 Sept. 2016. Web. 27 June 2016.

Zoladz, Lindsay. "Please, Don't Let Iggy Azalea Win the Best Rap Album Grammy." Vulture, 06 Feb 2015. Web. 27 June 2016.

Solomon, Akiba. "The Pseudoscience of 'Black Women Are Less Attractive.'" Colorlines, 17 May 2011. Web. 27 June 2016.

Harriot, Michael. "Black Bodies and the Last Frontier of Cultural Appropriation." Ebony, 20 May 2016. Web. 27 June 2016.

Richardson, Riche. "'The Bed Intruder'—News Video Goes Viral: Antoine Dodson as Internet Celebrity and Commodity." Technoculture: an online journal of technology in society, vol 4, 2014. Web. 27 June 2016.

It's Time to Own Our Shit and Change Everything

Kel, TaLynn. "My Lemonade Tastes Like Black Resistance." Breaking Normal, 11 July 2016. Web. 08 January 2017.

Kel, TaLynn. "Othering the Self – Learning to Recognize My Anti-Blackness." Black Girl Nerds, 02 March 2016. Web. 20 July 2016.

Rhodes, Isabella. "Growing Up a Blerd." Black Girl Nerds, 09 July 2016. Web. 20 July. 2016.

Hess, Amanda. "Sexists Don't Hate Women. They Just Prefer Men." Slate, 22 May 2014. Web. 20 July 2016.

The Complexities of Racism and Identity

Kel, TaLynn. "Can People Be Racist Against Their Own Race?." The Establishment, 18 Aug. 2016. Web. 20 August 2016.

McKenzie, Mia. "How to Tell the Difference Between Real Solidarity and 'Ally Theater.'" Black Girl Dangerous, 04 Nov. 2015.

Amen, Rael. "Jane Elliott speaks on racism white supremacy." YouTube, 01 July. 2016. Web. 20 Aug. 2016.

Mo. "On the peculiarities of the Negro brain." Science Blogs, 29 July 2007. Web. 20 Aug 2016. Web. 20 August 2016.

Moore, A. "8 Heartbreaking Cases Where Land Was Stolen from Black Americans Through Racism, Violence and Murder." Atlanta Black Star, 09 Oct. 2014. Web. 20 July 2016.

Larsen, Nella, Deborah E. McDowell, and Nella Larsen. Quicksand; And, Passing. New Brunswick, N.J: Rutgers University Press, 1986. Print.

Diaz, Natasha. "My Multiracial Identity Isn't A Party Trick." The Establishment, 10 July 2016. Web. 20 July 2016.

The Danger of Unchallenged Racism in Interracial Relationships

Kel, TaLynn. "Othering the Self – Learning to Recognize My Anti-Blackness." Black Girl Nerds, 02 March 2016. Web. 20 July 2016.

Kel, TaLynn. "My Husband's Unconscious Racism Nearly Destroyed Our Marriage." The Establishment, 05 May. 2016. Web. 20 August 2016.

Chelsie. "When Suddenly No Lives Matter." 2 boys 1 blog and me, 09 July 2016. Web. 20 August 2016.

Broadnax, Jamie. "Cosplay or No Cosplay: The Homicide of Darrien Hunt." Black Girl Nerds, 17 Sept. 2014. Web. 20 August 2016.

Graham, David A. "Sandra Bland and the Long History of Racism in Waller County, Texas." The Atlantic, 21 June 2015. Web. 20 Aug. 2016.

Neyfakh, Leon. "50-Year-Old Black Woman Who Died in Jail Was Denied Water and Medication, Court Filings Allege." Slate, 25 Feb. 2016. Web. 20 Aug. 2016.

Manuel-Logan, Ruth. "Police: Man Says He Killed Teen Seeking Help After Crash 'Accidentally.'" NewsOne, 2014. Web. 20 Aug. 2016.

Agorist, Matt. "Parents on a Date Were Asleep in Car When Cops Arrived and Killed Them Both." The Free Thought Project, 25. Feb 2016. Web. 20 Aug. 2016.

Tired of Whiteness

Ferner, Matt. "Here's How Many Cops Got Convicted of Murder Last Year For On-Duty Shootings." Huffington Post, 13 Jan. 2016. Web. 21 Sept. 2016.

Swaine, Jon. "GoFundMe defends Darren Wilson fundraising page despite racist postings." The Guardian, 22 Aug. 2014. Web. 21 Sept 2016.

Pyke, Alan. "The People Stopping Police Departments from Addressing Colin Kaepernick's Protest." Think Progress, 30 Aug. 2016. Web. 21 Sept. 2016.

Rich, Frank. "Matt Lauer's Gift to Donald Trump." New York Mag, 08 Sept. 2016. Web. 21 Sept. 2016.

Johnson, Kimberley. "No Jail Time for Rapist So He Can Enjoy The 'College Experience'." Liberals Unite, 22 Aug. 2016. Web. 21 Sept. 2016.

Grinberg, Emanuella; Shoichet, Catherine. "Brock Turner released from jail after serving 3 months for sexual assault." CNN, 03 Sept. 2016. Web. 21 Sept. 2016.

Guerra, Kristine. "Teen pleads guilty to sexual abuse of a 1-year-old girl, then a judge gives him no prison time." The Washington Post, 19 Sept. 2016. Web. 21 Sept. 2016.

Bazelon, Emily; Levin, Josh. "The Most Damning Verdict." Slate, 12 July 2012. Web. 21 Sept 2016.

Democracy Now! "No Charges in Ohio Police Killing of John Crawford as Wal-Mart Video Contradicts 911 Caller Account." Democracy Now! 25 Sept. 2014. Web. 21 Sept. 2016.

Bouie, Jamelle. "Michael Brown Wasn't a Superhuman Demon." Slate, 26 Nov. 2014. Web. 21 Sept. 2016.

Graham, David A. "Sandra Bland and the Long History of Racism in Waller County, Texas." The Atlantic, 21 June 2015. Web. 20 Aug. 2016.

Flynn, Sean. "The Tamir Rice Story: How to Make a Police Shooting Disappear." GQ, 14 July 2016. Web. 21 Sept. 2016.

McLaughlin, Eliot C. "Freddie Gray verdict: Officer Edward Nero not guilty." CNN, 24 May 2016. Web. 21 Sept. 2016.

Bellware, Kim. "Chicago Cop Who Killed Rekia Boyd Quits, Preserving His Cushy Retirement." Huffington Post, 17 Sept. 2016. Web. 21 Sept. 2016.

Stole, Bryn. "'Bad police work' in Alton Sterling death, but don't expect conviction." Sun Herald, 19 Sept. 2016. Web. 21 Sept. 2016.

Ortiz, Erik. "Philando Castile and Cop Who Killed Him Crossed Paths Before, Records Show," NBC News, 22 July 2016. Web. 21 Sept. 2016.

Felton, Ryan. "'Our kids can't play with toy guns': Tyre King police shooting a painful reminder." The Guardian, 20 Sept. 2016. Web. 21 Sept. 2016.

King, Elizabeth. "White Man in California Shoots at Cops With Gun, Gets Shot With Beanbags and Arrested." Complex, 17 Aug. 2016. Web. 21 Sept. 2016.

Jones, Jeremiah. "White Guy Shot TWO COPS. But Don't Worry He's Fine." Countercurrent News, 21 Aug. 2016. Web. 21 Sept. 2016.

NBC News. "Charleston Church Shooting." NBC News, 2016-2017. Web. 21 Sept. 2016.

Hughes, Trevor. "Planned Parenthood shooter 'happy' with his attack." USA Today, 11 April 2016. Web. 21 Sept. 2016.

CBS News. "Colorado movie theater massacre." CBS News, 2016. Web. 21 Sept. 2016.

You Are Not My White Savior

Florido, Adrian. "Why do black infants die so much more often than white infants?" 89.3 KPCC, 03 March 2014. Web. 25 Sept. 2016.

Schroeder, Michael O. "Racial Bias in Medicine Leads to Worse Care for Minorities." U.S. News and World Reports, 11 Feb. 2016. Web. 25 Sept. 2016.

Samarrai, Fariss. "Study Links Disparities in Pain Management to Racial Bias." University of Virginia, 04 April 2016. Web. 25 Sept. 2016.

Bouie, Jamelle. "How We Built the Ghettos." The Daily Beast, 13 March 2014. Web. 25 Sept. 2016.

Silverstein, Jason. "How Racism Is Bad for Our Bodies." The Atlantic, 12 March 2013. Web. 25 Sept. 2016.

Leslie Jones is the Least Protected Blackness of Us All

Cox, Carolyn. "The Ghostbusters Trailer Backlash Shows Men Believe in the Power of Representation (But Only When It Applies to Them)." The Mary Sue, 01 May 2016. Web. 23 Aug. 2016.

Ghostbusters (2016). Rotten Tomatoes, 2016. Web. 23 Aug. 2016.

Ghostbusters (2016). Box Office Mojo, 2016. Web. 23 Aug. 2016.

Riedel, Sam. "Why Busting 'Ghostbusters' Reboot Myths May No Longer Matter." The Establishment, 19 Aug 2016. Web. 23 Aug. 2016.

For Harriet. "Leslie Jones Quits Twitter After Spending a Day Battling Racist Twitter." For Harriet, 19, July 2016. Web. 23 Aug. 2016.

Bristol, Keir. "On Moya Bailey, Misogynoir, and Why Both Are Important." The Visibility Project, 27 May, 2014. Web. 23 Aug. 2016.

LaSha. "We Need to Talk About Leslie Jones and Colorism in Our Community." Ebony, 12 Aug 2016. Web. 23 Aug. 2016.

Lennard, Natasha. "'Why are black women less attractive?' asks Psychology Today." Salon, 17 May 2011. Web. 23 Aug. 2016.

Leicht, Angelica. "Suspects Arrested, Charged in #Jadapose Rape Case." Houston Press, 17 Oct. 2014. Web. 23 Aug. 2016.

Roberts, Monica. "Misgendering Attacks On A Black Woman's Femininity Aren't Funny." TransGriot, 02 June 2015. Web. 23 Aug. 2016.

Cooper, Brittney. "The world only has ugliness for black women. That's why Serena Williams is so important." Salon, 15 July 2015. Web. 23 Aug. 2016.

Azalia, Loy. "My struggle to protect black men when they've been my abuser." Blavity, August 2016. Web. 23 Aug. 2016.

Blay, Zeba. "'Confirmation' And the Silencing Of Black Women To Shield Black Men." Huffington Post, 15 April 2016. Web. 23 Aug. 2016.

Drayton, Tiffanie. "On Nate Parker's College Rape Case & Why Black Women Should Not Watch 'Birth of a Nation.'" Clutch, Aug. 2016. Web. 23 Aug. 2016.

Shackelford, Ashleigh. "Stop Excusing Black Men's Violence – Like Nate Parker's – for the Sake of Black Liberation." Wear Your Voice Magazine, 16 Aug. 2016. Web. 23 Aug. 2016.

Haimerl, Amy. "The fastest-growing group of entrepreneurs in America." Fortune, 29 June 2015. Web. 23 Aug. 2016.

Davis, Rachaell. "New Study Shows Black Women Are Among The Most Educated Group In The United States." Essence, 07 June 2016. Web. 23 Aug. 2016.

Kinks, Klassy. "White Hair Blog Claims Bantu Knots Were "Inspired" By Marc Jacobs, Black Twitter Goes Nuts." Black Girl Long Hair, 27 May 2015. Web. 23 Aug. 2016.

Wellington, Elizabeth. "When Black Girls Get Criticized and White Girls Get Celebrated." For Harriet, Oct. 2014. Web. 23 Aug. 2016.

Phillips, Kady. "Blavity Exclusive: Akilah Obviously on BuzzFeed and #StopBuzzThieves." Blavity, Aug. 2016. Web. 23 Aug. 2016.

Bowerman, Mary. "Is White Lives Matter a movement or white supremacist group?" USAToday, 22 Aug. 2016. Web. 23 Aug. 2016.

Kel, TaLynn. "When White People Consume Blackness for Personal Gain." The Establishment, 29 June 2016. Web. 23 Aug. 2016.

Wilson, Julee. "The Meaning Of #BlackGirlMagic, And How You Can Get Some of It." Huffington Post, 12 Jan. 2016. Web. 23 Aug. 2016.

Dear People Who Comment on My Facebook Posts to Silence Me

Gomez, Amanda. "Study finds higher expulsion rates for black students in South." PBS, 25 Aug. 2015. Web. 05 Sept. 2016.

Countercurrent News. "Police Admit They're 'Racist' During Arrest of Black Walmart Shoppers Who Were 'Walking Too Slow.'" Countercurrent News. 14 June 2015. Web. 05 Sept. 2016.

Allen, Nick. "Fatal shooting of black man Philando Castile by police during traffic stop in Minneapolis caught on video by girlfriend." The Telegraph, 07 July 2016. Web. 05 Sept. 2016.

The Grio. "Cops Taser black man mistaken for suspect, arrest him for asking questions." The Grio, 16 July 2016. Web. 05 Sept. 2016.

Vanity Fair. "Robert Downey Jr. Speaks About His Addictions." Vanity Fair, Oct. 2014. Web. 05 Sept. 2016.

Gauthier, Brendan. "Stanford rapist Brock Turner released from jail after serving just three months." Salon, 02 Sept. 2016. Web. 05 Sept. 2016.

McCormack, Simon. "White Ex-Police Chief Who Killed Unarmed Black Man Avoids Jail Time." Huffington Post, 01 Sept. 2016. Web. 05 Sept. 2016.

Morton, Clay. "Of 170 held after Waco biker shooting, all are now out of jail, with none charged in killings." Dallas News, 04 Oct. 2015. Web. 05 Sept. 2016.

Cahill, Tom. "Heavily Armed White Man Arrested Alive After Shooting at Police Officer." US Uncut, 07 July 2016. Web. 05 Sept. 2016.

Madrigal, Alexis. "The Racist Housing Policy That Made Your Neighborhood." The Atlantic, 22 May 2014. Web. 05 Sept. 2016.

King, Shaun. "King: It's payback time for Toyota, other lenders who charged blacks, Asians and Latinos higher interest rates." New York Daily News, 04 Feb. 2016. Web. 05 Sept. 2016.

Ganim, Sara; Sanchez, Ray. "Flint water crisis: New criminal charges are brought." CNN, 03 Aug. 2016. Web. 05 Sept 2016.

Demanding Black Forgiveness Is Just Another Way to Control Us

Bacon, John. "Police consider charges against Michael Brown's stepdad." USA Today, 02 Dec. 2014. Web. 08 Aug. 2016.

Berman, Mark. "'I forgive you.' Relatives of Charleston church shooting victims address Dylann Roof." The Washington Post, 19 June 2015. Web. 08 Aug. 2016.

ABC News Staff. "Michael Brown's Stepfather Apologizes for 'Burn' Outburst in Ferguson." ABC News, 03 Dec. 2014. Web. 08 Aug. 2016.

Relevant Staff. "Trayvon Martin's Parents: 'As Christians We Must Forgive Zimmerman.'" Relevant, 27 Aug. 2013. Web. 08 Aug. 2016.

Ortberg, Mallory; Wallace, Carvell. "You're Not Off The Hook: The White Myth Of Black Forgiveness." The Toast, 23 June 2015. Web. 08 Aug. 2016.

Kel, TaLynn. "My Husband's Unconscious Racism Nearly Destroyed Our Marriage." The Establishment, 26 May 2016. Web. 20 Aug. 2016.

White People, You Have a Lying Problem

Schwartz, Larry. "The 7 Biggest Liars in Presidential History." Alternet, 07 Feb. 2016. Web. 08 July 2016.

National Archives. "Statistical information about casualties of the Vietnam War." National Archives, August 2013. Web. 08 July 2016.

History.com Staff. "My Lai Massacre." History.com, 2009. Web. 08 July 2016.

Moore, A. "8 Successful and Aspiring Black Communities Destroyed by White Neighbors." Atlanta Black Star, 04 Dec. 2013. Web. 09 July. 2016.

Advocates for Youth Staff. "The Truth About Abstinence-Only Programs." Advocates for Youth, 2008. Web. 08 July 2016.

Myers, Lisa; NBC Investigative Unit. "Critics Question FEMA Director's Qualifications." MSNBC, 13 Sept. 2005. Web. 08 July 2016.

McCormack, Simon. "Brian Williams Investigation Uncovers More Alleged Lies." Huffington Post, 25 April 2015. Web. 08 July 2016.

Raphael, Ray. "Are U.S. History Textbooks Still Full of Lies and Half-Truths?" History News Network, 19 Sept. 2004. Web. 08 July 2016.

Blitz, Matt. "The Truth about Christopher Columbus." Today I Found Out, 26 Jan. 2016. Web. 08 July 2016.

Bouie Jamelle; Onion, Rebecca. "Slavery Myths Debunked." Slate, 29 Sept. 2015. Web. 08 July 2016.

Poniewozik, James "Why Brian Williams Lost His Job, and Why He Has a New One." Time, 10 June 2015. Web. 08 July 2016.

Kel, TaLynn. "My Husband's Unconscious Racism Nearly Destroyed Our Marriage." The Establishment, 26 May 2016. Web. 08 July 2016.

Stack, Liam. "Light Sentence for Brock Turner in Stanford Rape Case Draws Outrage." The New York Times, 06 June 2016. Web. 08 July 2016.

Apel, Therese. "2 Women in Truck That Ran Down Black Man Get Max Terms." USA Today, 10 April 2015. Web. 08 July 2016.

Why I Cut My Racist In-Laws Out of My Life

Kel, TaLynn. "My Husband's Unconscious Racism Nearly Destroyed Our Marriage." The Establishment, 26 May 2016. Web. 31 July 2016.

Kel, TaLynn. "White People, You Have A Lying Problem." The Establishment. 07 July 2016. Web. 31 July. 2016.

Wright, Kai. " Why Alton Sterling and Philando Castile Are Dead." The Nation, 07 July 2016. Web. 31 July 2016.

America, Stop Protecting Your Monsters

Kingkade, Tyler. "If Not For 2 Strangers, Brock Turner May Have Never Been Arrested." Huffington Post, 06 June 2016. Web. 14 Oct. 2016.

CBS News Staff. "Colorado Theater Massacre." CBS News, 2016. Web. 14 Oct. 2016.

Hughes, Trevor. "Planned Parenthood Shooter 'happy' with his attack." USA Today, 11 April 2016. Web. 21 Sept. 2016.

Schwartz, Gadi; Ortiz, Erik. "Brock Turner, Convicted Sexual Assault Offender, Released From Jail After 3 Months." NBC News, 02 Sept. 2016. Web. 14 Oct. 2016.

Cahill, Tom. "Montana father gets probation after he admits to raping 12-year-old daughter." US Uncut, 13 Oct. 2016. Web. 14 Oct. 2016.

Robles, Frances; Stewart, Nikita. "Dylann Roof's Past Reveals Trouble at Home and School." The New York Times, 16 July 2015. Web. 14 Oct. 2016.

Smith, Candace. "Trump's Female Supporters Back Him Despite Sexual Assault Accusations." ABC News, 15 Oct. 2016. Web. 14 Oct. 2016.

Shackelford, Ashleigh. "Stop Excusing Black Men's Violence – Like Nate Parker's – for the Sake of Black Liberation." Wear Your Voice Magazine, 16 Aug. 2016. Web. 14 Oct. 2016.

Raymond, Laurel. "Longest-Serving GOP Speaker In History Is A Liar And Serial Child Molester, Federal Judge Says." Think Progress, 27 April 2016. Web. 14 Oct. 2016.

Queally, James. "Oakland police to fire 4 officers, suspend 7 others, in sexual misconduct scandal." Los Angeles Times, 07 Sept. 2016, Web. 14 Oct, 2016.

Washington Blade Staff. "Arkansas Judge Resigns Amid Sex Scandal." Washington Blade, 11 May 2016. Web. 14 Oct. 2016.

Evans, Robert. "Why I Kept My Rape by A Priest A Secret (And Can't Anymore)." Cracked, 25 July 2016. Web. 14 Oct. 2016.

Fox 5 News Staff. "Pastor Charged with Rape of 10-Year Old Girl." Fox 5, 16 Sept. 2016. Web. 14 Oct. 2016.

ABC News Staff. "Priest Arrested for Child Rape." ABC News, 02 May 2016. Web. 14 Oct. 2016.

Lewis, Andy. "Roman Polanski Rape Victim Unveils Startling, Disturbing Photo for Book Cover (Exclusive)" The Hollywood Reporter, 24 July 2013. Web. 14 Oct. 2016.

Orth, Maureen. "10 Undeniable Facts about the Woody Allen Sexual Abuse Allegation." Vanity Fair, 07 Feb. 2014. Web. 14 Oct. 2016.

Cahill, Tom. "Montana father gets probation after he admits to raping 12-year-old daughter." US Uncut, 13 Oct. 2016. Web. 14 Oct. 2016.

Grinberg, Emanuella; Shoichet, Catherine E. "Brock Turner Released from Jail after Serving 3 Months for Sexual Assault." CNN, 02 Sept. 2016. Web. 14 Oct. 2016.

Johnson, Kimberley. "No Jail Time for Rapist So He Can Enjoy 'The College Experience." Liberals Unite, 22 Aug. 2016. Web. 14 Oct. 2016.

Guerra, Kristine. "Teen pleads guilty to sexual abuse of a 1-year-old girl, then a judge gives him no prison time." The Washington Post, 19 Sept. 2016. Web. 14 Oct. 2016.

Agorist, Matt. "Cops Beat Their Wives and Girlfriends at Double the National Rate, Still Receive Promotions." The Free Thought Project, 07 May 2014. Web. 14 Oct. 2016.

Bazelon, Emily; Levin, Josh. "The Most Damning Verdict."
Slate, 12 July 2012. Web. 14 Oct. 2016.

Cohen, Sarah; Ruiz, Rebecca; Childress, Sarah. "Departments
Are Slow to Police Their Own Abusers." The New York Times,
23 Nov. 2013. Web. 14 Oct. 2016.

Crimesider Staff. "New Charge for Tonya Couch, 'Affluenza'
Teen's Mom." CBS News, 26 May 2016. Web. 14 Oct, 2016.

Frazier, Charise. "'Affluenza' Teen's Attorney Seeks Early
Release." NewsOne, Sept. 2016. Web. 14 Oct. 2016.

Kel, TaLynn. "White People, You Have A Lying Problem." The
Establishment. 07 July 2016. Web. 14 Sept. 2016.

CNN. "Trump Supporters Standing by Their Man." CNN, 11 Oct.
2016. Web. 14 Oct. 2016.

Politifact Editors. "Donald Trump's File." Politifact, 2016. Web.
14 Oct. 2016.

Alexander, Michelle. "Why Hillary Clinton Doesn't Deserve the
Black Vote." The Nation, 10 Feb. 2016. Web. 14 Oct. 2016.

Timm, Trevor. "Trumps Many Many Threats to Sue the Press
Since Launching His Campaign." Columbia Journalism Review,
03 Oct. 2016. Web. 14 Oct. 2016.

Iaccarino, Anthony. "The Founding Fathers and Slavery."
Encyclopedia Britannica, 28 July 2016. Web. 14 Oct. 2016.

Ojanuga, Durrenda. "The Medical Ethics of the 'Father of Gynaecology', Dr. Marion Sims." Journal of Medical Ethics, 1993 vol 19: 28-31. Web. 14 Oct. 2016.

Goodman, Howard. "Studying prison experiments Research: For 20 years, a dermatologist used the inmates of a Philadelphia prison as the willing subjects of tests on shampoo, foot powder, deodorant, and later, mind-altering drugs and dioxin." The Baltimore Sun, 21 June 1998. Web. 14 Oct. 2016.

Human Rights Watch. "World Report: United States - Events of 2015." HRW.org, 2015. Web. 14 Oct. 2016.

Thirteen Media with Impact – WNET. "The Rise and Fall of Jim Crow." PBS Educational Broadcasting Corporation, 2002. Web. 14 Oct. 2016.

ACLU.com Editors. "Women's Rights." ACLU.com, 2016. Web. 14 Oct. 2016.

ACLU.com Editors. "Reproductive Freedom." ACLU.com, 2016. Web. 14 Oct. 2016.

ACLU.com Editors. "Reforming Police Practices." ACLU.com, 2016. Web. 14 Oct. 2016.

Thomas, Katie. "The Complex Math Behind Spiraling Prescription Drug Prices." The New York Times, 24 Aug. 2016. Web. 14 Oct. 2016.

Moore, Michael. "10 Things They Won't Tell You about the Flint Water Tragedy. But I Will." MichaelMoore.com, 29 Jan. 2016. Web. 14 Oct. 2016.

Judge, Monique. "State of Michigan Removes Flint's Ability to Sue Over Water Crisis." The Root, 20 Sept. 2016. Web. 14 Oct. 2016.

Blackface Isn't a Compliment

Blaque, Kat. "Are Zwarte Pieten Racist?" YouTube, 19 Oct. 2014. Web. 27 Sept. 2016.

Blaque, Kat. "Cultures are Not Costumes" YouTube, 08 Oct. 2014. Web. 27 Sept. 2016.

Blaque, Kat. "Veds 28: What Is Blackface?" YouTube, 29 Sept. 2014. Web. 27 Sept. 2016.

Kel, Talynn. "The Face that Paused a Thousand Meetings." Breaking Normal, 28 April 2016. Web. 27 Sept. 2016.

Biography.com Editors. "Trayvon Martin Biography." The Biography.com Website, 09 Feb. 2016. Web. 27 Sept. 2016.

Josefczyk, Aaron. "Community Gathers to Mourn 13-Year-Ole Tyre King Who Was Killed by Cops." The Huffington Post, 26 Sept. 2016. Web. 27 Sept. 2016.

Williams, Joseph P. "Tamir Rice Shooting: Not Just a Tragedy." U.S. News and World Reports, 29 Dec. 2015. Web. 27 Sept. 2016.

Kel, TaLynn. "White People, You Have A Lying Problem." The Establishment. 07 July 2016. Web. 27 Sept. 2016.

Kel, TaLynn. "When White People Consume Blackness for Personal Gain." The Establishment. 29 June 2016. Web. 27 Sept. 2016.

White People: Shut the Fuck Up About Black Voters

Eldridge, Ellen. "Georgia Militia Prepares for 'Fallout' After Election." Atlanta Journal Constitution, 04 Nov. 2016. Web. 08 Nov. 2016.

Reflections on the 2016 Election – Election Day

Fagan, Jeffrey; Braga, Anthony A.; Brunson, Rod K.; Pattavina, April. "An Analysis of Race and Ethnicity Patterns in Boston Police Department Field Interrogation, Observation, Frisk, and/or Search Reports." Raceandpolicing.issuelab.org, 15 June 2015. Web. 08 Nov. 2016.

Brown, Kara. "How Racism is Driving New York City's Gentrification." Jezebel, 12 May 2015. Web. 08 Nov. 2016.

Comissiong, Solomon. "Public Education in America: A Pillar of Institutional Racism." Black Agenda Report. 21 July 2009. Web. 08 Nov. 2016.

Hughes, Martin. "The Amazing Atheist Denies He's Racist…By Being Racist." Patheos, 30 June 2016. 08 Nov. 2016.

Holston, Paul. "Experts say white supremacists see Trump as 'last stand.'" PBS, 11 Aug. 2016. Web. 08 Nov. 2016.

Brown, Yawo. "The Subtle Linguistics of Polite White Supremacy." The Magical Negro.net, 14 Aug. 2015. Web. 08 Nov. 2016.

Keeping It Real About Interracial Relationships as a Person of Color

"No Prison Time for Ex-NYPD Officer Peter Liang in Fatal Shooting of Akai Gurley." Los Angeles Times, 19, April 2916. Web. 15 Nov. 2016.

Winn, Patrick. "Asia Embraces Blackface-Style Ads. Get Ready to Cringe." PRI, 01 July 2014. Web. 15 Nov. 2016.

Kel, Talynn. "One Punch Man." Breaking Normal, 22 Dec. 2015. Web. 15 Nov. 2016.

Pérez, Miriam Zoila. "4 Self-Care Resources for Days When the World is Terrible." Colorlines, 07 July 2016. Web. 09 Dec. 2016.

When White People Are Too Hateful to Realize They Screwed Up

When the Space You Promised Hurts Like Hell

The Breakfast Club Power 105.1 FM. "Trevor Noah Talks Tomi Lahren, Donald Trump, Racism in America & More." YouTube, 07 Dec. 2016. Web. 09 Dec. 2016.

Kel, TaLynn. "Becoming an Agent of Whiteness." The Establishment, 05 Dec. 2016. Web. 09 Dec. 2016.

Noah, Trevor. "Trevor Noah: Let's Not Be Divided. Divided People Are Easier to Rule." The New York Times, 05 Dec. 2016. Web. 09 Dec. 2016.

Viera, Bené. "Here's the problem with black men like Trevor Noah and Charlamagne Tha God." The Frisky, 07 Dec. 2016. Web. 09 Dec. 2016.

History.com Staff. "Harriet Tubman." History.com. Web. 09 Dec. 2016.

Loewen, James W.; Kaplan, Fran; Smith, Robert. "Sundown Towns: Racial Segregation Past and Present." America's Black Holocaust Museum. Web. 09 Dec. 2016.

Sanders, Brandee. "History's Lost Black Towns." The Root, 27 Jan. 2016. Web. 09 Dec. 2016.

The Establishment. "Every Day a Funeral." The Establishment, 20 Sept. 2016. Web. 09 Dec. 2016.

Moore, A. "8 Successful and Aspiring Black Communities Destroyed by White Neighbors." Atlanta Black Star, 04 Dec. 2013. Web. 09 Dec. 2016.

Oluo, Ijeoma. "You Don't Have To Like Me — You Just Have To Believe I'm A Human Being." The Establishment, 29 Nov. 2016. Web. 09 Dec. 2016.

www.ingramcontent.com/pod-product-compliance
Lightning Source LLC
Chambersburg PA
CBHW072035280526
45788CB00006B/2099